HBR'S 10 MUST READS

The definitive
management ideas
of the year from
Harvard Business Review.

2019

HBR's 10 Must Reads series is the definitive collection of ideas and best practices for aspiring and experienced leaders alike. These books offer essential reading selected from the pages of *Harvard Business Review* on topics critical to the success of every manager.

Titles include:

HBR's 10 Must Reads 2015
HBR's 10 Must Reads 2016
HBR's 10 Must Reads 2017
HBR's 10 Must Reads 2018
HBR's 10 Must Reads 2019
HBR's 10 Must Reads for New Managers
HBR's 10 Must Reads on Change Management
HBR's 10 Must Reads on Collaboration
HBR's 10 Must Reads on Communication
HBR's 10 Must Reads on Emotional Intelligence
HBR's 10 Must Reads on Entrepreneurship and Startups
HBR's 10 Must Reads on Innovation
HBR's 10 Must Reads on Leadership
HBR's 10 Must Reads on Leadership for Healthcare
HBR's 10 Must Reads on Leadership Lessons from Sports
HBR's 10 Must Reads on Making Smart Decisions
HBR's 10 Must Reads on Managing Across Cultures
HBR's 10 Must Reads on Managing People
HBR's 10 Must Reads on Managing Yourself
HBR's 10 Must Reads on Mental Toughness
HBR's 10 Must Reads on Sales
HBR's 10 Must Reads on Strategic Marketing
HBR's 10 Must Reads on Strategy
HBR's 10 Must Reads on Strategy for Healthcare
HBR's 10 Must Reads on Teams
HBR's 10 Must Reads: The Essentials

HBR'S 10 MUST READS

The definitive
management ideas
of the year from
Harvard Business Review.

2019

HARVARD BUSINESS REVIEW PRESS
Boston, Massachusetts

The web addresses referenced in this book were live and correct at the time of the book's publication but may be subject to change.

Library of Congress cataloging-in-publication data is forthcoming.

ISBN: 9781633696426
eISBN: 9781633696433

The paper used in this publication meets the requirements of the American National Standard for Permanence of Paper for Publications and Documents in Libraries and Archives Z39.48-1992.

Contents

Editors' Note   vii

The Overcommitted Organization   1
by *Mark Mortensen and Heidi K. Gardner*

Why Do We Undervalue Competent Management?   19
by *Raffaella Sadun, Nicholas Bloom, and John Van Reenen*

"Numbers Take Us Only So Far"   37
by *Maxine Williams*

The New CEO Activists   47
by *Aaron K. Chatterji and Michael W. Toffel*

Artificial Intelligence for the Real World   67
by *Thomas H. Davenport and Rajeev Ronanki*

Why Every Organization Needs an Augmented Reality Strategy   85
by *Michael E. Porter and James E. Heppelmann*

Thriving in the Gig Economy   109
by *Gianpiero Petriglieri, Susan Ashford, and Amy Wrzesniewski*

Managing Our Hub Economy   117
by *Marco Iansiti and Karim R. Lakhani*

The Leader's Guide to Corporate Culture   133
by *Boris Groysberg, Jeremiah Lee, Jesse Price, and J. Yo-Jud Cheng*

The Error at the Heart of Corporate Leadership   165
by *Joseph L. Bower and Lynn S. Paine*

Now What?   207
by *Joan C. Williams and Suzanne Lebsock*

About the Contributors   239
Index   243

Editors' Note

It's never easy to whittle down a year's worth of *Harvard Business Review*'s research, ideas, and advice to the few articles gathered in this volume, but this past year was particularly tough. In addition to staple HBR topics such as leadership and strategy, the complex and difficult issues we were turning over in our minds and discussing in boardrooms and on social media also filled the pages of HBR. Recurring themes included machine learning, the place of business in society, and the implications of intersectionality—where harassment and discrimination can affect any one of the multiple layers of our identity. The standout articles of the year covered an array of topics, from integrating cognitive technology with human work to speaking up—whether as a CEO activist or as a manager amid the #MeToo movement. Our authors gave you new lenses through which to view the evolving context in which we work. This collection of articles showcases these and other critical themes from the past year of *Harvard Business Review*.

We've all been working in teams for years. The challenge today is how to manage work and communication when you and everyone you work with are all on a half-dozen other teams too. **"The Overcommitted Organization"** affirms that some standard advice for working on teams still applies while also providing new strategies for managing this growing modern-day dilemma, from mapping overlap to sharing insights across projects to helping teams maintain progress when key members are yanked for "all hands on deck" emergencies. Authors Mark Mortensen and Heidi K. Gardner conduct research, teach, and consult on collaboration and leadership issues. They have identified several ways in which both team and organizational leaders can reduce the negative aspects of overlap and take advantage of the benefits, including skill sharing across teams, better time management, and opportunities to learn.

MBA students are taught that companies can't expect to compete on the basis of management competencies—they're too easy for rivals to copy, so they won't sustain competitive advantage over time. However, a decade-long research project undertaken by authors Raffaella Sadun, Nicholas Bloom, and John Van Reenen reveals that the conventional wisdom is flawed, raising the question **"Why Do**

We Undervalue Competent Management?"** In their study of 12,000 organizations the authors found vast differences in how companies execute 18 core management practices, including such basic ones as setting targets, running operations, and grooming talent. Those differences matter: Companies with strong managerial processes do significantly better on high-level metrics such as profitability, growth, and productivity. The authors identify the main challenges hindering the adoption of essential management practices, suggest solutions, and make the case that senior leaders should focus on operational excellence as a crucial complement to strategy.

To overcome organizational bias, leaders are relying on people analytics to make data-driven decisions and to hire and promote fairly. But some leaders who take this approach say they can't counteract or reverse bias with data: They can't "apply analytics to the challenges of underrepresented groups at work" because "the relevant data sets don't include enough people to produce reliable insights—the sample size, the n, is too small." In **"'Numbers Take Us Only So Far,'"** Facebook's global director of diversity, Maxine Williams, explains why data must be paired with qualitative research to give leaders the insights they need to increase diversity at all levels of their organizations. By drawing on industry or sector data, learning what other companies are doing, and deeply examining the experiences of their own employees, companies can advance their goals of improving diversity and inclusion.

CEOs have always lobbied publicly for political or social issues that are good for their business. But this year we saw a significant phenomenon emerge: **"The New CEO Activists."** Taking stands on issues that are not directly related to their business model and their success can hurt sales (or help them) when consumers respond with their wallets. So why take the risk? Duke's Aaron K. Chatterji and Harvard Business School's Michael W. Toffel offer a guide leaders can use in assessing whether to speak out and how, choosing which issues to weigh in on, and balancing the likelihood of having a positive effect with the possibility of a backlash.

Artificial intelligence and machine learning have generated lots of hype, but what do they mean for you and your business? In **"Artificial Intelligence for the Real World,"** Thomas H. Davenport and Rajeev Ronanki encourage readers to look at AI "through the lens of business capabilities rather than technologies." Instead of a transformative approach, the authors advise, companies should take an incremental approach to developing and implementing AI and focus on augmenting rather than replacing human capabilities. They assert that AI can support three important business needs: automating business processes, gaining insight through data analysis, and engaging with customers and employees. Their four-step framework for integrating AI technologies, along with the real-case examples they provide, will allow companies to explore how they might best use cognitive technologies.

For those who work outside the technology realm, the acronyms AI and AR can sound a bit like alphabet soup. We found value in reading the previous piece and **"Why Every Organization Needs an Augmented Reality Strategy"** together, because that can help define what those acronyms are and how they're used. AR—technologies that superimpose digital data and images on physical objects—has familiar entertainment applications, such as Snapchat and Pokémon Go. But AR is now being used in business in far more consequential ways; Michael E. Porter and James E. Heppelmann assert that it will become the new interface between humans and machines. They define AR, describe its evolving technology and applications, and discuss its importance. The authors provide both a primer for Luddites and an expansive review of the opportunities AR presents, from expected applications such as logistics and design to surprising ones such as allowing HR to tailor training according to an employee's experience or repeated errors.

Whether we're freelancers who have lost access to the security and support of traditional employers or corporate employees logging in from home offices, the way we work has changed. In **"Thriving in the Gig Economy,"** the organizational behavior professors Gianpiero Petriglieri, Susan Ashford, and Amy Wrzesniewski report on their study of freelance workers to understand what it takes to be successful in independent work. They found that the most effective independent workers "cultivate four types of connections—to *place, routines, purpose,* and *people*—that help them endure the emotional ups and downs of their work and gain energy and inspiration from their freedom." Addressing these core areas can help you stay motivated, boost your productivity and focus, and ward off feelings of rootlessness and isolation.

As individuals, we're working in new ways, but the context in which we work and our organizations grow—or fail—has changed too. **"Managing Our Hub Economy"** offers a fascinating, forward-looking, and sometimes chilling examination of the place of business in society. Hub firms such as Alibaba, Apple, and Amazon create real value for users but also concentrate data and power in the hands of a few companies that employ a tiny fraction of the workforce. Harvard Business School professors Marco Iansiti and Karim R. Lakhani argue that the hub economy will continue to spread across additional industries, concentrating power even more. "To remain competitive, companies will need to use their assets and capabilities differently, transform their core businesses, develop new revenue opportunities, and identify areas that can be defended from encroaching hub firms and others rushing in from previously disconnected economic sectors."

Another new perspective on an old issue is found in **"The Leader's Guide to Corporate Culture."** The conventional wisdom has it that leaders are expected to create and change strategy, but culture is ingrained, unchangeable, and "anchored in unspoken behaviors, mindsets, and social patterns." Not so, say Harvard Business School professor Boris Groysberg and his coauthors. They argue that it is possible to change your company's culture, but first you must understand how it works. By integrating findings from more than 100 of the most commonly used social and behavioral models, the authors created a framework that will allow you to model the impact of culture on your business and assess its alignment with your strategy. When properly managed, culture can help leaders achieve change and build organizations that will thrive in even the most trying times.

Most CEOs and boards are hyperfocused on creating wealth for their shareholders. But managing for the good of the stock is not always the same as managing for the good of the company—especially when it leads to a focus on the short term. In **"The Error at the Heart of Corporate Leadership,"** Joseph L. Bower and

Lynn S. Paine examine the foundations and flaws of agency theory, which views shareholders as the "owners" of a company and is behind the current widespread idea that corporate managers should make shareholder value their primary concern. The authors offer eight propositions to provide a company-centered model that would have at its core the health of the enterprise instead. Their model would return companies' attention to innovation, strategic renewal, and investment in the future.

Where do we go from here? The #MeToo movement and countless reports of sexual harassment in the workplace are transforming how we manage relationships at work. In **"Now What?"** the legal scholar Joan C. Williams and the feminist historian Suzanne Lebsock explore whether this is really the end of a harassment culture. Companies are moving away from quiet settlements with victims and toward firing abusers. But employers must still follow due process and evaluate the credibility of reports. They need clear policies and fair procedures for handling harassment. The authors surprised themselves with their closing advice: "If you are being sexually harassed, report it. We're not sure if we would have advised that, in such a blanket and unnuanced way, even a year ago."

The most important ideas of the year are at your fingertips in this volume. From ideas on managing your team, to issues for your board and senior executives, to harnessing artificial intelligence and augmented reality, to addressing meaty personnel issues such as diversity and harassment, the articles here will help you address the situations you're facing today and prepare for what lies on the horizon.

—The Editors

The definitive
management ideas
of the year from
Harvard Business Review.

2019

The Overcommitted Organization

by Mark Mortensen and Heidi K. Gardner

A SENIOR EXECUTIVE WE'LL CALL Christine is overseeing the launch of Analytix, her company's new cloud-based big-data platform, and she's expected to meet a tight go-live deadline. Until two weeks ago, her team was on track to do that, but it has since fallen seriously behind schedule. Her biggest frustration: Even though nothing has gone wrong with Analytix, her people keep getting pulled into other projects. She hasn't seen her three key engineers for days, because they've been busy fighting fires around a security breach on another team's product. Now she has to explain to the CEO that she can't deliver as promised—at a time when the company badly needs a successful launch.

Christine's story is hardly unique. Across the world, senior managers and team leaders are increasingly frustrated by conflicts arising from what we refer to as multiteaming—having their people assigned to multiple projects simultaneously. But given the significant benefits of multiteaming, it has become a way of organizational life, particularly in knowledge work. It allows groups to share individuals' time and brainpower across functional and departmental lines. It increases efficiency, too. Few organizations can afford to have their employees focus on just one project at a time and sit idle between tasks. So companies have optimized human capital somewhat as they would machines in factories, spreading expensive resources across teams that don't need 100% of those resources

100% of the time. As a result, they avoid costly downtime during projects' slow periods, and they can bring highly specialized experts in-house to dip in and out of critical projects as needed. Multiteaming also provides important pathways for knowledge transfer and the dissemination of best practices throughout organizations.

As clear and quantifiable as these advantages are, the costs are substantial and need to be managed, as Christine would attest. Organizations open themselves up to the risk of transmitting shocks across teams when shared members link the fates of otherwise independent projects. And teams discover that the constant entrance and exit of members weakens group cohesion and identity, making it harder to build trust and resolve issues. Individual employees pay a big price as well. They often experience stress, fatigue, and burnout as they struggle to manage their time and engagement across projects.

Over the past 15 years, we have studied collaboration in hundreds of teams, in settings as varied as professional services, oil and gas, high tech, and consumer goods. (See the sidebar "About the Research.") By carefully observing people during various stages of project-driven work, we have learned a tremendous amount about multiteaming. In this article we discuss why it is so prevalent in today's economy, examine the key problems that crop up for organizational and team leaders, and provide recommendations for how to solve them.

Why This Matters Now

Even though assigning employees to multiple projects at once is not new, the practice is especially widespread today. In a survey of more than 500 managers in global companies, we found that 81% of those working on teams worked on more than one concurrently. Other research places the number even higher—for example, 95% in knowledge-intensive industries.

Why is multiteaming practically ubiquitous? For several reasons.

First, organizations must draw on expertise in multiple disciplines to solve many large, complex problems. Businesses are tackling

Idea in Brief

The Pros

By assigning people to multiple teams at once, organizations make efficient use of time and brainpower. They also do a better job of solving complex problems and sharing knowledge across groups.

The Cons

Competing priorities and other conflicts can make it hard for teams with overlapping membership to stay on track. Group cohesion often suffers. And people who belong to many teams at once may experience burnout, which hurts engagement and performance.

The Fixes

Leaders can mitigate these risks by building trust and familiarity through launches and skills mapping, identifying which groups are most vulnerable to shocks, improving coordination across teams, and carving out more opportunities for learning.

cybersecurity risks that span departments as diverse as finance, supply chain, and travel. Energy companies are coordinating global megaprojects, including the opening of new deep-sea resource fields. Transportation and logistics firms are tasked with getting resources from point A to point B on time, irrespective of how remote those points are or what is being delivered. Large-scale manufacturing and construction endeavors, such as aircraft and city infrastructure projects, require tight collaboration between those producing the work and the agencies regulating it. In such contexts, organizations can't rely on generalists to come up with comprehensive, end-to-end solutions. They must combine the contributions of experts with deep knowledge in various domains. (For more on this, see "Getting Your Stars to Collaborate," HBR, January–February 2017.)

Second, with crowded markets and reduced geographic and industry barriers, organizations now face greater pressure to keep costs down and stretch resources. One client manager in a professional services firm noted, "To be really good stewards of client dollars, we don't want to pay for five weeks of a specialist's time when what we really need is an intense effort from that person in week five." That's why "bench time" between projects and even slow periods during projects have become increasingly rare. The instant

About the Research

Over the past 15 years, we've been measuring both the benefits and the trade-offs of multiteaming in areas such as human capital, resource utilization, quality management, and customer satisfaction. We have conducted:

- **In-depth studies** of eight global professional services firms where multiteaming is the norm, including statistical analyses of their staffing databases and personnel records.

- **A survey** of more than 500 midlevel managers in global companies, representing a wide range of industries and professions, to examine trends across organizations and geographies.

- **Ongoing research** at a 5,000-person technology and services company that is trying to optimize multiteaming. So far, this includes more than 50 interviews with team leaders and executives. We're also designing organizational experiments to test best practices and collect data on outcomes such as efficiency, staff burnout, and customer satisfaction.

- **Ongoing research** on agent-based modeling to understand the behavior of large systems of interconnected teams. We are also using simulations to model multiteaming, with a focus on understanding the relationship between team size, percentage of overlap among teams, and the number of teams each team member is on.

people are underutilized, their organizations put them to work on other things. In our research we found that even senior-level managers were flipping among seven or more projects in a single day—and as many as 25 in a given week. Compounding this, technology makes it easier to track downtime—even if it's just minutes—and assign employees work or loop them into projects during any lulls.

Third, organizational models are moving away from hierarchical, centralized staffing to give employees more choice in their projects and improve talent development, engagement, and retention. Indeed, in the gig economy, individuals have greater control than ever over the work they do (think open-source software programmers). This has made leading teams an even more critical skill. (For more on this, see "The Secrets of Great Teamwork," HBR, June 2016.) At the same time, it has brought multiteaming—and the associated risks—to a whole new level. More and more people have at-will contracts and work not only on multiple projects but for multiple organizations. In many cases, companies are sharing team members' time and smarts with market rivals.

Although most managers recognize the increasing prevalence of multiteaming, few have a complete understanding of how it affects their organizations, their teams, and individual employees. For instance, top leaders in one professional services firm were surprised to learn who in their organization was most squeezed by multiteaming. First-year associates worked on as many as six projects in a week, which at a glance seemed like a lot. But the number rose steeply with tenure—employees worked on as many as 15 projects a week once they had reached the six-year mark. More-experienced people were members of fewer concurrent teams, but the more senior they got, the more likely they were to lead many projects at the same time. (See the exhibit "Who's feeling the pain?") Interviews revealed that working on multiple teams was stressful—one person likened it to being "slapped about" by different project leaders—despite benefits such as bringing lessons from one project to bear on others.

It's a classic "blind men and elephant problem." Managers see some of the benefits and some of the drawbacks firsthand but rarely all at once, because those things play out through different mechanisms and at different levels. Imagine, for example, a sales manager who wants to provide better solutions for customers by incorporating insights from her team members' experiences on other projects. That's not going to happen if splitting each individual's time across five projects means her team doesn't have the bandwidth to sit down and share those great ideas in the first place. Or consider a project manager who is thinking about adding a third engineer to his team—just 10% of a full-time equivalent—to reduce the load on his two overworked lead engineers. He may not recognize that this sort of slicing and dicing is the reason his first two engineers are in danger of burnout—they are being pulled into too many competing projects. Examples like these abound.

For the most part, the benefits of multiteaming involve efficiency and knowledge flow, while the costs are largely intra- or interpersonal and psychological. That may be why the costs are tracked and

Who's feeling the pain?

At one professional services firm, the employees most squeezed by multiteaming were mid-tenure associates—they helped with more and more projects as they gained experience. But the more senior people became, the more likely they were to lead many projects at the same time.

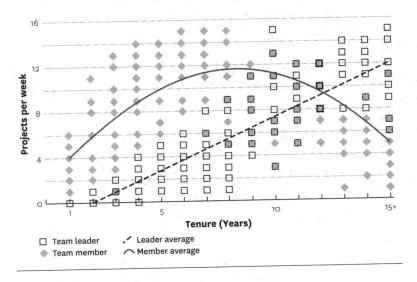

Projects per week vs. Tenure (Years)

Team leader · Leader average
Team member · Member average

managed less closely, if at all—and why they so often undermine the benefits without leaders' realizing it.

Managing the Challenges

Through our research and consulting, we have identified several ways that both team and organizational leaders can reduce the costs of multiteaming and better capitalize on its benefits. We'll outline them below.

Priorities for team leaders

Coordinating members' efforts (both within and across teams) and promoting engagement and adaptability are the key challenges for

Goals of multiteaming
(And the challenges that can undermine them)

Goals for teams	Challenges
Cost savings, because team members whose expertise is not required at the moment can bill their downtime to other projects	Weakened relationships and coherence within teams and projects
	Stress and burnout, particularly when members end up with assignments that exceed 100% time commitment
Process improvements as a result of importing best practices and insights through shared members	Interteam coordination costs so that schedules of projects with shared members don't collide
	Rocky transitions as members switch between *tasks* where their contributions are defined relative to other members' skills, adjust to different *roles* (boss on one team but subordinate on another), and learn new team *contexts* with unfamiliar routines, symbols, jokes, expectations, tolerance for ambiguity, and so on
	Reduced learning, because members lack time together to share knowledge and ideas
	Reduced motivation, because members have a small percentage of their time dedicated to any given project

Goals for organizations	Challenges
The capability to solve complex problems with members who have deep, specialized knowledge	Politics and tensions over shared human resources
Improved resource utilization across projects (no one is dedicated to a project that needs only 5% of his or her time)	Coordination costs of aligning timelines of projects even when they are not linked by content or workflow
	Weakened identification with the organization if people feel commoditized
Increased knowledge transfer and learning through shared membership	Increased risk as shocks affecting one team may pull shared members off other projects

team leaders. Focusing on those goals early on, before your team even meets for the first time, will help you establish stronger relationships, reduce coordination costs, ease the friction of transitions, ward off political skirmishes, and identify risks so that you can better mitigate them. Here's how to do it:

Launch the team well to establish trust and familiarity. When fully dedicated to one team, people learn about their teammates' outside lives—family, hobbies, life events, and the like. This enables them to coordinate better (they know, for example, that one teammate is off-line during kids' bedtimes or that another routinely hits the gym during lunch). More important, it forges strong bonds and interpersonal trust, which team members need in order to seek and offer constructive feedback, introduce one another to valuable network connections, and rely on one another's technical expertise.

When multiteaming, in contrast, people tend to be hyperfocused on efficiency and are less inclined to share personal information. If you don't engineer personal interactions *for* them, chances are they'll be left with an anemic picture of their teammates, which can breed suspicion about why others fail to respond promptly, how committed they are to team outcomes, and so on. So make sure team members spend some time in the beginning getting to know their colleagues. This will also help far-flung contributors give one another the benefit of the doubt later on. A Boston-based designer told us about his British counterpart:

"I used to think that Sylvia was frosty and elitist, because she never jumped into our brainstorming sessions. Instead, she sent missives afterward, sometimes only to the project director. Then we spent a few days working together in person while I was in London, and I came to appreciate that she's an introvert who just needs time to process ideas before responding. Plus, because she had never met any of us, it was really hard for her to keep track of who had said what on the calls; she recognized only the leader's unique accent."

After the designer shared that "aha" with the team leader, the group switched to video calls so that everyone could see Sylvia's "thinking face" and she could feel confident that she was responding to the right people when making comments.

Formally launching the team—in person, if at all possible—helps a lot, especially if members open up about their own development goals. At McKinsey each team member, including the leader, explains how he or she expects to use that project to build or improve a critical skill. This level of openness not only encourages people to display some vulnerability (which is practically the definition of trust) but also gives members concrete ideas about how they can help one another.

The launch may feel like an unnecessary step if people know one another and everyone is ready to dive in, but research shows that team kickoffs can improve performance by up to 30%, in part because they increase peer-to-peer accountability. By clarifying roles and objectives up front and establishing group norms, you're letting people know what to expect from their colleagues. That's needed on any team, of course, but it's especially critical in organizations where people belong to several teams at once and must absorb *many* sets of roles, objectives, and norms to do good work across the board.

On teams that people frequently join or leave, you'll need to periodically "re-kick" to onboard new members and assess whether agreed-upon processes and expectations still make sense. A good rule of thumb is to do this whenever 15% of the team has changed.

Map everyone's skills. Figure out the full portfolio of capabilities that each person brings to the project—both technical skills and broader kinds of knowledge, such as familiarity with the customer's decision-making process, or a knack for negotiation, or insights about an important target market. Make sure everyone knows how each teammate contributes. This increases the chances that members will learn from one another. The pride people take in sharing their knowledge and the cohesion fostered by peer mentoring are often as valuable as the actual knowledge shared.

As with launching, it's tempting to skip mapping if many members have worked together before. But we've found that even familiar teams are likely to hold outdated assumptions about individuals' potential contributions and often disagree about their teammates' expertise. As a result, they may argue about which roles members should play or bristle at assignments, thinking they're unfair or a bad fit. People may also waste time seeking outside resources when a teammate already has the needed knowledge, which demotivates those whose skills have been overlooked.

Sherif, a tax expert, experienced these problems when he joined with four colleagues to pitch a new client. "We'd all worked together on prior projects over the years—enough, we assumed, to know one another's 'sweet spots,'" he told us. "Over time, though, I grew more and more frustrated that two of my partners kept adding bits of regulatory advice to the pitch document—that's why I was on the team! I was handling nearly the exact same issue for a current client. I felt undermined, and the more they tried to sideline me, the more cantankerous I got." A few days before the client meeting, the group talked it out and discovered that Sherif had been honing his specialist expertise on projects the others hadn't been part of. They simply didn't realize what he had to offer. "We'd all been running in so many directions at the same time that our individual knowledge was changing quickly," he says. "No wonder we had friction."

Skills mapping could have prevented this. It also streamlines communication (no need to "reply all" if you know who's actually responsible for an issue). And it equips members to hold one another accountable for high-quality, on-time delivery, which is otherwise tricky when people are frequently coming and going. Creating the expectation of peer accountability relieves you as the team leader from some of that day-to-day oversight, freeing you up to scan the environment for potential shocks from other teams, for example, or to handle some of the inevitable negotiations about shared resources.

Manage time across teams. As you form a team, explicitly talk about everyone's competing priorities up front. By preemptively

THE OVERCOMMITTED ORGANIZATION

identifying crunch periods across projects, you can revamp dead-lines or plan on spending more hands-on time yourself at certain points. Making the topic "discussable" so that people won't feel guilty about conflicts allows the team to openly and productively handle these issues when they come up later.

Establishing the right rhythm of meetings will make it easier to manage time across teams and address competing priorities. At the outset, you'll want to schedule several full-team meetings at criti-cal junctures. (Research shows, for instance, that the halfway point in any project is a vital moment for a check-in, because that's when people shift into a higher gear, acutely aware that their time is lim-ited.) Make attendance truly mandatory, and ensure it by giving each team member a piece of the meetings to run—even if it's just for 10 minutes. Check in early to see that all members have cleared meet-ing dates with their other teams. Ideally, the organizational culture will support formal check-in meetings as a high priority. If not, you may need to coordinate with other team leaders before putting a schedule together.

When you plan other team meetings, invite exactly who's needed and no one else, to minimize scheduling conflicts with other teams. Most of the time, you won't need everyone. Meet in subteams when-ever possible. Don't forget to leverage technology: Instead of using precious live meeting time for updates, send a three-line e-mail or keep an online dashboard updated so that people can track progress as needed. Although technology doesn't replace face-to-face interac-tion, it can tide you over when a full meeting is too costly. And be cre-ative: Younger team members are more likely to watch a 30-second video update than to read a two-page memo. Brief, spontaneous check-ins with team members over Skype or FaceTime can keep you updated on their competing deadlines; this visual interaction makes it more likely that you'll pick up cues about their stress and motiva-tion levels, too.

Create a learning environment. Learning makes work feel more meaningful, and it's supposed to be a major benefit of multiteaming—but it often gets crowded out by time pressures.

There are other obstacles as well: Even if you've worked to build trust and personal connections, it's harder for multiteamers to give effective feedback than it is for dedicated team members, because people whose time is divided among several projects are less likely to regularly observe their teammates' actions or to be present at a time that "feels right" to offer critiques. Members who see only a small slice of a project may lack the context to fully understand what kind of feedback is appropriate. They also tend to focus on short-term tasks and to communicate with one another only when required.

Carrie, for example, was promoted to run the development office of a major metropolitan hospital, and her new 20-person staff was splitting its time among dozens of projects each week. After six months she realized, "We were all living in a feedback desert. I literally hadn't had a single comment in half a year about how I could do my job better, despite clear examples of projects that hadn't lived up to expectations." To change the tone, she modeled seeking input and responding to it constructively. "Doing so day in and day out, I started to create an environment where people shared their concerns to get help as soon as they needed it," she says. "Over time, it felt safe enough to put in more-formal processes to review projects and allow everyone to learn from errors without fear of retribution or blame."

You can also designate team members from different functions or offices to colead parts of the project so that they benefit from greater cross-contact; a formal assignment makes it more likely that they'll devote time to learning from each other. Similarly, pair a highly experienced team member with someone more junior and help them understand what both can gain from the exchange—it's not just one-way learning flowing down to the junior person.

Foster curiosity by posing "What if . . . ?" questions when it's likely that different members' backgrounds will provide new insights. If you get a question that you know another member could answer more fully, given his or her experience, redirect the asker and prompt the expert to do a bit of tutoring.

Boost motivation. On traditional, fixed teams, a strong sense of cohesion and group identity motivates members. But leaders in multiteaming environments need to leverage more of an exchange relationship. The ability to get jazzed about a project naturally flags when members spend only a small amount of time on it. Their inner accountant asks, "If I'll get only 10% of the credit, how much time and effort should I devote to this?" Figure out what your ten-percenters really value and frame the work in terms of those rewards. For example, if you have a Millennial who is eager to develop transferable skills, you might occasionally take time during meetings to have team members share and learn something new, or hold a workshop at the end of the project in which members cross-train.

Remember, too, that a sense of fairness drives many behaviors. If people feel they are pulling their weight while others slack off, they quickly become demotivated. When team members are tugged in many directions, it's often difficult for each one to recognize and appreciate how hard the others are working. As the leader, keep publicly acknowledging various members' contributions so that they become visible to the whole team, spawning a greater awareness of the collective efforts.

Like Christine, the frustrated leader of the Analytix software team, you might be feeling the strain of sharing valuable talent with other teams. Before you reach the breaking point, take these steps to clarify and manage your interdependency with other teams. They will help you avoid conflicts when that's possible, defuse them when it's not, and set an example of better collaboration with other team leaders—peers who face the same challenges you do.

Priorities for organizational leaders

If you're leading an organization where multiteaming is prevalent, you'll need to keep a close eye on how—and how many—members are shared across teams. We've found that you can reduce organizational risk and boost innovation by following these steps:

Map and analyze human capital interdependence. Patterns of team overlap range from highly concentrated (a large proportion of members are shared by just a few teams) to highly dispersed (the sharing is spread out across many teams).

Each pattern has its own implications for risk management. When a surprise problem jolts one team, the cry "All hands on deck" pulls shared members off their other teams—with disproportionately large effects on teams that have a concentrated overlap in members. When the overlap is more dispersed, the shock will be felt by more teams but to a lesser extent by each one. (See the exhibit "Who takes the hit?")

There are implications for knowledge transfer as well. Best practices travel from one project to the next as team members share what's working—and what isn't—on their other projects. Highly concentrated overlap makes it easier to spread ideas from one team to another; highly dispersed overlap makes it easier to spread them to more teams.

Who takes the hit?

When a couple of teams share many members, a shock to one group severely jolts the other, because people shift their efforts from ongoing work to firefighting.

When many teams share just one or two members, a shock to one group has a minor impact on the others—but the effects ripple throughout the organization.

Keep an accurate map of the links among teams in your organization through periodic updates from managers and team members. The frequency of these check-ins will depend on the life cycles of your teams. You'll need them more often if teams and assignments change week to week, less often if you've got yearlong projects with stable membership. This bird's-eye view will help you see which teams fail to pick up on new trends because they're too isolated, for instance, and which are so tightly interconnected that they aren't mitigating the risks of their shared membership.

The question we get most often about mapping interdependence is "What's the right amount?" Unfortunately, there's no magic answer—either for overlap between teams or for the number of teams per individual. Both targets depend highly on context. When teams are very similar in their tasks and culture, transitioning between them is relatively easy, so you can have a large amount of overlap and members can be on more of them. Transitioning across teams with very different tasks or cultures should be kept to a minimum, however—it's a bigger, costlier shift. Interestingly, the reverse holds true when workloads differ across teams, because members aren't in high demand from all teams at the same time (they aren't as susceptible to burnout as, say, tax advisers in April are).

Once you've done all this analysis, it's time to address the shortcomings you've uncovered—which brings us to the next two steps.

Promote knowledge flows. Pay close attention to teams that share few or no members with others—whether that's by design or by accident. These "islands" will require help staying informed about what's working elsewhere in the organization, sharing their knowledge and ideas, and deciding who would be the best resource to apply to a given task.

Your goal here is to establish knowledge transfer as a cultural norm, which involves getting employees to recognize that everyone wins when they take the time to share insights across projects. As with any cultural shift, it's important to lead by example and to reward those who follow suit. That's simple to say—but not so simple to do. To make it easier, highlight the benefits of sharing, and provide processes and technology to facilitate it, such as brown-bag lunches and online forums. One tech firm we worked with made a point of celebrating project breakthroughs that were attributed to transferred best practices. R&D teams at a manufacturing company shared monthly testimonials from individuals who had gained new insights through cross-staffing. In both cases the objective was to make the benefits of knowledge transfer clear—and to counter the ever-present pressure for people to keep their heads down and focus on immediate tasks.

Buffer against shocks. How can you prevent shocks in one team from being transmitted to others? Often you can't—but knowing how teams are connected through shared membership allows you to anticipate *where* some shocks may be transferred and to design small amounts of slack into the system to absorb them. This doesn't mean having people sit around twiddling their thumbs just in case. Rather, you're enabling them to shift their attention when needed. One engineering firm we worked with had identified several skilled "firefighters" and assigned them to long-term projects that wouldn't suffer if they had to address urgent problems elsewhere. This had the added benefit of providing those individuals with exciting challenges that were a welcome change of pace from their day-to-day work.

It takes a critical eye and a clear set of strategic priorities to determine which projects can be disrupted and which can't. Sometimes it makes sense to give certain projects "protected" status, exempting members of those teams from answering others' firefighting calls. Overall, the idea is to be responsive to immediate problems without sacrificing teams' ongoing needs. Of course, even if you've built slack into team design, you may occasionally have to jump in with extra resources to save critical projects that take a hit. But your other teams will feel less pain when you do.

None of this is easy. You may need to work with HR or IT to establish processes or systems that will allow you to track multiteaming more accurately across the organization. You may even need to create a new role to define and coordinate these efforts effectively. And people may resist the increased oversight—it can feel like micro-management to team leaders and members who are accustomed to having freer rein, particularly in entrepreneurial cultures. Still, in the end such investments are worthwhile; it's actually more costly to allow the trade-offs of multiteaming to go unchecked. If you're open about the problems you're trying to solve with all this transparency, people are less likely to feel surveilled or constrained by it and more likely to see the upside.

———

Nearly every knowledge worker these days is a member of multiple concurrent teams. Together, organizational and team leaders can make the most of that trend by creating an environment where multiteamers will thrive. Some of this involves managing interdependence risks, articulating and navigating groups' competing priorities, and removing obstacles to strategic coordination across groups. And some entails building stronger connections and greater trust among people who spend only a small fraction of their time together.

All around, it's a significant investment of time and effort. But organizations pay a much higher price when they neglect the costs of multiteaming in hot pursuit of its benefits.

Originally published in September–October 2017. Reprint R1705C

Why Do We Undervalue Competent Management?

by Raffaella Sadun, Nicholas Bloom, and John Van Reenen

IN MBA PROGRAMS, students are taught that companies can't expect to compete on the basis of internal managerial competencies because they're just too easy to copy. Operational effectiveness—doing the same thing as other companies but doing it exceptionally well—is not a path to sustainable advantage in the competitive universe. To stay ahead, the thinking goes, a company must stake out a distinctive strategic position—doing something different than its rivals. This is what the C-suite should focus on, leaving middle and lower-level managers to handle the nuts and bolts of managing the organization and executing plans.

Michael Porter articulated the difference between strategy and operational effectiveness in his seminal 1996 HBR article, "What Is Strategy?" The article's analysis of strategy and the strategist's role is rightly influential, but our research shows that simple managerial competence is more important—and less imitable—than Porter argued.

If you look at the data, it becomes clear that core management practices can't be taken for granted. There are vast differences in how well companies execute basic tasks like setting targets and grooming talent, and those differences matter: Firms with strong managerial processes perform significantly better on high-level metrics such as productivity, profitability, growth, and longevity. In addition, the differences in the quality of those processes—and in performance— persist over time, suggesting that competent management is not easy to replicate.

Nobody has ever argued that operational excellence doesn't matter. But we contend that it should be treated as a crucial complement to strategy—and that this is true now more than ever. After all, if a firm can't get the operational basics right, it doesn't matter how brilliant its strategy is. On the other hand, if firms have sound fundamental management practices, they can build on them, developing more-sophisticated capabilities—such as data analytics, evidence-based decision making, and cross-functional communication—that are essential to success in uncertain, volatile industries.

Achieving managerial competence takes effort, though: It requires sizable investments in people and processes throughout good times and bad. These investments, we argue, represent a major barrier to imitation.

In this article we'll review our research findings and then discuss the obstacles that often prevent executives from devoting sufficient resources to improving management skills and practices. Throughout, we'll show that such investments are a powerful way to become more competitive. If the world has really entered a "new normal" of low productivity growth, as Robert Gordon and others have argued, pushing managerial capital up a level could be the best route out of the performance doldrums.

The Research

Over the past century, scholars have learned a great deal about how core management processes affect a company's performance. For example, researchers such as Kim Clark, Bob Hayes, and David Garvin documented differences within factories, industries, and companies. But a lack of big data encompassing many firms,

Idea in Brief

The Conventional Wisdom

It's a truism among strategists that you can't compete on the basis of better management processes because they're easily copied. Operational excellence is table stakes in the competitive marketplace.

What the Data Shows

There are three problems with this thinking. First, effective management processes are highly correlated with measures of strategic success. Second, differences in process quality persist over time.

Third, there's little evidence that best-in-class processes can be imitated. GM tried for years to adopt Toyota's superior production system and failed miserably.

Implications

Organizations need competent management just as much as they need analytical brilliance. We should stop teaching business school students that operational issues are beneath the CEO—and should encourage firms to invest in strengthening management throughout the organization.

industries, and countries inhibited the statistical study of management practices. In the past decade, however, we have developed ways to robustly measure core management practices, and we can now show that their adoption accounts for a large fraction of performance differences across firms and countries.

As we've described in earlier articles in HBR, in 2002 we began an in-depth study of how organizations in 34 countries use (or don't use) core management practices. Building on a survey instrument that was initially developed by John Dowdy and Stephen Dorgan at McKinsey, we set out to rate companies on their use of 18 practices in four areas: operations management, performance monitoring, target setting, and talent management. (See the sidebar "Core Managerial Practices" for a detailed list. Though these don't represent the full set of important managerial practices, we have found that they're good proxies for general operational excellence.) The ratings ranged from poor to nonexistent at the low end (say, for performance monitoring using metrics that did not indicate directly whether overall business objectives were being met) to very sophisticated at the high end (for performance monitoring that continuously tracked

Core Managerial Practices

In our research, we assess the sophistication with which organizations manage the four broad dimensions—and the 18 specific aspects—of management shown below. The list varies slightly depending on sector (this one is for manufacturers). It's not exhaustive, but companies that manage these fundamentals well tend to have high levels of overall operational excellence.

Operations Management

- Use of lean techniques
- Reasons for adopting lean processes

Performance Monitoring

- Process documentation
- Use of key performance indicators
- KPI reviews
- Discussion of results
- Consequences for missing targets

Target Setting

- Choice of targets
- Connection to strategy, extent to which targets cascade down to individual workers
- Time horizon
- Level of challenge
- Clarity of goals and measurement

Talent Management

- Talent mindset at the highest levels
- Stretch goals
- Management of low performance
- Talent development
- Employee value proposition
- Talent retention

and communicated metrics, both formally and informally, to all staff with an array of visual tools).

Our aim was to gather reliable data that was fully comparable across firms and covered a large, representative sample of enterprises around the world. We realized that to do that, we needed to manage the data collection ourselves, which we did with the help of a large team of people from the Centre for Economic Performance at the London School of Economics. To date the team has interviewed managers from more than 12,000 companies about their practices. On the basis of the information gathered, we rate every organization on each management practice, using a 1 to 5 scale in which higher scores indicate greater adoption. Those ratings are then averaged to produce an overall management score for each company. (For more details, see the sidebar "About the Research.")

That data has led us to two main findings: First, achieving operational excellence is still a massive challenge for many organizations. Even well-informed and well-structured companies often struggle with it. This is true across countries and industries—and in spite of the fact that many of the managerial processes we studied are well known.

The dispersion of management scores across firms was wide. Big differences across countries were evident, but a major fraction of the variation (approximately 60%) was actually within countries. (See the exhibit "Management quality varies across—and within—countries.") The discrepancies were substantial even within rich countries like the United States.

In our entire sample we found that 11% of firms had an average score of 2 or less, which corresponds to very weak monitoring, little effort to identify and fix problems within the organization, almost no targets for employees, and promotions and rewards based on tenure or family connections. At the other end of the spectrum we identified clear management superstars across all the countries surveyed: Six percent of the firms in our sample had an average score of 4 or greater. In other words they had rigorous performance monitoring, systems geared to optimize the flow of information across and within functions, continuous improvement programs that supported short- and long-term targets, and performance systems

About the Research

Our research project, World Management Survey, has examined the adoption and use of management practices across more than 12,000 firms and 34 countries. We measure each organization's performance on 18 specific practices in four areas: operations management, performance monitoring, target setting, and talent management. To do that, we have experienced interviewers speak by phone with a firm's plant managers, asking everyone the same 18 open-ended questions and following up with more questions until they have a good sense of the firm's habits. A listener, who doesn't have information about the organization's financial performance, independently scores the organization on each question and each practice.

So far we've conducted more than 20,000 interviews and surveyed companies in four sectors: manufacturing, health care, retail, and higher education. More information about our methodology is available on our website, worldmanagementsurvey.com, where readers can also download the survey, fill in their own responses, and compare their organizations against the benchmarks in our data set. Obviously, the results won't be as complete, or as trustworthy, as they'd be if the organization were being independently assessed, but the process can provide a useful broad-strokes view.

---

that rewarded and advanced great employees and helped underperformers turn around or move on.

By interviewing several companies multiple times throughout the past decade, we were able to observe that these large differences in the adoption of core management practices were long-lasting. This isn't really surprising: According to our estimates, the costs involved in improving management practices are as high as those associated with capital investments such as buildings and equipment.

One of our findings may surprise readers: These differences show up within companies, too. A project conducted with the U.S. Census revealed that variations in management practices inside firms across their plants accounted for about one-third of total variations across all plant locations. This was particularly true in large firms, where practices can differ a great deal across plants, divisions, and regions. Even the biggest and most successful firms typically fail to implement best practices throughout the whole organization. Some parts of it are effectively managed, but other parts struggle.

Management quality varies across—and within—countries

Some countries get higher average ratings than others on the use of management processes. But as data from this sample of countries shows, in-country variation is even more striking. The black bars indicate what percentage of firms in each country fell into each scoring range (1 equaled the worst and 5 the best performance). The gray bars show total global percentages.

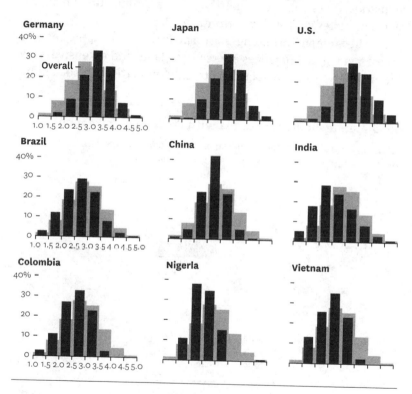

Our second major finding was that the large, persistent gaps in basic managerial practices we documented were associated with large, persistent differences in firm performance. As we've noted, our data shows that better-managed firms are more profitable, grow faster, and are less likely to die. Indeed, moving a firm from the worst 10% to the best 10% of management practices is associated with a $15 million increase in profits, 25% faster annual growth, and 75% higher productivity. Better-managed firms also spend 10 times as much on R&D and increase their patenting by a factor of 10 as well—which suggests that they're not sacrificing innovation to efficiency. They also attract more talented employees and foster better worker well-being. These patterns were evident in all countries and industries. (For a sample of metrics, see the exhibit "Good management correlates with strong performance.")

But these empirical findings raise a major question: If the benefits of core managerial practices are really so large and extensive, why doesn't every company focus on strengthening them? Also, a more

Good management correlates with strong performance

The companies scoring in the top decile on management outperformed on a variety of strategic measures. Performance by decile:

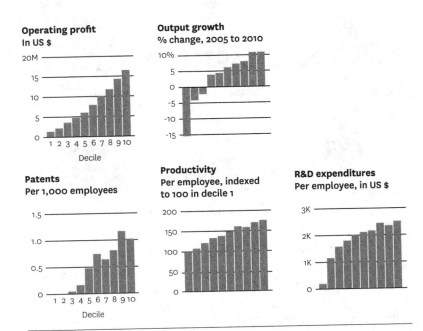

existential issue (which we'll address toward the end of the article) is, What should executives, business schools, and policy makers take away from this body of research?

What Causes the Differences?

Some of the variation in management practice is driven by external factors. The intensity of competition is one; competition creates a strong incentive to reduce inefficiencies and kills off badly managed firms. Labor regulations play a role as well; they can make it difficult to give opportunities to employees on the basis of merit or to adopt performance-related compensation. On the flip side, regulators may be in a position to create incentives for employee training or support firms that prioritize managerial competence.

We've also observed that inconsistencies often result from stubborn blind spots and deficiencies within companies. Here are the things that typically hinder the adoption of essential management practices:

False perceptions
Our research indicates that a surprisingly large number of managers are unable to objectively judge how badly (or well) their firms are run. (Similar biases show up in other settings. For example, 70% of students, 80% of drivers, and 90% of university teachers rate themselves as "above average.")

Consider the average response we got to the question "On a scale from 1 to 10, how well managed is your firm?," which we posed to each manager at the end of the survey interview. (See the exhibit "Overconfidence is a problem for managers.") Most managers have a very optimistic assessment of the quality of their companies' practices. Indeed, the median answer was a 7. Furthermore, we found zero correlation between perceived management quality and actual quality (as indicated by both their firms' management scores and their firms' performance), suggesting that self-assessments are a long way from reality.

Overconfidence is a problem for managers

At the end of every interview, we ask managers to say how well they think their organizations are run and to score them on a scale from 1 (worst) to 10 (best). Overall, their responses are far more positive than warranted.

Percentage of managers giving each score

This large gap is problematic, because it implies that even managers who really need to improve their practices often don't take the initiative, in the false belief that they're doing just fine.

In a variant of this problem, managers may overestimate the costs of introducing new practices or underestimate how much difference they could make. This was a situation we encountered in a field experiment that one of us conducted with 28 Indian textile manufacturers. Accenture had been hired by a Stanford–World Bank project to improve their management practices, but many proposed enhancements—such as quality control systems, employee rewards, and production planning—were not implemented because of skepticism about their benefits. Consultants trying to introduce methods that are standard in most U.S. or Japanese factories were met with claims that "it will never work here" or "we do things our way." Yet the firms that adopted the methods boosted their performance.

Perception problems are hard but not impossible to eradicate. The key is to improve the quality of information available to managers so that they have an objective way to evaluate their relative performance.

As our survey shows, self-reported metrics are likely to be at best very noisy—they're imperfect indicators of what really happens on the ground. There are various reasons why. A common issue is that employees don't raise problems for fear of being blamed for those they identify. That dynamic deprives managers of critical knowledge needed to understand a firm's gaps.

In our experience, managers can address this issue by proactively creating opportunities for candid—and blame-free—discussions with their employees. That's the approach followed by Danaher, a large U.S. conglomerate known for its relentless (and effective) adoption of the Danaher Business System (DBS)—a tool kit of managerial processes modeled on the Toyota Production System—across its many subsidiaries. Danaher typically initiates the relationship with a newly acquired subsidiary through a series of hands-on, structured interactions between senior Danaher managers and the acquisition's top executives, which challenge the latter to identify managerial gaps that may be preventing the business from fulfilling its potential. People taking part in these open conversations—especially those with longer tenure—describe them as eye-opening experiences that significantly change attitudes toward core management processes.

Governance structure

In other cases, managers may be fully aware of the need to improve their practices but pass on this opportunity for fear that change may jeopardize private objectives. This problem is particularly common in firms that are owned and run by families, as you can see in the exhibit "Family-run firms tend to have weaker management." Even when we cut the data by firm size, sector of activity, and country, family-run enterprises still had the lowest average management scores.

Family-run firms tend to have weaker management

Average score by type of ownership (1 = worst; 5 = best)

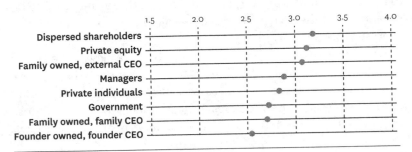

Why are family firms so reluctant to embrace strong management processes? One explanation—which finds support in our research—is that their adoption may have significant personal costs to family members. New practices may require hiring or delegating authority to talent outside the family circle. (Indeed, we've seen that higher management scores tend to go hand-in-hand with more-decentralized decision making.)

An example of this is Gokaldas Exports, a family- owned business founded in 1979 that had grown into India's largest apparel exporter by 2004. Gokaldas was a highly successful firm with 30,000 workers, was valued at approximately $215 million, and exported nearly 90% of its production. Its founder, Jhamandas Hinduja, had bequeathed control of the company to three sons, each of whom brought his own son into the business. Nike, a major customer, wanted Gokaldas to introduce lean management practices; it put the company in touch with consultants who could help make that happen. Yet the CEO was resistant. It took rising competition from Bangladesh, multiple visits to see lean manufacturing in action at firms across Asia and the United States, and finally the intervention of other family members (one of whom we taught in business school) to overcome his reluctance.

Self-reflection exercises can help family CEOs clarify whether they value their firms' long-term success more than "being the boss"—even if success means sharing the glory with other managers. In our experience a candid evaluation of one's priorities is crucial—managers are often oblivious to the fact that their own desire for control may be inhibiting the growth and success of their organizations.

In addition, family executives—and especially owners—should understand that introducing new managerial capabilities within the firm does not necessarily entail a loss of control. It is more likely to create a different role for them—but not necessarily fewer responsibilities.

That is what happened at Moleskine, based in Milan, Italy. Launched in 1997 by three friends, Moleskine went from being a niche notebook producer to a market leader in the space of a few years. Its success created a dilemma for its founders: While it was clear that the company had tremendous potential to grow further, they also recognized the pressing need to professionalize its operations. The founders searched for a private equity firm that could provide the necessary capital and expertise and help them find a new CEO. Eventually, they chose Syntegra Capital and Arrigo Berni, an experienced chief executive who had held leadership roles at family-owned producers of luxury products. Berni brought new rigor to strategy development and operations and at the same time crafted a role for the founders that made the most of their commercial and design expertise. Thanks to this successful partnership—and an IPO in 2013—Moleskine was able to deepen its competitive advantage and develop new growth opportunities globally.

Skill deficits

Good management practices require capabilities (such as numeracy and analytical skills) that may be lacking in a firm's workforce, especially in emerging economies. Indeed, our data shows that the average management score is significantly higher at firms with better-educated employees. Being located near a leading university or business school is also strongly associated with better management scores. Superior performance is likelier when executive education can be had nearby, it seems. While to some extent the availability of skills is shaped by a firm's specific context, managers can play a critical role by recognizing the importance of employees' basic skills and providing internal training programs.

Organizational politics and culture

Even when top managers correctly perceive what needs to be done, are motivated to make changes, and have the right skills, the adoption of core management processes can be a challenge. Videojet, a subsidiary acquired by Danaher, provides a case in point. In 2005, Videojet launched a new internal initiative that required the engineering and sales teams to collaborate on developing an innovative printer. The Videojet executives decided to use core DBS managerial processes—which up to that point had been used almost exclusively within manufacturing—to structure regular debriefing and problem-solving sessions between the two teams.

Unfortunately, preexisting divides between engineers and salespeople meant that the structured interactions, which had been effective in driving continuous improvement in manufacturing, became perfunctory meetings. For example, just before the product launch, a member of the sales team raised concerns about some technical aspects of the new printer, which in his eyes could seriously compromise its success. The core DBS processes had been introduced to help teams identify and address precisely this type of concern. Whereas in manufacturing, employees were encouraged to stop the production line to flag quality problems in real time so that they could be isolated and fixed, in this instance the feedback was ignored and interpreted by the rest of the team as a boycotting attempt rather than a constructive suggestion. Shortly after this episode, the printer was launched to a poor market reception, which confirmed the gravity of the issues the salesperson had raised. Thanks to this experience, Videojet executives understood that they would need to work more consciously to foster interactions between diverse pockets of expertise within the firm. They continued to use the DBS tools but also committed to frequent, longer structured interactions and collective sign-offs between engineers and salespeople during the various product development stages. Videojet launched a very successful printer just a couple of years after the initial failed product launch and has since become an exemplar in the use of DBS tools for product development.

Sometimes the organization at large resists change. Susan Helper and Rebecca Henderson provide a fascinating account of the difficulties GM encountered in implementing the Toyota Production System during the 1980s and 1990s. Even in the face of mounting competition, GM found it hard to adopt Toyota's superior management methods, mainly because of adversarial relationships with suppliers and blue-collar workers. Employees, for example, thought that any productivity enhancement from the new practices would just lead to head-count reductions and would more generally put employees under greater pressure. This distrust inhibited GM's ability to negotiate for the working arrangements needed to introduce the new practices (such as teams and joint problem solving).

Videojet's and GM's experiences illustrate a fundamental issue: Management practices often rely on a complicated shared understanding among people within the firm. The inability to foster it can easily kill the efforts of the most able and well-intentioned managers. On the other hand, once such an understanding is in place, it's very difficult for competitors to replicate.

A question that managers face is how to create this common understanding. Changing individual incentives is unlikely to work, since the adoption of new processes usually requires the cooperation of teams of people; it's difficult to disentangle the rewards to be assigned to a single employee. And adoption is hard to measure, so it would be challenging to tie an individual bonus to the implementation of a certain practice. As organizational economists know, simple contractual solutions are hardly effective in these situations.

But managers have a different weapon at their disposal, which in our experience can potentially be more effective. It's their presence. The successful adoption stories that we've encountered in our research often took place in organizations where someone very high up signaled the importance of change through personal involvement, constant communication, message reinforcement, and visibility. "Walking the talk" matters enormously and can drastically affect the odds of success for change initiatives.

This idea is supported by a large-scale research project on the relationship between management and CEO behavior that Raffaella conducted with a different team of researchers at the London School of Economics and Columbia University. After a painstaking exercise in which they codified the agendas of more than 1,200 CEOs of manufacturing firms in six countries, they found that management quality was significantly higher in organizations in which CEOs dedicated a larger portion of their time to employees than to outside stakeholders.

Though core management practices may appear to be relatively simple—in that they often rely on nontechnological investments—they are not light switches that can be flipped on and off at will. They require a profound commitment from the top, an understanding of the types of skills required for adoption, and—ultimately—a fundamental shift in mentality at all levels of the organization.

Next Steps

Our findings have implications for how managers are trained. Today business students are encouraged to judge case studies about operational effectiveness as "nonstrategic" and to see these issues as not pertinent to the role of the CEO. But it's unwise to teach future leaders that strategic decision making and basic management processes are unrelated, and that the first is far more important to competitive success than the second.

Indeed, our work suggests that the management community may have badly underestimated the benefits of core management practices—as well as the investment needed to strengthen them—by relegating them to the domain of "easy to replicate." Managers should certainly dedicate their time to fundamental strategic choices, but they should not suppose that fostering strong managerial practices is below their pay grade. Just as the ability to discern competitive shifts is important to firm performance, so too is the ability to make sure that operational effectiveness is truly part of the organization's DNA.

One frequent suggestion in this era of flattened organizations is that everyone has to be a strategist. But we'd suggest that everyone also needs to be a manager. Core management practices, established thoughtfully, can go a long way toward plugging the execution gap and ensuring that strategy gets the best possible chance to succeed.

Originally published in September–October 2017. Reprint R1705K

"Numbers Take Us Only So Far"

by Maxine Williams

I WAS ONCE EVICTED from an apartment because I was black. I had secured a lovely place on the banks of Lake Geneva through an agent and therefore hadn't met the owner in person before signing the lease. Once my family and I moved in and the color of my skin was clear to see, the landlady asked us to leave. If she had known that I was black, I was told, she would never have rented to me.

Terrible as it felt at the time, her directness was useful to me. It meant I didn't have to scour the facts looking for some other, nonracist rationale for her sudden rejection.

Many people have been denied housing, bank loans, jobs, promotions, and more because of their race. But they're rarely told that's the reason, as I was—particularly in the workplace. For one thing, such discrimination is illegal. For another, executives tend to think—and have a strong desire to believe—that they're hiring and promoting people fairly when they aren't. (Research shows that individuals who view themselves as objective are often the ones who apply the most unconscious bias.) Though managers don't cite or (usually) even perceive race as a factor in their decisions, they use ambiguous assessment criteria to filter out people who aren't like them, research by Kellogg professor Lauren Rivera shows. People in marginalized racial and ethnic groups are deemed more often than whites to be "not the right cultural fit" or "not ready" for high-level roles; they're taken out of the running because their "communication style" is somehow off the mark. They're left only with lingering suspicions that their identity is the real issue, especially when decision makers' bias is masked by good intentions.

I work in the field of diversity. I've also been black my whole life. So I know that underrepresented people in the workplace yearn for two things: The first is to hear that they're not crazy to suspect, at times, that there's a connection between negative treatment and bias. The second is to be offered institutional support.

The first need has a clear path to fulfillment. When we encounter colleagues or friends who have been mistreated and who believe that their identity may be the reason, we should acknowledge that it's fair to be suspicious. There's no leap of faith here—numerous studies show how pervasive such bias still is.

But how can we address the second need? In an effort to find valid, scalable ways to counteract or reverse bias and promote diversity, organizations are turning to people analytics—a relatively new field in business operations and talent management that replaces gut decisions with data-driven practices. People analytics aspires to be "evidence based." And for some HR issues—such as figuring out how many job interviews are needed to assess a candidate, or determining how employees' work commutes affect their job satisfaction—it is. Statistically significant findings have led to some big changes in organizations. Unfortunately, companies that try to apply analytics to the challenges of underrepresented groups at work often complain that the relevant data sets don't include enough people to produce reliable insights—the sample size, the n, is too small. Basically they're saying, "If only there were more of you, we could tell you why there are so few of you."

Companies have access to more data than they realize, however. To supplement a small n, they can venture out and look at the larger context in which they operate. But data volume alone won't give leaders the insight they need to increase diversity in their organizations. They must also take a closer look at the individuals from underrepresented groups who work for them—those who barely register on the analytics radar.

Idea in Brief

Though executives tend to think—and want to believe—they're hiring and promoting fairly, bias still creeps into their decisions. They often use ambiguous criteria to filter out people who aren't like them or deem people from minority groups to be "not the right cultural fit," leaving those employees with the uneasy feeling that their identity might be the real issue.

Companies need to acknowledge that it's fair for employees from underrepresented groups to be suspicious about bias, says Williams, Facebook's global director of diversity. They also must find ways to give those workers more support. To that end, many organizations are turning to people analytics, which aspires to replace gut decisions with data-driven ones. Unfortunately, firms often say that they don't have enough people from marginalized groups in their data sets to produce reliable insights.

But there are things employers can do to supplement small n's: draw on industry or sector data; learn from what's happening in other companies; and deeply examine the experiences of individuals who work for them, talking with them to gather critical qualitative information. If firms are systematic and comprehensive in these efforts, they'll have a better chance of improving diversity and inclusion.

Supplementing the n

Nonprofit research organizations are doing important work that sheds light on how bias shapes hiring and advancement in various industries and sectors. For example, a study by the Ascend Foundation showed that in 2013 white men and white women in five major Silicon Valley firms were 154% more likely to become executives than their Asian counterparts were. And though both race and gender were factors in the glass ceiling for Asians, race had 3.7 times the impact that gender did.

It took two more years of research and analysis—using data on several hundred thousand employees, drawn from the EEOC's aggregation of all Bay Area technology firms and from the individual reports of 13 U.S. tech companies—before Ascend determined how bias affected the prospects of blacks and Hispanics. Among those groups it again found that, overall, race had a greater negative impact than gender on advancement from the professional to the executive level. In the Bay Area white women fared worse than white men but much better than all Asians, Hispanics, and blacks. Minority women faced the biggest obstacle to entering the executive ranks. Black and Hispanic women were severely challenged by both their low numbers at the professional level and their lower chances of rising from professional to executive. Asian women, who had more representation at the professional level than other minorities, had the lowest chances of moving up from professional to executive. An analysis of national data found similar results.

By analyzing industry or sector data on underrepresented groups—and examining patterns in hiring, promotions, and other decisions about talent—we can better manage the problems and risks in our own organizations. Tech companies may look at the Ascend reports and say, "Hey, let's think about what's happening with our competitors' talent. There's a good chance it's happening here, too." Their HR teams might then add a layer of career tracking for women of color, for example, or create training programs for managing diverse teams.

Another approach is to extrapolate lessons from other companies' analyses. We might look, for instance, at Red Ventures, a Charlotte-based digital media company. Red Ventures is diverse by several measures. (It has a Latino CEO, and about 40% of its employees are people of color.) But that doesn't mean there aren't problems to solve. When I met with its top executives, they told me they had recently done an analysis of performance reviews at the firm and found that internalized stereotypes were having a negative effect on black and Latino employees' self-assessments. On average, members of those two groups rated their performance 30% lower than their managers did (whereas white male employees scored their performance 10% higher than their managers did). The study also uncovered a correlation between racial isolation and negative self-perception. For example, people of color who worked in engineering generally rated themselves lower than those who worked in sales, where there were more blacks and Latinos. These patterns were consistent at all levels, from junior to senior staff.

In response, the HR team at Red Ventures trained employees in how to do self-assessments, and that has started to close the gap for blacks and Latinos (who more recently rated themselves 22% lower than their managers did). Hallie Cornetta, the company's VP of human capital, explained that the training "focused on the importance of completing quantitative and qualitative self-assessments honestly, in a way that shows how employees personally view their performance across our five key dimensions, rather than how they assume their manager or peers view their performance." She added: "We then shared tangible examples of what 'exceptional' versus 'solid' versus 'needs improvement' looks like in these dimensions to remove some of the subjectivity and help minority—and all—employees assess with greater direction and confidence."

Getting Personal

Once we've gone broader by supplementing the n, we can go deeper by examining individual cases. This is critical. Algorithms and statistics do not capture what it feels like to be the only black or Hispanic team member or the effect that marginalization has on individual employees and the group as a whole. We must talk openly with people, one-on-one, to learn about their experiences with bias, and share our own stories to build trust and make the topic safe for discussion. What we discover through those conversations is every bit as important as what shows up in the aggregated data.

An industry colleague, who served as a lead on diversity at a tech company, broke it down for me like this: "When we do our employee surveys, the Latinos always say they are happy. But I'm Latino, and I know that we are often hesitant to rock the boat. Saying the truth is too risky, so we'll say what you want to hear—even if you sit us down in a focus group. I also know that those aggregated numbers where there are enough of us for the n to be significant don't reflect the heterogeneity in our community. Someone who is light-skinned and grew up in Latin America in an upper-middle-class family probably is very happy and comfortable indeed. Someone who is darker-skinned and grew up working-class in America is probably not feeling that same sense of belonging. I'm going to spend time and effort trying to build solutions for the ones I know are at a disadvantage, whether the data tells me that there's a problem with all Latinos or not."

This is a recurring theme. I spoke with 10 diversity and HR professionals at companies with head counts ranging from 60 to 300,000, all of whom are working on programs or interventions for the people who don't register as "big" in big data. They rely at least somewhat on their own intuition when exploring the impact of marginalization. This may seem counter to the mission of people analytics, which is to remove personal perspective and gut feelings from the talent equation entirely. But to discover the effects of bias in our organizations—and to identify complicating factors within groups, such as class and colorism among Latinos and others—we need to collect and analyze qualitative data, too. Intuition can help us find it. The diversity and HR folks described using their "spidey sense" or knowing there is "something in the water"—essentially, understanding that bias is probably a factor, even though people analytics doesn't always prove causes and predict outcomes. Through conversations with employees—and sometimes through focus groups, if the resources are there and participants feel it's safe to be honest—they reality-check what their instincts tell them, often drawing on their own experiences with bias. One colleague said, "The combination of qualitative and quantitative data is ideal, but at the end of the day there is nothing that data will tell us that we don't already know as black people. I know what my experience was as an African-American man who worked for 16 years in roles that weren't related to improving diversity. It's as much heart as head in this work."

A Call to Action

The proposition at the heart of people analytics is sound—if you want to hire and manage fairly, gut-based decisions are not enough. However, we have to create a new approach, one that also works for small data sets—for the marginalized and the underrepresented.

Here are my recommendations:

First, analysts must challenge the traditional minimum confident n, pushing themselves to look beyond the limited hard data. They don't have to prove that the difference in performance ratings between blacks and whites is "statistically significant" to help managers understand the impact of bias in performance reviews. We already know from the breadth and depth of social science research about bias that it is pervasive in the workplace and influences ratings, so we can combine those insights with what we hear and see on the ground and simply start operating as if bias exists in our companies. We may have to place a higher value on the experiences shared by five or 10 employees—or look more carefully at the descriptive data, such as head counts for underrepresented groups and average job satisfaction scores cut by race and gender—to examine the impact of bias at a more granular level.

In addition, analysts should frequently provide confidence intervals—that is, guidance on how much managers can trust the data if the n's are too small to prove statistical significance. When managers get that information, they're more likely to make changes in their hiring and management practices, even if they believe— as most do—that they are already treating people fairly. Suppose, for example, that as Red Ventures began collecting data on self-assessments, analysts had a 75% confidence level that blacks and Latinos were underrating themselves. The analysts could then have advised managers to go to their minority direct reports, examine the results from that performance period, and determine together whether the self-reviews truly reflected their contributions. It's a simple but collaborative way to address implicit bias or stereotyping that you're reasonably sure is there while giving agency to each employee.

Second, companies also need to be more consistent and comprehensive in their qualitative analysis. Many already conduct interviews and focus groups to gain insights on the challenges of the underrepresented; some even do textual analysis of written performance reviews, exit interview notes, and hiring memos, looking for language that signals bias or negative stereotyping. But we have to go further. We need to find a viable way to create and process more-objective performance evaluations, given the internalized biases of both employees and managers, and to determine how those biases affect ratings.

This journey begins with educating all employees on the real-life impact of bias and negative stereotypes. At Facebook we offer a variety of training programs with an emphasis on spotting and counteracting bias, and we keep reinforcing key messages post-training, since we know these muscles take time to build. We issue reminders at critical points to shape decision making and behavior. For example, in our performance evaluation tool, we incorporate prompts for people to check word choice when writing reviews and self-assessments. We remind them, for instance, that terms like "cultural fit" can allow bias to creep in and that they should avoid describing women as "bossy" if they wouldn't describe men who demonstrated the same behaviors that way. We don't yet have data on how this is influencing the language used—it's a new intervention—but we will be examining patterns over time.

Perhaps above all, HR and analytics departments must value both qualitative and quantitative expertise and apply mixed-method approaches everywhere possible. At Facebook we're building cross-functional teams with both types of specialists, because no single research method can fully capture the complex layers of bias that everyone brings to the workplace. We view all research methods as trying to solve the same problem from different angles. Sometimes we approach challenges from a quantitative perspective first, to uncover the "what" before looking to the qualitative experts to dive into the "why" and "how." For instance, if the numbers showed that certain teams were losing or attracting minority employees at higher rates than others (the "what"), we might conduct interviews, run focus groups, or analyze text from company surveys to understand the "why," and pull out themes or lessons for other parts of the company. In other scenarios we might reverse the order of those steps. For example, if we repeatedly heard from members of one social group that they weren't seeing their peers getting recognized at the same rate as people in other groups, we could then investigate whether numerical trends confirmed those observations, or conduct statistical analyses to figure out which organizational circumstances were associated with employees' being more or less likely to get recognized.

Cross-functional teams also help us reap the benefits of cognitive diversity. Working together stretches everyone, challenging team members' own assumptions and biases. Getting to absolute "whys" and "hows" on any issue, from recruitment to engagement to performance, is always going to be tough. But we believe that with this approach, we stand the best chance of making improvements across the company. As we analyze the results of Facebook's Pulse survey, given twice a year to employees, and review Performance Summary Cycle inputs, we'll continue to look for signs of problems as well as progress.

Evidence of discrimination or unfair outcomes may not be as certain or obvious in the workplace as it was for me the time I was evicted from my apartment. But we can increase our certainty, and it's essential that we do so. The underrepresented people at our companies are not crazy to perceive biases working against them, and they can get institutional support.

Originally published in November–December 2017. Reprint R1706L

The New CEO Activists

by Aaron K. Chatterji and Michael W. Toffel

WHEN WE FIRST STARTED STUDYING CEO activism, three years ago, we never imagined how significant this phenomenon would become. At the time a small but growing band of executives were taking public stands on political and social issues unrelated to their companies' bottom lines. Since then, controversies over laws affecting transgender people in North Carolina, police shootings in Missouri, and executive orders on immigration have drawn increasing numbers of CEOs into contentious public debates. More recently, the White House's withdrawal from the Paris climate accord, response to the clash between white supremacists and counterprotesters in Charlottesville, Virginia, and decision to rescind Deferred Action for Childhood Arrivals have galvanized many U.S. corporate leaders to speak out and take action.

Of course, corporations have long played an active role in the U.S. political process. They lobby, make contributions to candidates, and fund political action committees and campaigns on various issues in an effort to shape public policies to their benefit. But CEO activism is something new. Until recently, it was rare for corporate leaders to plunge aggressively into thorny social and political discussions about race, sexual orientation, gender, immigration, and the environment. The so-called Michael Jordan dictum that Republicans buy sneakers too reminds executives that choosing sides on divisive issues can hurt sales, so why do it? Better to weigh in on what traditionally have been seen as business issues, such as taxes and trade, with technocratic arguments rather than moral appeals.

But the world has changed. Political partisanship and discourse grow ever more extreme, and the gridlock in Washington, D.C., shows no sign of easing. Political and social upheaval has provoked frustration and outrage, inspiring business leaders like Tim Cook of Apple, Howard Schultz of Starbucks, and Marc Benioff of Salesforce—among many others—to passionately advocate for a range of causes. "Our jobs as CEOs now include driving what we think is right," Bank of America's CEO, Brian Moynihan, told the *Wall Street Journal*. "It's not exactly political activism, but it is action on issues beyond business."

The world is taking notice. CEO activism has gotten lots of media attention lately, and public relations firms are now building entire practices around it. While this phenomenon has largely

How CEOs respond: three types of tactics

Traditional	Nonconfrontational
	Lobby behind the scenes
	Contribute to campaigns
	Communicate internally with employees
	Do nothing
Activism	**Raising awareness**
	Issue a statement or tweet
	Write an op-ed
	Seek to spur public action via trade associations
	Exerting economic influence
	Relocate business activities
	Pause business expansion
	Fund political and activist groups

Idea in Brief

The Situation

More and more CEOs are taking a stand on divisive social issues—a dramatic departure from tradition.

The Reason

They're frustrated with the growing political turmoil and paralysis in the government. Stakeholders, furthermore, are starting to expect corporate leaders to speak out.

The Upshot

CEO activism can have unintended consequences. In this article, the authors look at recent examples of such advocacy and piece together a playbook for executives.

been confined to the United States, there's little reason to doubt that it could develop into a global force. We believe that the more CEOs speak up on social and political issues, the more they will be expected to do so. And increasingly, CEO activism has strategic implications: In the Twitter age, silence is more conspicuous—and more consequential.

All this activity raises big questions that we will attempt to address: Does CEO activism actually change hearts and minds? What are the risks and potential rewards? And what is the playbook for corporate leaders considering speaking out?

Why CEOs Speak Up

CEOs are weighing in on controversial topics for several reasons. Some point to their corporate values to explain their advocacy, as BOA's Moynihan and Dan Schulman of PayPal did when taking a stand against a North Carolina law requiring people to use the bathrooms corresponding with the gender on their birth certificates, which became a referendum on transgender rights.

Other CEOs argue that companies should have a higher purpose beyond maximizing shareholder value—a concept that has been gaining traction in the business world. As Benioff told *Time,* "Today CEOs need to stand up not just for their shareholders, but their employees, their customers, their partners, the community, the environment, schools, everybody."

Activism in action

Corporate leader	Issue	Action taken
Marc Benioff CEO, Salesforce	*Antidiscrimination*	In 2015, Benioff tweeted his opposition to Indiana's Religious Freedom Restoration Act and suspended corporate travel to the state; he later spoke out against North Carolina's bathroom bill and developed a reputation for rallying other business leaders to speak out.
Dan Cathy CEO, Chick-fil-A	*Same-sex marriage*	In 2012, Cathy publicly opposed same-sex marriage on a radio show; his corporation's foundation also donated to anti-LGBTQ organizations.
David and Barbara Green Cofounders, Hobby Lobby	*Health care/ religious freedom*	The Greens filed a highly publicized lawsuit in 2012 to oppose Affordable Care Act–mandated birth control coverage.
Peter Lewis Late chairman, Progressive Insurance	*Marijuana decriminalization*	In 2011, Lewis wrote an opinion piece for Forbes supporting decriminalization; he also donated $3 million to marijuana legalization campaigns.
John Mackey CEO, Whole Foods Market	*Health care*	In 2009, Mackey wrote an editorial criticizing the Affordable Care Act.
Paul Polman CEO, Unilever	*Climate change*	Polman has delivered many public speeches supporting government policies to address climate change.
Jim Rogers Former CEO, Duke Energy	*Climate change*	In 1990, Rogers (as CEO of Public Service Indiana, which eventually became part of Duke Energy) testified before Congress in support of Clean Air Act amendments; he later lobbied Congress to support climate change legislation.
Hamdi Ulukaya CEO, Chobani	*Refugee crisis*	In 2014, Ulukaya pledged to donate $2 million to refugees. He also hired refugees to work at Chobani's manufacturing plants and wrote an op-ed for CNN in support of refugees.

Source: Michael W. Toffel, Aaron K. Chatterji, and Julia Kelley, "CEO Activism (a)," Harvard Business School Case 617-001, March 2017.

And for many leaders, speaking out is a matter of personal conviction. David Green, the founder and CEO of Hobby Lobby, a family-owned chain of crafts stores, cited his religious beliefs when opposing the Obamacare requirement that health insurance for employees include coverage for the morning-after pill among all other forms of birth control.

Some leaders have commented that a greater sense of corporate purpose has become important to Millennials, whether they be employees or customers. Indeed, research from Weber Shandwick and KRC Research finds that large percentages of Millennials believe that CEOs have a responsibility to speak out on political and social issues and say that CEO activism is a factor in their purchasing decisions.

Sometimes leaders point to multiple motivations. "I just think it's insincere to not stand up for those things that you believe in," Jeff Immelt, the former CEO of GE, has said. "We're also stewards of our companies; we're representatives of the people that work with us. And I think we're cowards if we don't take a position occasionally on those things that are really consistent with what our mission is and where our people stand."

The Tactics of CEO Activists

Though they're motivated by diverse interests—external, internal, and deeply personal—activist CEOs generally employ two types of tactics: raising awareness and leveraging economic power.

Raising awareness

For the most part, this involves making public statements—often in the news media, more frequently on Twitter—to garner support for social movements and help usher in change. In such statements business leaders are communicating to stakeholders where they stand on a whole slate of issues that would not have been on the CEO's agenda a generation ago. For example, Goldman Sachs's CEO, Lloyd Blankfein, and Biogen's former CEO George Scangos have spoken out publicly on government policies that affect the rights of LGBTQ individuals. On the socially conservative side of the spectrum, Chick-fil-A's CEO, Dan Cathy, has denounced gay marriage.

In some cases, several CEOs have worked together to raise awareness. For example, days before the United Nations climate-change-agreement negotiations took place in Paris in late 2015, the CEOs of 14 major food companies—Mars, General Mills, Coca-Cola, Unilever, Danone Dairy North America, Hershey, Ben & Jerry's, Kellogg, PepsiCo, Nestlé USA, New Belgium Brewing, Hain Celestial, Stonyfield Farm, and Clif Bar—cosigned an open letter calling on government leaders to create a strong accord that would "meaningfully address the reality of climate change." Similarly, nearly 100 CEOs cosigned an amicus brief to encourage federal judges to overturn Trump's executive order banning citizens from seven Muslim-majority countries from entering the United States.

Collective action can have greater impact than acting alone. Take what happened with Trump's economic councils. Though Merck's CEO, Kenneth Frazier, received a lot of press when he resigned from the president's American Manufacturing Council in response to Trump's remarks blaming white supremacists and counterprotesters equally for the violence in Charlottesville, it was only after CEOs jumped ship en masse from that group and from Trump's Strategic and Policy Forum that the president disbanded both councils—a move that was widely viewed as a defeat for Trump.

Leveraging economic power

Some of the more powerful cases of CEO activism have involved putting economic pressure on states to reject or overturn legislation. For example, in response to Indiana's Religious Freedom Restoration Act (RFRA), which some viewed as anti-LGBTQ, Bill Oesterle, then the CEO of Angie's List, canceled its planned expansion in Indianapolis, and Benioff threatened to halt all Salesforce employee travel to the state. Other leaders joined the protest, including the president of the National College Athletic Association, Mark Emmert, who suggested that the bill's passage could affect the location of future tournaments and that the association might consider moving its headquarters out of Indianapolis. Under pressure, then-governor Mike Pence approved a revised version of the law, which forbade businesses from denying service to customers because of their sexual orientation.

In response to North Carolina's bathroom law, Schulman canceled PayPal's plans for a new global operations center in Charlotte, which would have created more than 400 skilled jobs. As many other CEOs followed suit, the potential damage mounted: The Associated Press has estimated that the bathroom law controversy will cost the state more than $3.76 billion in lost business over a dozen years.

Companies and their leaders also wield economic power by donating to third-party groups that promote their favored causes. To help fight Trump's immigration ban, for example, the car-sharing company Lyft pledged $1 million to the American Civil Liberties Union, which is challenging the ban in court. In response to the Charlottesville protest and Trump's reaction to it, James Murdoch, the chief executive of 21st Century Fox, donated $1 million to the Anti-Defamation League, a group that fights bigotry.

How effective are these approaches? The trend of corporate leaders taking a public stand on issues not necessarily related to their businesses is relatively new, so there's little empirical evidence of its impact. But we do have limited anecdotal evidence that it can shape public policy—as it did in the case of Indiana's RFRA. When legislators passed a similar religious freedom bill in Georgia, threats to stop filming in the state from leaders of many studios and networks—including Disney, CBS, MGM, and Netflix—and similar kinds of warnings from Benioff and other CEOs were seen as instrumental in moving the governor to veto it. And leaders of the National Basketball Association, NCAA, and Atlantic Coast Conference have been credited with forcing North Carolina to revise its bathroom law.

To move beyond anecdotal evidence, we set out to investigate in a scientific, rigorous way whether CEOs can help win public support for policies, thus affecting legislators' votes and whether governors sign or veto bills. Our findings demonstrate that CEOs can indeed play an important role in shaping the public's views on political and social issues. (See the sidebar "Our Research: Does CEO Activism

Our Research: Does CEO Activism Influence Public Opinion?

Some of the experiments we conducted investigated whether and how CEO activism might affect public opinion. In one, we developed a survey asking people if they supported or opposed Indiana's Religious Freedom Restoration Act (RFRA), at a time when the controversy over it was still very much in the news. In some cases, we first told them that many were concerned that the law might allow discrimination against gays and lesbians. In other cases we attributed those concerns to Apple's CEO, Tim Cook; to Bill Oesterle, who was then CEO of Indiana-based Angie's List; or to the mayor of Indianapolis.

The market research company Civic Science deployed our survey on the hundreds of third-party websites (newspapers, entertainment sites, and so on) with which it partners, gathering 3,418 responses from across the United States. Among those in the baseline condition, who were not told of any discrimination concern, 50% of respondents favored the law—evidence of how split the country is on such legislation. Support for the law dipped to about 40% among respondents who answered the question after being presented with discrimination concerns, regardless of who expressed them—a CEO or a politician—or even if they weren't attributed to anyone in particular.

Influence Public Opinion?") Moreover, as we'll discuss, we find that when CEOs communicate a stance on such issues, it can spur like-minded consumers to purchase more of their products.

The Risks and Potential Rewards

In today's politically charged atmosphere, mere affiliations with political leaders or causes can be risky. A few weeks into Trump's term, Under Armour's CEO, Kevin Plank, faced criticism after referring to the president as "a real asset for the country" in an interview. One of his star pitchmen, the Golden State Warriors player Stephen Curry, expressed his displeasure publicly. The hashtag #BoycottUnderArmour began appearing on Twitter, and other Under Armour endorsers, including ballerina Misty Copeland, echoed Curry. The company had to take out a full-page newspaper ad clarifying Plank's

These results imply that public opinion, at least in this study, was shaped more by the message than by the messenger. There are two ways to interpret this: You can infer that CEOs have no special ability to influence public opinion. After all, their statements had no more effect than politicians' or unattributed statements. On the other hand, the results show that CEOs can be as persuasive as political leaders. CEOs can attract media attention, especially when they speak out on contentious social and environmental issues that are not obviously connected to their bottom lines, which heightens their authenticity. Given that CEOs can sway public opinion, we assume that they can shape public policy, too.

Our study went a bit further to see whether CEO activism would affect people differently depending on their preexisting policy preferences. We found that Cook's discrimination remarks further eroded (already-low) RFRA support among same-sex marriage advocates but had no impact on the much more pro-RFRA views of same-sex marriage opponents. It's important to be aware of whose opinions CEO activism is likely to shift—and whose are likely to be unmoved. In fact, recent research has found that CEOs' political endorsements can significantly affect the campaign contributions of their employees, which suggests that CEO activism might be especially influential with a CEO's own employees.

comments and stating his opposition to Trump's immigration ban. But that response did not stop Under Armour's stock from being downgraded as one analyst wondered whether the gaffe would "make it nearly impossible to effectively build a cool urban lifestyle brand in the foreseeable future."

CEO activism has sometimes led to charges of hypocrisy. For example, a few conservative websites have criticized Benioff and Cook for denouncing religious freedom laws while Salesforce and Apple continue to do business in countries that persecute LGBTQ individuals. And some activism efforts have come off as clumsy: Consider the widespread ridicule that greeted Howard Schultz's Race Together campaign, in which Starbucks baristas were instructed to write that phrase on all drink cups in an effort to combat racism.

On the other hand, activism can burnish a corporate leader's reputation. In the aftermath of the violence in Charlottesville, the

CEOs who resigned from Trump's economic councils (a group that included Plank) were widely praised. The applause for Merck's Frazier, the first to step down, was particularly effusive. "Mr. Frazier, thank you for your courageous stand," tweeted U.S. representative Keith Ellison. The Anne Frank Center for Mutual Respect was even more emphatic, tweeting "A HERO: Ken Frazier."

This controversy also highlighted the risk of silence, which may be viewed as a sign of tacit approval. The *New York Times* and CNBC published lists of which CEOs remained on the president's various economic councils, with CNBC noting that "with each new resignation, those left on the council faced increased scrutiny." Oracle's CEO had similarly been put on the spot when a group of workers from that company launched a petition urging their employer to join numerous other companies in opposing Trump's immigration ban. Their effort attracted national attention, with *USA Today* observing, "More than 130 tech companies—from Apple to Zynga—have signed the amicus brief. Oracle and IBM have not."

Still, CEOs should keep in mind that reactions to activism can cut both ways. While Benioff's advocacy has been widely praised, he admitted to CBS News that Colin Powell, the former secretary of state and a retired four-star general—and now a Salesforce director—warned him: "The farther you go up the tree, the more your backside is going to be exposed, and you'd better be careful." After Chick-fil-A's Cathy spoke out against gay marriage, the chain faced consumer picket lines and a boycott—but also a countervailing "Chick-fil-A Appreciation Day," which attracted large crowds of customers. Indeed, in a Weber Shandwick survey 40% of respondents said they would be more likely to purchase from a company if they agreed with the CEO's position, but 45% said they'd be less likely to if they disagreed with the CEO's view.

We conducted our own experiment to assess the influence of CEO activism on U.S. consumers' behavior. In it, we asked a nationally representative group of respondents about their intent to buy Apple products in the near future. To some, we first provided a statement describing CEO Tim Cook's opinion that Indiana's religious freedom bill was discriminatory against LGBTQ individuals;

to others, we provided a generic statement about Cook's management philosophy. To the rest, we provided no statement at all; we simply asked about purchasing intent. We randomly deployed these three conditions and received 2,176 responses. The people in the group exposed to Cook's activism, we found, expressed significantly higher intent to buy Apple products in the near future than those in the other two groups. Learning about Cook's activism increased intent to purchase among supporters of same-sex marriage but did not erode intent among its opponents. These results indicate that CEO activism can generate goodwill for the company but need not alienate those who disagree with the CEO. But this most likely does not apply to all companies. Apple products are especially sticky, so while Cook's remarks might not provoke a backlash against iPhones, other business leaders should consider whether the political makeup of their consumers and the nature of their products might lead to a different result. It's critical for every CEO to proceed thoughtfully.

The CEO Activist's Playbook

Drawing on our empirical research and interviews with CEO activists and their stakeholders, we have developed a guide for leaders who are deciding whether to speak out and how.

What to weigh in on

Smart CEO activists typically choose their issues; the issues do not choose them. To avoid being blindsided by a news story or awkwardly weighing in on a topic they know little about, CEOs should sit down with their executive teams, including their chief communications officers, and decide what issues matter to them and why. This discussion should include reflection on why championing the selected causes would have greater social impact than championing other causes. (On occasion, however, there's no time for this kind of deliberation, such as when corporate leaders felt they quickly needed to make it clear they had no tolerance for racism after Charlottesville.)

Executives must balance the likelihood of having an effect and other potential benefits—such as pleasing employees and consumers—against the possibility of a backlash. As part of this assessment, CEOs should explicitly consider how their statements and actions will be received in a politically polarized atmosphere. A 2016 Global Strategy Group report shows that when companies are associated with political issues, customers view this connection through the lens of their party affiliation. (See the exhibit "A polarized response.") According to the study, twice as many Democrats viewed Schultz's Race Together campaign positively as viewed it negatively, but three times as many Republicans viewed it unfavorably as viewed it favorably. Cook's advocacy for gay marriage produced similar responses. Championship of less divisive issues, such as parental leave and STEM education, however, is more likely to improve the brand image of the CEO's company among both Democrats and Republicans, the study showed.

CEOs should also consider the extent to which the public believes a CEO voice is appropriate on a given topic. The Global Strategy Group study found that Democrats and Republicans both thought it was fitting for companies to take public stances on economic issues like minimum wage and parental leave. However, there was much less consensus about the appropriateness of weighing in on social issues such as abortion, gun control, LGBTQ equality, and immigration. (See the exhibit "Is it appropriate to take a stand? What consumers think.")

Immigration has proven a particularly complex issue, as the experiences of Chobani's CEO, Hamdi Ulukaya, and Carbonite's CEO, Mohamad Ali, illustrate. Immigrants to the United States themselves, both publicly opposed the Trump administration's restrictions. Both have been praised for their stances, but Ulukaya was also threatened and his company faced a boycott, while Ali's remarks prompted no discernible backlash. This difference could be attributed to Ulukaya's focus on the moral need t o provide job opportunities for refugees, whereas Ali placed more emphasis on immigrants as job creators whose work also benefits native-born citizens. It's important to note, however, that while speaking out

A polarized response

Democrats and Republicans can have very different reactions to corporate activism.

The chart below shows how each company's stance on a social issue affected its overall favorability ratings with Democrats and Republicans. The percentages indicate the net change in support from members of each party in response to the activist stance.

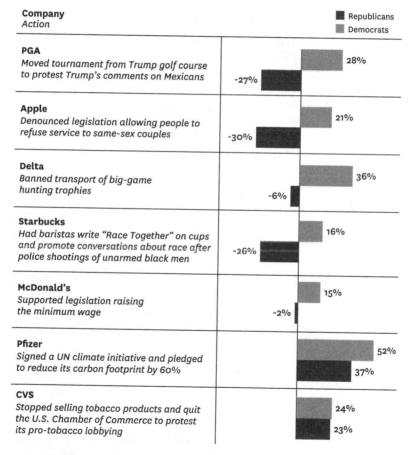

Company
Action

■ Republicans
▨ Democrats

PGA
Moved tournament from Trump golf course to protest Trump's comments on Mexicans
28%
-27%

Apple
Denounced legislation allowing people to refuse service to same-sex couples
21%
-30%

Delta
Banned transport of big-game hunting trophies
36%
-6%

Starbucks
Had baristas write "Race Together" on cups and promote conversations about race after police shootings of unarmed black men
16%
-26%

McDonald's
Supported legislation raising the minimum wage
15%
-2%

Pfizer
Signed a UN climate initiative and pledged to reduce its carbon footprint by 60%
52%
37%

CVS
Stopped selling tobacco products and quit the U.S. Chamber of Commerce to protest its pro-tobacco lobbying
24%
23%

Source: "Business & Politics: Do They Mix?" Third Annual Study, January 2016, a survey of 803 U.S. adults by Global Strategy Group.

Is it appropriate to take a stand? What consumers think

A Global Strategy Group survey showed that Americans tend to approve of corporate activism on economic issues more than activism on social issues.

Percentage of respondents who thought it was appropriate for companies to take a stance on each issue

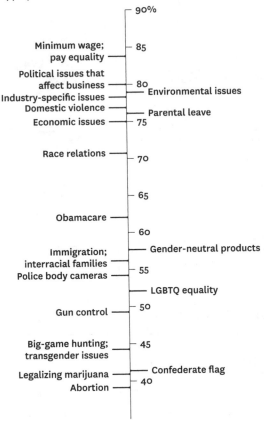

Source: "Business & Politics: Do They Mix?" Third Annual Study, January 2016, a survey of 803 U.S. Adults by Global Strategy Group.

on controversial topics might provoke an adverse reaction, it is also likely to attract media coverage, which increases the opportunity for a CEO's views to be heard in the first place.

To influence public policy, the message has to be authentic to both the individual leader and the business. There should be a compelling narrative for why *this* issue matters to *this* CEO of *this* business at *this* time. The issue selection is also a crucial time to "get smart" about the underlying details. CEOs can quickly get in over their heads if they start speaking publicly about complex issues and are pressed by knowledgeable journalists and commentators. Because the credibility of business leaders rests on the perception that they make decisions after careful analysis, CEO activists can be effective only if they really understand the issue under debate.

When to weigh in

Once the issue is selected, the CEO activist has to understand if there are key moments when speaking out might actually make a difference. Is it while a piece of legislation is being considered, or is it afterward?

We have observed that a CEO activist's chances of blocking a particular policy are typically better than his or her chances of reversing legislation that has been enacted. As we have seen with the Republican Party's efforts to repeal the Affordable Care Act in recent months, the U.S. legislative system was designed to be slow moving and deliberative. This institutional feature makes it difficult not only to pass sweeping new legislation but to repeal existing laws as well.

Also, consider the news cycle. As we noted earlier, being the first CEO to quit one of the president's economic councils earned Frazier (and Merck) significant positive media coverage. When other CEOs quit in rapid succession over the next 48 hours, their stories were lumped together. Frazier's actions will likely be remembered more than those of the CEOs who followed him. Of course, there was a downside to all the attention: President Trump struck back directly at Frazier, tweeting an insult and citing Merck's responsibility for high drug prices. To date, there's no evidence that this has hurt Merck's business.

Implications for Democracy

CEO activism may be giving businesses and their leaders even more influence in a political system in which their money can already buy access to power. Some people, including North Carolina's lieutenant governor, who supported the bathroom bill while facing an onslaught of CEO activism, have gone further, characterizing it as corporate bullying. One Georgia state senator, who sponsored that state's religious freedom bill, lamented, "Marc Benioff is the ringleader for big-business CEOs who use economic threats to exercise more power over public policy than the voters who use the democratic process." From this perspective, CEO activism can be viewed as endangering democracy's ideal that each citizen should have an equal say in influencing policy outcomes.

There is of course another angle on this that considers CEO activism within the current environment of political influence. As we've noted, CEO activism is an unusually transparent way for corporate leaders to try to affect policy—in contrast to behind-the-scenes efforts to work with legislators, trade associations, and think tanks. Because CEO activism is highly visible, employees, customers, and the media can decide how to respond to it. There is also a political divide here. (To be sure, certain controversies transcend politics.) Some progressives have been appreciative of recent CEO activism while decrying the activities of business leaders like the Koch brothers. As a result, many conservatives see a double standard at play. Most of the CEO activists have been espousing liberal views, but it remains to be seen how widespread activism from conservative business leaders would be received.

How to weigh in

CEO activism differs from traditional corporate engagement in politics precisely because it is visible and high profile. The CEO needs to decide whether he or she wants all that attention or if the cause would be better advanced by a coalition of CEOs. More than 160 CEOs and business leaders chose to sign a letter by the Human Rights Campaign opposing the North Carolina bathroom law. In taking this approach, they mitigated the risk of consumer backlash and amplified the newsworthiness and thus the impact of their activism. Collective action can also make it more difficult for critics to target individual corporate leaders and thus can be perceived as less risky. But it is slower by design and is likely to be less effective in associating a particular leader and corporate brand with a particular cause.

CEOs also may choose not to weigh in at all. Some leaders may feel that they do not understand the issue well enough, hold an unpopular view, or simply want to focus on other areas. All of those are credible reasons to hold back. But executives should expect that employees, the media, and other interested parties may ask why the CEO has not spoken out, and should be ready to explain the rationale.

The inside game

It's a good idea to make sure that internal stakeholders are aligned with CEO activism—or at least aware of it ahead of time. When Frazier was considering resigning from Trump's economic council, he reached out to his board members, who subsequently defended his decision and praised his courage and integrity. Our interviews suggest that not all CEOs consult with their directors or employees before taking public stands, which may imperil their efforts.

Though CEOs first have to decide whether they're speaking for themselves or their organizations, they should recognize that any statements they make will nonetheless be associated with their companies. We have seen almost no CEOs successfully separate themselves from their firms in this way. Given that, we advise setting up a rapid response team composed of representatives from the board, investors, senior management (including the chief communications officer), and employees to act as a kitchen cabinet on CEO activism. Seeking broad consensus across the organization could prevent CEO activism from being timely, which is often critical to attract attention to a message, but if the CEO can at least inform his or her cabinet about what to expect and why, it should greatly reduce the risk that key stakeholders will be unprepared for any backlash.

Predicting the reaction and gauging the results

CEO activists should prepare thoughtful responses to those who disagree with them. After Target modified its bathroom policy to accommodate transgender customers, hundreds of thousands of people signed a petition in protest. The literature tells us that when easy alternatives to a product or service are available, boycotts are more effective. Target is particularly vulnerable in this regard. Thus it's not surprising that the retail chain, which has many stores in politically conservative areas of the United States, has taken action to assuage the criticism by spending $20 million creating single-occupancy bathrooms in its stores. On the other hand, Nordstrom's customer base of affluent urban women did not threaten to abandon the upscale department store chain when President Trump attacked it for distancing itself from Ivanka Trump's apparel line.

Companies generally lack good data on the political beliefs of their customers, but this information would be useful in assessing potential reactions to CEO activism. CEOs and their companies are likely to know more about the political beliefs of their employees and can better predict their responses, however. Will employees rally to the cause or go public with their disapproval—as more than a thousand IBM employees did after CEO Virginia Rometty met with President Trump?

CEO activism also risks a backlash from politicians. Trump has tweeted his disagreement with numerous companies and their management decisions, marshaling millions of Twitter followers and creating public relations headaches. CEOs and their teams should be gaming out the likely response from supporters and critics in their own organizations, the media, and the political sphere.

It's imperative to hold postmortems, too, and answer the question: Did I make a difference? Metrics to assess the impact of activism should be established ahead of time, whether they be retweets, media mentions, public opinion polls, or actual policy shifts. Big swings in public opinion are rare, so it makes sense to set realistic goals, track intermediate outcomes, and measure progress over time.

CEO activism could become a first-order strategic issue. As more and more business leaders choose to speak out on contentious political and social matters, CEOs will increasingly be called on to help shape the debate about such issues. Many will decide to stay out of the fray, but they should still expect to be peppered with questions from employees, the media, and other stakeholders about the hot-button topics of day.

We believe CEOs need a playbook in this new world. To effectively engage in CEO activism, they should select issues carefully, reflect on the best times and approaches to get involved, consider the potential for backlash, and measure results. By following these guidelines, CEO activists can be more effective on the issues they care about most.

Further Reading

- **"Why Apple's Tim Cook and Other CEOs Are Speaking Out on Police Shootings,"** Aaron K. Chatterji, *Fortune,* July 16, 2016

- **"Do CEO Activists Make a Difference? Evidence from a Quasi-Field Experiment,"** Aaron K. Chatterji and Michael W. Toffel, working paper, July 2017

- **"Starbucks' 'Race Together' Campaign and the Upside of CEO Activism,"** Aaron K. Chatterji and Michael W. Toffel, *Harvard Business Review,* March 24, 2015

- **"The Power of C.E.O. Activism,"** Aaron K. Chatterji and Michael W. Toffel, *New York Times,* April 1, 2016

- **"Is It Safe for CEOs to Voice Strong Political Opinions?"** Leslie Gaines-Ross, *Harvard Business Review,* June 23, 2016

- **"Business & Politics: Do They Mix?"** Global Strategy Group, annual studies, 2013–2016

- **"The Dawn of CEO Activism,"** Weber Shandwick, with KRC Research, 2016

Originally published in January–February 2018. Reprint R1801E

Artificial Intelligence for the Real World

by Thomas H. Davenport and Rajeev Ronanki

IN 2013, THE MD ANDERSON CANCER CENTER launched a "moon shot" project: diagnose and recommend treatment plans for certain forms of cancer using IBM's Watson cognitive system. But in 2017, the project was put on hold after costs topped $62 million—and the system had yet to be used on patients. At the same time, the cancer center's IT group was experimenting with using cognitive technologies to do much less ambitious jobs, such as making hotel and restaurant recommendations for patients' families, determining which patients needed help paying bills, and addressing staff IT problems. The results of these projects have been much more promising: The new systems have contributed to increased patient satisfaction, improved financial performance, and a decline in time spent on tedious data entry by the hospital's care managers. Despite the setback on the moon shot, MD Anderson remains committed to using cognitive technology—that is, next-generation artificial intelligence—to enhance cancer treatment, and is currently developing a variety of new projects at its center of competency for cognitive computing.

The contrast between the two approaches is relevant to anyone planning AI initiatives. Our survey of 250 executives who are familiar with their companies' use of cognitive technology shows that three-quarters of them believe that AI will substantially transform their companies within three years. However, our study of

152 projects in almost as many companies also reveals that highly ambitious moon shots are less likely to be successful than "low-hanging fruit" projects that enhance business processes. This shouldn't be surprising—such has been the case with the great majority of new technologies that companies have adopted in the past. But the hype surrounding artificial intelligence has been especially powerful, and some organizations have been seduced by it.

In this article, we'll look at the various categories of AI being employed and provide a framework for how companies should begin to build up their cognitive capabilities in the next several years to achieve their business objectives.

Three Types of AI

It is useful for companies to look at AI through the lens of business capabilities rather than technologies. Broadly speaking, AI can support three important business needs: automating business processes, gaining insight through data analysis, and engaging with customers and employees. (See the exhibit "Cognitive projects by type.")

Process automation

Of the 152 projects we studied, the most common type was the automation of digital and physical tasks—typically back-office administrative and financial activities—using robotic process automation

---

Cognitive projects by type

We studied 152 cognitive technology projects and found that they fell into three categories.

Robotics & cognitive automation:	Cognitive insight:	Cognitive engagement:
71	57	24

Idea in Brief

The Problem

Cognitive technologies are increasingly being used to solve business problems, but many of the most ambitious AI projects encounter setbacks or fail.

The Approach

Companies should take an incremental rather than a transformative approach and focus on

augmenting rather than replacing human capabilities.

The Process

To get the most out of AI, firms must understand which technologies perform what types of tasks, create a prioritized portfolio of projects based on business needs, and develop plans to scale up across the company.

technologies. RPA is more advanced than earlier business-process automation tools, because the "robots" (that is, code on a server) act like a human inputting and consuming information from multiple IT systems. Tasks include:

- transferring data from e-mail and call center systems into systems of record—for example, updating customer files with address changes or service additions;

- replacing lost credit or ATM cards, reaching into multiple systems to update records and handle customer communications;

- reconciling failures to charge for services across billing systems by extracting information from multiple document types; and

- "reading" legal and contractual documents to extract provisions using natural language processing.

RPA is the least expensive and easiest to implement of the cognitive technologies we'll discuss here, and typically brings a quick and high return on investment. (It's also the least "smart" in the sense that these applications aren't programmed to learn and improve,

The business benefits of AI

We surveyed 250 executives who were familiar with their companies' use of cognitive technologies to learn about their goals for AI initiatives. More than half said their primary goal was to make existing products better. Reducing head count was mentioned by only 22%.

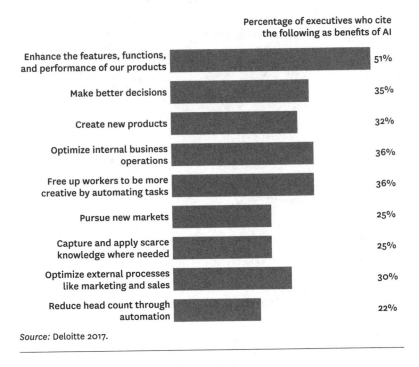

Percentage of executives who cite
the following as benefits of AI

Enhance the features, functions, and performance of our products	51%
Make better decisions	35%
Create new products	32%
Optimize internal business operations	36%
Free up workers to be more creative by automating tasks	36%
Pursue new markets	25%
Capture and apply scarce knowledge where needed	25%
Optimize external processes like marketing and sales	30%
Reduce head count through automation	22%

Source: Deloitte 2017.

though developers are slowly adding more intelligence and learning capability.) It is particularly well suited to working across multiple back-end systems.

At NASA, cost pressures led the agency to launch four RPA pilots in accounts payable and receivable, IT spending, and human resources—all managed by a shared services center. The four projects worked well—in the HR application, for example, 86% of transactions were completed without human intervention—and are being

The challenges of AI

Executives in our survey identified several factors that can stall or derail AI initiatives, ranging from integration issues to scarcity of talent.

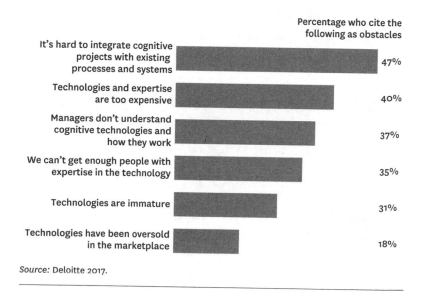

Percentage who cite the following as obstacles

It's hard to integrate cognitive projects with existing processes and systems	47%
Technologies and expertise are too expensive	40%
Managers don't understand cognitive technologies and how they work	37%
We can't get enough people with expertise in the technology	35%
Technologies are immature	31%
Technologies have been oversold in the marketplace	18%

Source: Deloitte 2017.

rolled out across the organization. NASA is now implementing more RPA bots, some with higher levels of intelligence. As Jim Walker, project leader for the shared services organization notes, "So far it's not rocket science."

One might imagine that robotic process automation would quickly put people out of work. But across the 71 RPA projects we reviewed (47% of the total), replacing administrative employees was neither the primary objective nor a common outcome. Only a few projects led to reductions in head count, and in most cases, the tasks in question had already been shifted to outsourced workers. As technology improves, robotic automation projects are likely to lead to some job losses in the future, particularly in the offshore business-process outsourcing industry. If you can outsource a task, you can probably automate it.

Cognitive insight

The second most common type of project in our study (38% of the total) used algorithms to detect patterns in vast volumes of data and interpret their meaning. Think of it as "analytics on steroids." These machine-learning applications are being used to:

- predict what a particular customer is likely to buy;

- identify credit fraud in real time and detect insurance claims fraud;

- analyze warranty data to identify safety or quality problems in automobiles and other manufactured products;

- automate personalized targeting of digital ads; and

- provide insurers with more-accurate and detailed actuarial modeling.

Cognitive insights provided by machine learning differ from those available from traditional analytics in three ways: They are usually much more data-intensive and detailed, the models typically are trained on some part of the data set, and the models get better—that is, their ability to use new data to make predictions or put things into categories improves over time.

Versions of machine learning (deep learning, in particular, which attempts to mimic the activity in the human brain in order to recognize patterns) can perform feats such as recognizing images and speech. Machine learning can also make available new data for better analytics. While the activity of data curation has historically been quite labor-intensive, now machine learning can identify probabilistic matches—data that is likely to be associated with the same person or company but that appears in slightly different formats—across databases. GE has used this technology to integrate supplier data and has saved $80 million in its first year by eliminating redundancies and negotiating contracts that were previously managed at the business unit level. Similarly, a large bank used this technology to extract data on terms from supplier contracts and match it with invoice numbers, identifying tens of millions of dollars in products and services not supplied. Deloitte's audit practice is using cognitive insight to extract terms from contracts, which enables an audit to address a much higher proportion of documents, often 100%, without human auditors' having to painstakingly read through them.

Cognitive insight applications are typically used to improve performance on jobs only machines can do—tasks such as programmatic ad buying that involve such high-speed data crunching and automation that they've long been beyond human ability—so they're not generally a threat to human jobs.

Cognitive engagement

Projects that engage employees and customers using natural language processing chatbots, intelligent agents, and machine learning were the least common type in our study (accounting for 16% of the total). This category includes:

- intelligent agents that offer 24/7 customer service addressing a broad and growing array of issues from password requests to technical support questions—all in the customer's natural language;

- internal sites for answering employee questions on topics including IT, employee benefits, and HR policy;

- product and service recommendation systems for retailers that increase personalization, engagement, and sales— typically including rich language or images; and

- health treatment recommendation systems that help providers create customized care plans that take into account individual patients' health status and previous treatments.

The companies in our study tended to use cognitive engagement technologies more to interact with employees than with customers. That may change as firms become more comfortable turning customer interactions over to machines. Vanguard, for example, is piloting an intelligent agent that helps its customer service staff answer frequently asked questions. The plan is to eventually allow customers to engage with the cognitive agent directly, rather than with the human customer-service agents. SEBank, in Sweden, and the medical technology giant Becton, Dickinson, in the United States, are using the lifelike intelligent-agent avatar Amelia to serve as an internal employee help desk for IT support. SEBank has recently made Amelia available to customers on a limited basis in order to test its performance and customer response.

Companies tend to take a conservative approach to customer-facing cognitive engagement technologies largely because of their immaturity. Facebook, for example, found that its Messenger chatbots couldn't answer 70% of customer requests without human intervention. As a result, Facebook and several other firms are restricting bot-based interfaces to certain topic domains or conversation types.

Our research suggests that cognitive engagement apps are not currently threatening customer service or sales rep jobs. In most of the projects we studied, the goal was not to reduce head count but to handle growing numbers of employee and customer interactions without adding staff. Some organizations were planning to hand over routine communications to machines, while transitioning customer-support personnel to more-complex activities such as handling customer issues that escalate, conducting extended unstructured dialogues, or reaching out to customers before they call in with problems.

As companies become more familiar with cognitive tools, they are experimenting with projects that combine elements from all three categories to reap the benefits of AI. An Italian insurer, for example, developed a "cognitive help desk" within its IT organization. The system engages with employees using deep-learning technology (part of the cognitive insights category) to search frequently asked questions and answers, previously resolved cases, and documentation to come up with solutions to employees' problems. It uses a smart-routing capability (business process automation) to forward the most complex problems to human representatives, and it uses natural language processing to support user requests in Italian.

Despite their rapidly expanding experience with cognitive tools, however, companies face significant obstacles in development and implementation. On the basis of our research, we've developed a four-step framework for integrating AI technologies that can help companies achieve their objectives, whether the projects are moon shoots or business-process enhancements.

1. Understanding the Technologies

Before embarking on an AI initiative, companies must understand which technologies perform what types of tasks, and the strengths and limitations of each. Rule-based expert systems and robotic process automation, for example, are transparent in how they do their work, but neither is capable of learning and improving. Deep learning, on the other hand, is great at learning from large volumes of labeled data, but it's almost impossible to understand how it creates the models it does. This "black box" issue can be problematic in highly regulated industries such as financial services, in which regulators insist on knowing why decisions are made in a certain way.

We encountered several organizations that wasted time and money pursuing the wrong technology for the job at hand. But if they're armed with a good understanding of the different technologies, companies are better positioned to determine which might best address specific needs, which vendors to work with, and how quickly a system can be implemented. Acquiring this understanding requires ongoing research and education, usually within IT or an innovation group.

In particular, companies will need to leverage the capabilities of key employees, such as data scientists, who have the statistical and big-data skills necessary to learn the nuts and bolts of these technologies. A main success factor is your people's willingness to learn. Some will leap at the opportunity, while others will want to stick with tools they're familiar with. Strive to have a high percentage of the former.

If you don't have data science or analytics capabilities in-house, you'll probably have to build an ecosystem of external service providers in the near term. If you expect to be implementing longer-term AI projects, you will want to recruit expert in-house talent. Either way, having the right capabilities is essential to progress.

Given the scarcity of cognitive technology talent, most organizations should establish a pool of resources—perhaps in a centralized function such as IT or strategy—and make experts available to high-priority projects throughout the organization. As needs and talent proliferate, it may make sense to dedicate groups to particular business functions or units, but even then a central coordinating function can be useful in managing projects and careers.

2. Creating a Portfolio of Projects

The next step in launching an AI program is to systematically evaluate needs and capabilities and then develop a prioritized portfolio of projects. In the companies we studied, this was usually done in workshops or through small consulting engagements. We recommend that companies conduct assessments in three broad areas.

Identifying the opportunities

The first assessment determines which areas of the business could benefit most from cognitive applications. Typically, they are parts of the company where "knowledge"—insight derived from data analysis or a collection of texts—is at a premium but for some reason is not available.

- **Bottlenecks.** In some cases, the lack of cognitive insights is caused by a bottleneck in the flow of information; knowledge exists in the organization, but it is not optimally distributed. That's often the case in health care, for example, where knowledge tends to be siloed within practices, departments, or academic medical centers.

- **Scaling challenges.** In other cases, knowledge exists, but the process for using it takes too long or is expensive to scale. Such is often the case with knowledge developed by financial advisers. That's why many investment and wealth management firms now offer AI-supported "robo-advice" capabilities that provide clients with cost-effective guidance for routine financial issues.

In the pharmaceutical industry, Pfizer is tackling the scaling problem by using IBM's Watson to accelerate the laborious process of drug-discovery research in immuno-oncology, an emerging approach to cancer treatment that uses the body's immune system to help fight cancer. Immuno-oncology drugs can take up to 12 years to bring to market. By combining a sweeping literature review with Pfizer's own data, such as lab reports, Watson is helping researchers to surface relationships and find hidden patterns that should speed the identification of new drug targets, combination therapies for study, and patient selection strategies for this new class of drugs.

- **Inadequate firepower.** Finally, a company may collect more data than its existing human or computer firepower can adequately analyze and apply. For example, a company may have massive amounts of data on consumers' digital behavior but lack insight about what it means or how it can be strategically applied. To address this, companies are using machine learning to support tasks such as programmatic buying of personalized digital ads or, in the case of Cisco Systems and IBM, to create tens of thousands of "propensity models" for determining which customers are likely to buy which products.

Determining the use cases

The second area of assessment evaluates the use cases in which cognitive applications would generate substantial value and contribute to business success. Start by asking key questions such as: How critical to your overall strategy is addressing the targeted problem? How difficult would it be to implement the proposed AI solution—both technically and organizationally? Would the benefits from launching the application be worth the effort? Next, prioritize the use cases according to which offer the most short- and long-term value, and which might ultimately be integrated into a broader platform or suite of cognitive capabilities to create competitive advantage.

Selecting the technology

The third area to assess examines whether the AI tools being considered for each use case are truly up to the task. Chatbots and intelligent agents, for example, may frustrate some companies because most of them can't yet match human problem solving beyond simple scripted cases (though they are improving rapidly). Other technologies, like robotic process automation that can streamline simple processes such as invoicing, may in fact slow down more-complex production systems. And while deep learning visual recognition systems can recognize images in photos and videos, they require lots of labeled data and may be unable to make sense of a complex visual field.

In time, cognitive technologies will transform how companies do business. Today, however, it's wiser to take incremental steps with the currently available technology while planning for transformational change in the not-too-distant future. You may ultimately want to turn customer interactions over to bots, for example, but for now it's probably more feasible—and sensible—to automate your internal IT help desk as a step toward the ultimate goal.

3. Launching Pilots

Because the gap between current and desired AI capabilities is not always obvious, companies should create pilot projects for cognitive applications before rolling them out across the entire enterprise.

Proof-of-concept pilots are particularly suited to initiatives that have high potential business value or allow the organization to test different technologies at the same time. Take special care to avoid "injections" of projects by senior executives who have been influenced by technology vendors. Just because executives and boards of directors may feel pressure to "do something cognitive" doesn't mean you should bypass the rigorous piloting process. Injected projects often fail, which can significantly set back the organization's AI program.

If your firm plans to launch several pilots, consider creating a cognitive center of excellence or similar structure to manage them. This approach helps build the needed technology skills and capabilities within the organization, while also helping to move small pilots into broader applications that will have a greater impact. Pfizer has more than 60 projects across the company that employ some form of cognitive technology; many are pilots, and some are now in production.

At Becton, Dickinson, a "global automation" function within the IT organization oversees a number of cognitive technology pilots that use intelligent digital agents and RPA (some work is done in partnership with the company's Global Shared Services organization). The global automation group uses end-to-end process maps to guide implementation and identify automation opportunities. The group also uses graphical "heat maps" that indicate the organizational activities most amenable to AI interventions. The company has successfully implemented intelligent agents in IT support processes, but as yet is not ready to support large-scale enterprise processes, like order-to-cash. The health insurer Anthem has developed a similar centralized AI function that it calls the Cognitive Capability Office.

Business-process redesign

As cognitive technology projects are developed, think through how workflows might be redesigned, focusing specifically on the division of labor between humans and the AI. In some cognitive projects, 80% of decisions will be made by machines and 20% will be made by humans; others will have the opposite ratio. Systematic redesign of workflows is necessary to ensure that humans and machines augment each other's strengths and compensate for weaknesses.

The investment firm Vanguard, for example, has a new "Personal Advisor Services" (PAS) offering, which combines automated investment advice with guidance from human advisers. In the new system, cognitive technology is used to perform many of the traditional tasks of investment advising, including constructing a customized portfolio, rebalancing portfolios over time, tax loss harvesting, and tax-efficient investment selection. Vanguard's human advisers serve as "investing coaches," tasked with answering investor questions, encouraging healthy financial behaviors, and being, in Vanguard's words, "emotional circuit breakers" to keep investors on plan. Advisers are encouraged to learn about behavioral finance to perform these roles effectively. The PAS approach has quickly gathered more than $80 billion in assets under management, costs are lower than those for purely human-based advising, and customer satisfaction is high. (See the exhibit "One company's division of labor.")

One company's division of labor

Vanguard, the investment services firm, uses cognitive technology to provide customers with investment advice at a lower cost. Its Personal Advisor Services system automates many traditional tasks of investment advising, while human advisers take on higher-value activities. Here's how Vanguard redesigned its work processes to get the most from the new system.

Cognitive technology	Adviser
Generates a financial plan	Understands investment goals
Provides goals-based forecasting in real time	Customizes an implementation plan
Rebalances portfolio to target mix	Provides investment analysis and retirement planning
Minimizes taxes	Develops retirement income and Social Security drawdown strategies
Tracks aggregated assets in one place	Serves as a behavioral coach
Engages clients virtually	Monitors spending to encourage accountability
	Offers ongoing wealth and financial-planning support
	Addresses estate-planning considerations

Source: Vanguard Group.

Vanguard understood the importance of work redesign when implementing PAS, but many companies simply "pave the cow path" by automating existing work processes, particularly when using RPA technology. By automating established workflows, companies can quickly implement projects and achieve ROI—but they forgo the opportunity to take full advantage of AI capabilities and substantively improve the process.

Cognitive work redesign efforts often benefit from applying design-thinking principles: understanding customer or end-user needs, involving employees whose work will be restructured, treating designs as experimental "first drafts," considering multiple alternatives, and explicitly considering cognitive technology capabilities in the design process. Most cognitive projects are also suited to iterative, agile approaches to development.

4. Scaling Up

Many organizations have successfully launched cognitive pilots, but they haven't had as much success rolling them out organization-wide. To achieve their goals, companies need detailed plans for scaling up, which requires collaboration between technology experts and owners of the business process being automated. Because cognitive technologies typically support individual tasks rather than entire processes, scale-up almost always requires integration with existing systems and processes. Indeed, in our survey, executives reported that such integration was the greatest challenge they faced in AI initiatives.

Companies should begin the scaling-up process by considering whether the required integration is even possible or feasible. If the application depends on special technology that is difficult to source, for example, that will limit scale-up. Make sure your business process owners discuss scaling considerations with the IT organization before or during the pilot phase: An end run around IT is unlikely to be successful, even for relatively simple technologies like RPA.

The health insurer Anthem, for example, is taking on the development of cognitive technologies as part of a major modernization of its existing systems. Rather than bolting new cognitive apps onto legacy technology, Anthem is using a holistic approach that maximizes the value being generated by the cognitive applications, reduces the overall cost of development and integration, and creates a halo effect on legacy systems. The company is also redesigning processes at the same time to, as CIO Tom Miller puts it, "use cognitive to move us to the next level."

In scaling up, companies may face substantial change-management challenges. At one U.S. apparel retail chain, for example, the pilot project at a small subset of stores used machine learning for online product recommendations, predictions for optimal inventory and rapid replenishment models, and—most difficult of all—merchandising. Buyers, used to ordering product on the basis of their intuition, felt threatened and made comments like "If you're going to trust this, what do you need me for?" After the pilot, the buyers went as a group to the chief merchandising officer and requested that the program be killed. The executive pointed out that the results were positive and warranted expanding the project. He assured the buyers that, freed of certain merchandising tasks, they could take on more high-value work that humans can still do better than machines, such as understanding younger customers' desires and determining apparel manufacturers' future plans. At the same time, he acknowledged that the merchandisers needed to be educated about a new way of working.

If scale-up is to achieve the desired results, firms must also focus on improving productivity. Many, for example, plan to grow their way into productivity—adding customers and transactions without adding staff. Companies that cite head count reduction as the primary justification for the AI investment should ideally plan to realize that goal over time through attrition or from the elimination of outsourcing.

The Future Cognitive Company

Our survey and interviews suggest that managers experienced with cognitive technology are bullish on its prospects. Although the early successes are relatively modest, we anticipate that these technologies will eventually transform work. We believe that companies that are adopting AI in moderation now—and have aggressive implementation plans for the future—will find themselves as well positioned to reap benefits as those that embraced analytics early on.

Through the application of AI, information-intensive domains such as marketing, health care, financial services, education, and professional services could become simultaneously more valuable and less expensive to society. Business drudgery in every industry and function—overseeing routine transactions, repeatedly answering the same questions, and extracting data from endless documents—could become the province of machines, freeing up human workers to be more productive and creative. Cognitive technologies are also a catalyst for making other data-intensive technologies succeed, including autonomous vehicles, the Internet of Things, and mobile and multichannel consumer technologies.

The great fear about cognitive technologies is that they will put masses of people out of work. Of course, some job loss is likely as smart machines take over certain tasks traditionally done by humans. However, we believe that most workers have little to fear at this point. Cognitive systems perform tasks, not entire jobs. The human job losses we've seen were primarily due to attrition of workers who were not replaced or through automation of outsourced work. Most cognitive tasks currently being performed augment human activity, perform a narrow task within a much broader job, or do work that wasn't done by humans in the first place, such as big-data analytics.

Most managers with whom we discuss the issue of job loss are committed to an augmentation strategy—that is, integrating human and machine work, rather than replacing humans entirely. In our survey, only 22% of executives indicated that they considered reducing head count as a primary benefit of AI.

We believe that every large company should be exploring cognitive technologies. There will be some bumps in the road, and there is no room for complacency on issues of workforce displacement and the ethics of smart machines. But with the right planning and development, cognitive technology could usher in a golden age of productivity, work satisfaction, and prosperity.

Further Reading

- **"Big Idea: The Business of Artificial Intelligence,"** by Erik Brynjolfsson and Andrew McAfee, HBR.org/ai
- **"Inside Facebook's AI Workshop,"** by Scott Berinato, HBR.org/ai
- **"AI Can Be a Troublesome Teammate,"** by Kurt Gray, HBR.org/ai

Originally published in January–February 2018. Reprint R1801H

Why Every Organization Needs an Augmented Reality Strategy

by Michael E. Porter and James E. Heppelmann

THERE IS A FUNDAMENTAL DISCONNECT between the wealth of digital data available to us and the physical world in which we apply it. While reality is three-dimensional, the rich data we now have to inform our decisions and actions remains trapped on two-dimensional pages and screens. This gulf between the real and digital worlds limits our ability to take advantage of the torrent of information and insights produced by billions of smart, connected products (SCPs) worldwide.

Augmented reality, a set of technologies that superimposes digital data and images on the physical world, promises to close this gap and release untapped and uniquely human capabilities. Though still in its infancy, AR is poised to enter the mainstream; according to one estimate, spending on AR technology will hit $60 billion in 2020. AR will affect companies in every industry and many other types of organizations, from universities to social enterprises. In the coming months and years, it will transform how we learn, make decisions, and interact with the physical world. It will also change how enterprises serve customers, train employees, design and create products, and manage their value chains, and, ultimately, how they compete.

In this article we describe what AR is, its evolving technology and applications, and why it is so important. Its significance will grow exponentially as SCPs proliferate, because it amplifies their power to create value and reshape competition. AR will become the new interface between humans and machines, bridging the digital and physical worlds. While challenges in deploying it remain, pioneering organizations, such as Amazon, Facebook, General Electric, Mayo Clinic, and the U.S. Navy, are already implementing AR and seeing a major impact on quality and productivity. Here we provide a road map for how companies should deploy AR and explain the critical choices they will face in integrating it into strategy and operations.

What Is Augmented Reality?

Isolated applications of AR have been around for decades, but only recently have the technologies required to unleash its potential become available. At the core, AR transforms volumes of data and analytics into images or animations that are overlaid on the real world. Today most AR applications are delivered through mobile devices, but increasingly delivery will shift to hands-free wearables such as head-mounted displays or smart glasses. Though many people are familiar with simple AR entertainment applications, such as Snapchat filters and the game Pokémon Go, AR is being applied in far more consequential ways in both consumer and business-to-business settings. For example, AR "heads-up" displays that put navigation, collision warning, and other information directly in drivers' line of sight are now available in dozens of car models. Wearable AR devices for factory workers that superimpose production-assembly or service instructions are being piloted at thousands of companies. AR is supplementing or replacing traditional manuals and training methods at an ever-faster pace.

More broadly, AR enables a new information-delivery paradigm, which we believe will have a profound impact on how data is structured, managed, and delivered on the internet. Though the web transformed how information is collected, transmitted, and

Idea in Brief

The Problem

While the physical world is three-dimensional, most data is trapped on 2-D screens and pages. This gulf between the real and digital worlds limits our ability to make the best use of the volumes of information available to us.

The Solution

Augmented reality solves this problem by superimposing digital images and data on real objects.

By putting information directly into the context in which we'll apply it, AR speeds our ability to absorb and act on it.

The Outcome

Pioneering organizations, including GE, Mayo Clinic, and the U.S. Navy, are using AR to improve productivity, quality, and training. By combining the strengths of humans and machines, AR will dramatically increase value creation.

accessed, its model for data storage and delivery—pages on flat screens—has major limits: It requires people to mentally translate 2-D information for use in a 3-D world. That isn't always easy, as anyone who has used a manual to fix an office copier knows. By superimposing digital information directly on real objects or environments, AR allows people to process the physical and digital simultaneously, eliminating the need to mentally bridge the two. That improves our ability to rapidly and accurately absorb information, make decisions, and execute required tasks quickly and efficiently.

AR displays in cars are a vivid illustration of this. Until recently, drivers using GPS navigation had to look at a map on a flat screen and then figure out how to apply it in the real world. To take the correct exit from a busy rotary, for example, the driver needed to shift his or her gaze between the road and the screen and mentally connect the image on the map to the proper turnoff. AR heads-up displays lay navigational images directly over what the driver sees through the windshield. This reduces the mental effort of applying the information, prevents distraction, and minimizes driver error, freeing people to focus on the road. (For more on this, see the sidebar "Enhancing Human Decision Making.")

Converging physical and digital

Augmented reality reduces the mental effort needed to connect digital information about the physical world with the context it applies to.

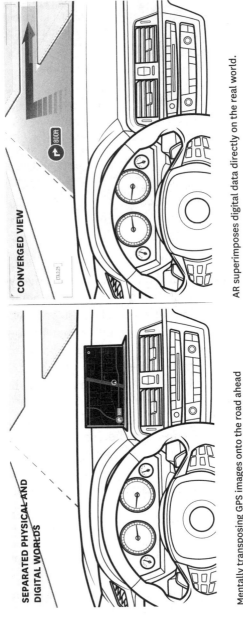

SEPARATED PHYSICAL AND DIGITAL WORLDS

Mentally transposing GPS images onto the road ahead is demanding and prone to errors.

CONVERGED VIEW

AR superimposes digital data directly on the real world.

Enhancing Human Decision Making

At its core, the power of augmented reality grows out of the way humans process information. We access information through each of our five senses—but at different rates. Vision provides us with the most information by far: An estimated 80% to 90% of the information humans get is accessed through vision.

The ability to absorb and process information is limited by our mental capacity. The demand on this capacity is referred to as "cognitive load." Each mental task we undertake reduces the capacity available for other, simultaneous tasks.

Cognitive load depends on the mental effort required to process a given type of information. For example, reading instructions from a computer screen and acting on them creates a greater cognitive load than hearing those same instructions, because the letters must be translated into words and the words interpreted. Cognitive load also depends on "cognitive distance," or the gap between the form in which information is presented and the context in which it is applied. Consider what happens when someone refers to a smartphone for directions while driving. The driver must consume the information from the screen, retain that information in working memory, translate the directions into the physical environment in front of him, and then act on those directions, all while operating the vehicle. There is significant cognitive distance between the digital information on the screen and the physical context in which information is applied. Dealing with this distance creates cognitive load.

The combination of the speed at which information is transmitted and absorbed and the cognitive distance involved in applying it lies at the root of the much-repeated phrase "A picture is worth a thousand words." When we look at the physical world, we absorb a huge amount and variety of information almost instantaneously. By the same token, an image or picture that superimposes information on the physical world, placing it in context for us, reduces cognitive distance and minimizes cognitive load.

This explains why AR is so powerful. There is no better graphical user interface than the physical world we see around us when it is enhanced by a digital overlay of relevant data and guidance where and when they are needed. AR eliminates dependence on out-of-context and hard-to-process 2-D information on pages and screens while greatly improving our ability to understand and apply information in the real world.

AR is making advances in consumer markets, but its emerging impact on human performance is even greater in industrial settings. Consider how Newport News Shipbuilding, which designs and builds U.S. Navy aircraft carriers, uses AR near the end of its manufacturing process to inspect a ship, marking for removal steel construction structures that are not part of the finished carrier. Historically, engineers had to constantly compare the actual ship with complex 2-D blueprints. But with AR, they can now see the final design superimposed on the ship, which reduces inspection time by 96%—from 36 hours to just 90 minutes. Overall, time savings of 25% or more are typical for manufacturing tasks using AR.

AR's Key Capabilities

As we've previously explained (see "How Smart, Connected Products Are Transforming Competition," HBR, November 2014), the SCPs spreading through our homes, workplaces, and factories allow users to monitor product operations and conditions in real time, control and customize product operations remotely, and optimize product performance using real-time data. And in some cases, intelligence and connectivity allow SCPs to be fully autonomous.

AR powerfully magnifies the value created by those capabilities. Specifically, it improves how users visualize and therefore access all the new monitoring data, how they receive and follow instructions and guidance on product operations, and even how they interact with and control the products themselves.

Visualize

AR applications provide a sort of X-ray vision, revealing internal features that would be difficult to see otherwise. At the medical device company AccuVein, for instance, AR technology converts the heat signature of a patient's veins into an image that is superimposed on the skin, making the veins easier for clinicians to locate. This dramatically improves the success rate of blood draws and other vascular procedures. AR more than triples the likelihood of a successful needle stick on the first try and reduces the need for "escalations" (calling for assistance, for example) by 45%.

Bosch Rexroth, a global provider of power units and controls used in manufacturing, uses an AR-enhanced visualization to demonstrate the design and capabilities of its smart, connected CytroPac hydraulic power unit. The AR application allows customers to see 3-D representations of the unit's internal pump and cooling options in multiple configurations and how subsystems fit together.

Instruct and guide

AR is already redefining instruction, training, and coaching. These critical functions, which improve workforce productivity, are inherently costly and labor-intensive and often deliver uneven results. Written instructions for assembly tasks, for instance, are frequently hard and time-consuming to follow. Standard instructional videos aren't interactive and can't adapt to individual learning needs. In-person training is expensive and requires students and teachers to meet at a common site, sometimes repeatedly. And if the equipment about which students are being taught isn't available, they may need extra training to transfer what they've learned to a real-world context.

AR addresses those issues by providing real-time, on-site, step-by-step visual guidance on tasks such as product assembly, machine operation, and warehouse picking. Complicated 2-D schematic representations of a procedure in a manual, for example, become interactive 3-D holograms that walk the user through the necessary processes. Little is left to the imagination or interpretation.

At Boeing, AR training has had a dramatic impact on the productivity and quality of complex aircraft manufacturing procedures. In one Boeing study, AR was used to guide trainees through the 50 steps required to assemble an aircraft wing section involving 30 parts. With the help of AR, trainees completed the work in 35% less time than trainees using traditional 2-D drawings and documentation. And the number of trainees with little or no experience who could perform the operation correctly the first time increased by 90%.

AR-enabled devices can also transmit what an on-site user is seeing to a remote expert, who can respond with immediate guidance. In effect, this instantly puts the expert at the user's side, regardless of location. This capability not only improves worker performance but substantially reduces costs—as Lee Company, which sells and services building systems, has discovered. It uses AR to help its field technicians with installations and repairs. A remote expert can see what the tech is viewing through his or her AR device, guide the tech through the work to be done, and even annotate the tech's view with instructions. Getting expert support from a central location in real time has increased Lee's tech utilization dramatically. And, by reducing the number of repeat visits, Lee saves more than $500 per technician per month in labor and travel costs. The company calculates a return of $20 on every dollar invested in AR.

Interact
Traditionally, people have used physical controls such as buttons, knobs, and, more recently, built-in touchscreens to interact with products. With the rise of SCPs, apps on mobile devices have increasingly replaced physical controls and allowed users to operate products remotely.

AR takes the user interface to a whole new level. A virtual control panel can be superimposed directly on the product and operated using an AR headset, hand gestures, and voice commands. Soon, users wearing smart glasses will be able to simply gaze at or point to a product to activate a virtual user interface and operate it. A worker wearing smart glasses, for instance, will be able to walk a line of factory machines, see their performance parameters, and adjust each machine without physically touching it.

The interact capability of AR is still nascent in commercial products but is revolutionary. Reality Editor, an AR app developed by the Fluid Interfaces group at MIT's Media Lab, provides a glimpse of how it is rapidly evolving. Reality Editor makes it easy to add an interactive AR experience to any SCP. With it, people can point a smartphone or a tablet at an SCP (or, eventually, look at it through smart glasses), "see" its digital interfaces and the capabilities that can be programmed, and link those capabilities to hand gestures or voice commands or even to another smart product. For example, Reality Editor can allow a user to see a smart light bulb's controls for color and intensity and set up voice commands like "bright" and "mood" to activate them. Or different settings of the bulb can be linked to buttons on a smart light switch the user can place anywhere that's convenient.

The technologies underpinning these capabilities are still emerging, but the accuracy of voice commands in noisy environments is improving, and advances in gesture and gaze tracking have been rapid. GE has already tested the use of voice commands in AR experiences that enable factory workers to perform complex wiring processes in wind turbines—and has achieved a 34% increase in productivity.

Combining AR and Virtual Reality

AR's well-known cousin, virtual reality, is a complementary but distinct technology. While AR superimposes digital information on the physical world, VR replaces physical reality with a computer-generated environment. Though VR is used mostly for entertainment applications, it can also replicate physical settings for training purposes. It is especially useful when the settings involved are hazardous or remote. Or, if the machinery required for training is not available, VR can immerse technicians in a virtual environment using holograms of the equipment. So when needed, VR adds a fourth capability—simulate—to AR's core capabilities of visualize, instruct, and interact.

AR will be far more widely applied in business than VR will. But in some circumstances, combining AR and VR will allow users to transcend distance (by simulating faraway locations), transcend time (by reproducing historical contexts or simulating possible future situations), and transcend scale (by allowing users to engage with environments that are either too small or too big to experience directly). What's more, bringing people together in shared virtual environments can enhance comprehension, teamwork, communication, and decision making.

Ford, for example, is using VR to create a virtual workshop where geographically dispersed engineers can collaborate in real time on holograms of vehicle prototypes. Participants can walk around and go inside these life-size 3-D holograms, working out how to refine design details such as the position of the steering wheel, the angle of the dashboard, and the location of instruments and controls without having to build an expensive physical prototype and get everyone to one location to examine it.

The U.S. Department of Homeland Security is going a step further by combining AR instructions with VR simulations to train personnel in responding to emergency situations such as explosions. This reduces costs and—in cases in which training in real environments would be dangerous—risk. The energy multinational BP overlays AR training procedures on VR simulations that replicate specific drilling conditions, like temperature, pressure, topography, and ocean currents, and that instruct teams on operations and help them practice coordinated emergency responses to disasters without high costs or risk.

How AR Creates Value

AR creates business value in two broad ways: first, by becoming part of products themselves, and second, by improving performance across the value chain—in product development, manufacturing, marketing, service, and numerous other areas.

AR as a product feature

The capabilities of AR play into the growing design focus on creating better user interfaces and ergonomics. The way products convey important operational and safety information to users has increasingly become a point of differentiation (consider how mobile apps have supplemented or replaced embedded screens in products like Sonos audio players). AR is poised to rapidly improve such interfaces.

Dedicated AR heads-up displays, which have only recently been incorporated into automobiles, have been a key feature in elite military products, such as fighter jets, for years and have been adopted in commercial aircraft as well. These types of displays are too expensive and bulky to integrate into most products, but wearables such as smart glasses are a breakthrough interface with wide-ranging implications for all manufacturers. With smart glasses, a user can see an AR display on any product enabled to communicate with them.

If you view a kitchen oven through smart glasses, for example, you might see a virtual display that shows the baking temperature, the minutes remaining on the timer, and the recipe you are following. If you approach your car, an AR display might show you that it is locked, that the fuel tank is nearly full, and that the left-rear tire's pressure is low.

Because an AR user interface is purely software based and delivered via the cloud, it can be personalized and can continually evolve. The incremental cost of providing such an interface is low, and manufacturers also stand to save considerable amounts when traditional buttons, switches, and dials are removed. Every product manufacturer needs to carefully consider the disruptive impact that this next-generation interface may have on its offering and competitive positioning.

AR and the value chain

The effects of AR can already be seen across the value chain, but they are more advanced in some areas than in others. In general, visualize and instruct/guide applications are now having the greatest impact on companies' operations, while the interact capability is still emerging and in pilot testing.

Product development. Though engineers have been using computer-aided design (CAD) capabilities to create 3-D models for 30 years, they have been limited to interacting with those models through 2-D windows on their computer screens, which makes it harder for them to fully conceptualize designs. AR allows 3-D models to be superimposed on the physical world as holograms, enhancing engineers' ability to evaluate and improve designs. For example, a life-size 3-D hologram of a construction machine can be positioned on the ground, and engineers can walk around it, peer under and over it, and even go inside it to fully appreciate the sight lines and ergonomics of its design at full scale in its intended setting.

AR also lets engineers superimpose CAD models on physical prototypes to compare how well they match. Volkswagen is using this technique—which makes any difference between the latest design and the prototype visually obvious—to check alignment in digital design reviews. This improves the accuracy of the quality assurance process, in which engineers previously had to painstakingly compare 2-D drawings with prototypes, and makes it five to 10 times faster.

We expect that in the near future AR-enabled devices such as phones and smart glasses, with their embedded cameras, accelerometers, GPS, and other sensors, will increasingly inform product design by exposing when, where, and how users actually interact with the product—how often a certain repair sequence is initiated, for example. In this way the AR interface will become an important source of data.

Manufacturing. In manufacturing, processes are often complex, requiring hundreds or even thousands of steps, and mistakes are costly. As we've learned, AR can deliver just the right information the moment it's needed to factory workers on assembly lines, reducing errors, enhancing efficiency, and improving productivity.

In factories, AR can also capture information from automation and control systems, secondary sensors, and asset management systems and make visible important monitoring and diagnostic data about each machine or process. Seeing information such as efficiency and defect rates in context helps maintenance technicians understand problems and prompts factory workers to do proactive maintenance that may prevent costly downtime.

Iconics, which specializes in automation software for factories and buildings, has begun to integrate AR into its products' user interfaces. By attaching relevant information to the physical location where it will be best observed and understood, the AR interfaces enable more-efficient monitoring of machines and processes.

Logistics. Warehouse operations are estimated to account for about 20% of all logistics costs, while picking items from shelves represents up to 65% of warehouse costs. In most warehouses, workers still perform this task by consulting a paper list of things to collect and then searching for them. This method is slow and error-prone.

The logistics giant DHL and a growing number of other companies are using AR to enhance the efficiency and accuracy of the picking process. AR instructions direct workers to the location of each product to be pulled and then suggest the best route to the next product. At DHL this approach has led to fewer errors, more-engaged workers, and productivity gains of 25%. The company is now rolling out AR-guided picking globally and testing how AR can enhance other types of warehouse operations, such as optimizing the position of goods and machines in layouts. Intel is also using AR in warehouses and has achieved a 29% reduction in picking time, with error rates falling to near zero. And the AR application is allowing new Intel workers to immediately achieve picking speeds 15% faster than those of workers who've had only traditional training.

Marketing and sales. AR is redefining the concept of showrooms and product demonstrations and transforming the customer experience. When customers can see virtually how products will look or function in a real setting before buying them, they have more-accurate expectations, more confidence about their purchase decisions, and greater product satisfaction. Down the road, AR may even reduce the need for brick-and-mortar stores and showrooms altogether.

When products can be configured with different features and options—which can make them difficult and costly to stock—AR is a particularly valuable marketing tool. The construction products company AZEK, for instance, uses AR to show contractors and consumers how its decking and paver products look in various colors and arrangements. Customers can also see the simulations in context: If you look at a house through a phone or a tablet, the AR app can add a deck onto it. The experience reduces any uncertainty customers might feel about their choices and shortens the sales cycle.

In e-commerce, AR applications are allowing online shoppers to download holograms of products. Wayfair and IKEA both offer libraries with thousands of 3-D product images and apps that integrate them into a view of an actual room, enabling customers to see how furniture and decor will look in their homes. IKEA also uses its app to collect important data about product preferences in different regions.

After-sales service. This is a function where AR shows huge potential to unlock the value-creating capabilities of SCPs. AR assists technicians serving customers in the field in much the same way it helps workers in factories: by showing predictive analytics data generated by the product, visually guiding them through repairs in real time, and connecting them with remote experts who can help optimize procedures. For example, an AR dashboard might reveal to a field technician that a specific machine part will most likely fail within a month, allowing the tech to preempt a problem for the customer by replacing it now.

At KPN, a European telecommunications service provider, field engineers conducting remote or on-site repairs use AR smart glasses to see a product's service-history data, diagnostics, and location-based information dashboards. These AR displays help them make better decisions about how to resolve issues, producing an 11% reduction in overall costs for service teams, a 17% decrease in work-error rates, and higher repair quality.

Xerox used AR to connect field engineers with experts instead of providing service manuals and telephone support. First-time fix rates increased by 67%, and the engineers' efficiency jumped by 20%. Meanwhile, the average time it took to resolve problems dropped by two hours, so staffing needs fell. Now Xerox is using AR to connect remote technical experts directly with customers. This has increased by 76% the rate at which technical problems are resolved by customers without any on-site help, cutting travel costs for Xerox and minimizing downtime for customers. Perhaps not surprisingly, Xerox has seen its customer satisfaction rates rise to 95%.

Human resources. Early AR adopters like DHL, the U.S. Navy, and Boeing have already discovered the power of delivering step-by-step visual worker training on demand through AR. AR allows instruction to be tailored to a particular worker's experience or to reflect the prevalence of particular errors. For example, if someone repeatedly makes the same kind of mistake, he can be required to use AR support until his work quality improves. At some companies, AR has reduced the training time for new employees in certain kinds of work to nearly zero and lowered the skill requirements for new hires.

This is especially advantageous for the package delivery company DHL, which faces surges in demand during peak seasons and is heavily dependent on the effective hiring and training of temporary workers. By providing real-time training and hands-on guidance on navigating warehouses and properly packing and sorting materials, AR has reduced DHL's need for traditional instructors and increased the onboarding speed for new employees.

AR and Strategy

AR will have a widespread impact on how companies compete. As we've explained in our previous HBR articles, SCPs are changing the structure of almost all industries as well as the nature of competition within them—often expanding industry boundaries in the process. SCPs give rise to new strategic choices for manufacturers, ranging from what functionality to pursue and how to manage data rights and security, to whether to expand a company's scope of products and compete in smart systems.

The increasing penetration of AR, along with its power as the human interface with SCP technologies, raises some new strategic questions. While the answers will reflect each company's business and unique circumstances, AR will become more and more integral to every firm's strategy.

Here are the essential questions companies face:

1. **What is the range of AR opportunities in the industry, and in what sequence should they be pursued?** Companies must weigh AR's potential impact on customers, product capabilities, and the value chain.

2. **How will AR reinforce a company's product differentiation?** AR opens up multiple differentiation paths. It can create companion experiences that expand the capabilities of products, give customers more information, and increase product loyalty. AR interfaces that enhance products' functionality or ease of use can be big differentiators, as can those that substantially improve product support, service,

and uptime. And AR's capacity to provide new kinds of feedback on how customers use products can help companies uncover further opportunities for product differentiation.

The right differentiation path will depend on a company's existing strategy; what competitors are doing; and the pace of technology advances, especially in hardware.

3. Where will AR have the greatest impact on cost reduction? AR enables new efficiencies that every firm must explore. As we've noted, it can significantly lower the cost of training, service, assembly, design, and other parts of the value chain. It can also substantially cut manufacturing costs by reducing the need for physical interfaces.

Each company will need to prioritize AR-driven cost-reduction efforts in a way that's consistent with its strategic positioning. Firms with sophisticated products will need to capitalize on AR's superior and low-cost interface, while many commodity producers will focus on operational efficiencies across the value chain. In consumer industries and retail, marketing-related visualize applications are the most likely starting point. In manufacturing, instruct applications are achieving the most immediate payoff by addressing inefficiencies in engineering, production, and service. And AR's interact capability, though still emerging, will be important across all industries with products that have customization and complex control capabilities.

4. Should the company make AR design and deployment a core strength, or will outsourcing or partnering be sufficient? Many firms are scrambling to access the digital talent needed for AR development, which is in short supply. One skill in great demand is user experience or user interface (UX/UI) design. It's critical to present 3-D digital information in ways that make it easy to absorb and act on; companies want to avoid making a stunning but unhelpful AR experience that defeats its core purpose. Effective AR experiences also require the right content, so people who know how to create and manage it—another novel skill—are crucial too. Digital modeling capabilities and knowledge of how to apply them in AR applications are key as well.

Over time we expect companies to create teams dedicated to AR, just as they set up such teams to build and run websites in the 1990s and 2000s. Dedicated teams will be needed to establish the infrastructure that will allow this new medium to flourish and to develop and maintain the AR content. Many firms have started to build AR skills in-house, but few have mastered them yet.

Whether to hire and train AR employees or partner with specialty software and services companies is an open question for many. Some companies have no choice but to treat AR talent as a strategic asset and invest in acquiring and developing it, given AR's potentially large impact on competition in their business. However, if AR is important but not essential to competitive advantage, firms can partner with specialty software and services companies to leverage outside talent and technology.

The challenges, time, and cost involved in building the full set of AR technologies we have described are significant, and specialization always emerges in each component. In the early stages of AR, the number of technology and service suppliers has been limited, and companies have built internal capabilities. However, best-of-breed AR vendors with turnkey solutions are starting to appear, and it will become increasingly difficult for in-house efforts to keep up with them.

5. How will AR change communications with stakeholders? AR complements existing print and 2-D digital communication approaches and in some cases can replace them altogether. Yet we see AR as much more than just another communication channel. It is a fundamentally new means of engaging with people. Just consider the novel way it helps people absorb and act on information and instructions.

The web, which began as a way to share technical reports, ultimately transformed business, education, and social interaction. We expect that AR will do the same thing for communication—changing it in ways far beyond what we can envision today. Companies will need to think creatively about how they can use this nascent channel.

Deploying AR

AR applications are already being piloted and deployed in products and across the value chain, and their number and breadth will only grow.

Every company needs an implementation road map that lays out how the organization will start to capture the benefits of AR in its business while building the capabilities needed to expand its use. When determining the sequence and pace of adoption, companies must consider both the technical challenges and the organizational skills involved, which vary from context to context. Specifically, organizations need to address five key questions:

1. Which development capabilities will be required? Some AR experiences involve more complexity than others. Experiences that allow people to visualize products in different configurations or settings—like those created by IKEA, Wayfair, and AZEK—are a relatively easy place for companies to start. Consumers just need to be encouraged to download and launch AR apps, and only a mobile device is needed to use them.

Instruction applications, like the ones Boeing and GE employ in manufacturing, are more difficult to build and use. They require the capacity to develop and maintain dynamic 3-D digital content and often benefit greatly from the use of head-mounted displays or smart glasses, which are still in the early stages of development.

Apps that produce interactive experiences, which create significant value for both consumers and businesses, are the most challenging to develop. They also involve less-mature technology, such as voice or gesture recognition, and the need to integrate with software that controls SCPs. Most companies will start with static visualizations of 3-D models, but they should build the capability to move quickly into dynamic instructional experiences that have greater strategic impact.

2. How should organizations create digital content? Every AR experience, from the least to the most sophisticated, requires content. In some cases it's possible to repurpose existing digital content, such as product designs. Over time, however, more-complex, dynamic contextual experiences must be built from scratch, which requires specialized expertise.

Simple applications, such as an AR-enhanced furniture catalog, may need only basic product representations. More-sophisticated business instruction applications, however, such as those used for machine repair, will require accurate and highly detailed digital product representations. Companies can create these by adapting CAD models used in product development or by using digitization techniques such as 3-D scanning. The most sophisticated AR experiences also need to tap real-time data streams from enterprise business systems, SCPs, or external data sources and integrate them into the content. To prepare for broadening the AR portfolio, companies should take an inventory of existing 3-D digital assets in CAD and elsewhere and invest in digital modeling capabilities.

3. How will AR applications recognize the physical environment? To accurately superimpose digital information on the physical world, AR technologies must recognize what they're looking at. The simplest approach is to determine the location of the AR device using, say, GPS and show relevant information for that location without anchoring it to a specific object. This is known as an "unregistered" AR experience. Vehicle heads-up navigation displays typically work this way.

Higher-value "registered" experiences anchor information to specific objects. They can do this through markers, such as bar codes, logos, or labels, which are placed on the objects and scanned by the user with an AR device. A more powerful approach, however, uses technology that recognizes objects by comparing their shape to a catalog of 3-D models. This allows a maintenance technician, for example, to instantly recognize and interact with any type of equipment he or she is responsible for maintaining and to do so from any angle. While markers are a good starting point, shape-recognition technologies are advancing quickly, and organizations will need the capability to use them to tap into many of the highest-value AR applications.

4. What AR hardware is required? AR experiences aimed at broad consumer audiences have typically been designed for smartphones, taking advantage of their simplicity and ubiquity. For more-sophisticated experiences, companies use tablets, which offer larger screens, better graphics, and greater processing power. Since tablet penetration is lower, companies will often provide them to users. For certain high-value applications—notably those in aircraft and automobiles—manufacturers are building dedicated AR heads-up displays into their products—a costly approach.

Eventually, however, most AR applications for service, manufacturing, and even product interfaces will require head-mounted displays that free users' hands. This technology is currently both immature and expensive, but we expect that affordable smart glasses will become widely available in the next few years and will play a major part in releasing AR's full power. Microsoft, Google, and Apple now offer AR technologies optimized for their own devices. However, most organizations should take a cross-platform approach that allows AR experiences to be deployed across multiple brands of phones and tablets and should make sure they're ready for smart glasses when they arrive.

5. Should you use a software-development or a content-publishing model? Many early AR experiences have been delivered through stand-alone software applications that are downloaded, complete with digital content, to a phone or a tablet. This approach creates reliable, high-resolution experiences and allows organizations to make apps that don't require internet connectivity. The problem with this model is that any change to the AR experience requires software developers to rewrite the app, which can create expensive bottlenecks.

An emerging alternative uses commercial AR-publishing software to create AR content and host it in the cloud. The AR experience can then be downloaded on demand using a general-purpose app running on an AR device. Like website content, the AR content can be updated or supplemented without changing the software itself—an important benefit when large amounts of information and frequent content changes are involved. The content-publishing model will become common as more and more machines and products include real-time AR interaction and control. A content-publishing capability is essential to scaling AR up across the organization.

The Broader Impact

The digital revolution, with its SCPs and explosion of data, is unleashing productivity and unlocking value across the economy. Increasingly, the constraint is not a lack of data and knowledge but how to assimilate and act on them—in other words, the interface with humans. AR is emerging as a leading solution to this challenge.

At the same time, the rapid evolution of machine learning and automation is raising serious concerns about human opportunity. Will there be enough jobs for everyone, especially for people without advanced education and knowledge? In a world of artificial intelligence and robots, will humans become obsolete?

It is easy to conclude that new technology diminishes human opportunity. Yet new inventions have been replacing human labor for centuries, and they have led to growth in employment, not a decline. Technology has dramatically increased our productivity and our standard of living. It has given rise to new kinds of offerings that meet new needs and require new types of workers. Many of today's jobs involve products and services that did not even exist a hundred years ago. A lesson of history is that today's digital revolution will generate new waves of innovation and new kinds of work that we cannot yet imagine.

The role of humans in this future is misunderstood. People have unique strengths that machines and algorithms will not replicate anytime soon. We have sophisticated motor skills—well beyond what robots are capable of today—that allow us to do the subtle manipulation that's needed in, say, replacing a machine part or wiring a turbine. Even relatively less skilled work, such as drawing blood, pruning a garden, or repairing a flat tire, requires human dexterity and defies automation. Human cognition adapts instantaneously to novel situations; people easily adjust the way they interpret information, solve problems, exercise judgment, and take action to suit their circumstances. Humans have flexibility, imagination, intuition, and creative ability that for the foreseeable future are beyond the reach of any machine.

How Does Augmented Reality Work?

Augmented reality starts with a camera-equipped device—such as a smartphone, a tablet, or smart glasses—loaded with AR software. When a user points the device and looks at an object, the software recognizes it through computer vision technology, which analyzes the video stream.

The device then downloads information about the object from the cloud, in much the same way that a web browser loads a page via a URL. A fundamental difference is that the AR information is presented in a 3-D "experience" superimposed on the object rather than in a 2-D page on a screen. What the user sees, then, is part real and part digital.

AR can provide a view of the real-time data flowing from products and allow users to control them by touchscreen, voice, or gesture. For example, a user might touch a stop button on the digital graphic overlay within an AR experience—or simply say the word "stop"—to send a command via the cloud to a product. An operator using an AR headset to interact with an industrial robot might see superimposed data about the robot's performance and gain access to its controls.

As the user moves, the size and orientation of the AR display automatically adjust to the shifting context. New graphical or text information comes into view while other information passes out of view. In industrial settings, users in different roles, such as a machine operator and a maintenance technician, can look at the same object but be presented with different AR experiences that are tailored to their needs.

A 3-D digital model that resides in the cloud—the object's "digital twin"— serves as the bridge between the smart object and the AR. This model is created either by using computer-aided design, usually during product development, or by using technology that digitizes physical objects. The twin then collects information from the product, business systems, and external sources to reflect the product's current reality. It is the vehicle through which the AR software accurately places and scales up-to-date information on the object.

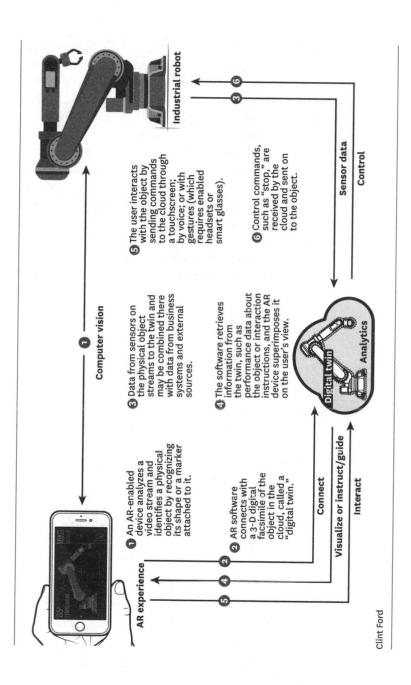

Industrial robot

Computer vision

1 An AR-enabled device analyzes a video stream and identifies a physical object by recognizing its shape or a marker attached to it.

3 Data from sensors on the physical object streams to the twin and may be combined there with data from business systems and external sources.

4 The software retrieves information from the twin, such as performance data about the object or interaction instructions, and the AR device superimposes it on the user's view.

5 The user interacts with the object by sending commands to the cloud through a touchscreen; by voice; or with gestures (which requires enabled headsets or smart glasses).

6 Control commands, such as "stop," are received by the cloud and sent on to the object.

Digital twin

Analytics

Sensor data

Control

AR experience

2 AR software connects with a 3-D digital facsimile of the object in the cloud, called a "digital twin."

Connect

Visualize or instruct/guide

Interact

Clint Ford

While the advances in artificial intelligence and robotics are impressive, we believe that combining the capabilities of machines with humans' distinctive strengths will lead to far greater productivity and more value creation than either could generate alone. What's needed to realize this opportunity is a powerful human interface that bridges the gap between the digital and physical worlds. We see AR as a historic innovation that provides this. It helps humans enhance their own capabilities by taking full advantage of new digital knowledge and machine capabilities. It will profoundly change training and skill development, allowing people to perform sophisticated work without protracted and expensive conventional instruction—a model that is inaccessible to so many today. AR, then, enables people to better tap into the digital revolution and all it has to offer.

Originally published in November–December 2017. Reprint R1706B

Thriving in the Gig Economy

by Gianpiero Petriglieri, Susan Ashford, and Amy Wrzesniewski

HAVE YOU EVER BEEN ON a trapeze?" That's how Martha, an independent consultant, responded when we asked her to describe her work in the five years since she'd left a global consulting firm to set out on her own. She had recently tried the art, which she saw as a good metaphor for her life: the void she felt when between assignments; the exhilaration of landing the next engagement; the discipline, concentration, and grace that mastering her profession required. Trapeze artists seem to take huge risks, she explained, but a safety system—including nets, equipment, and fellow performers—supports them: "They appear to be on their own, but they're not."

Martha (whose name, like others in this article, has been changed) is part of a burgeoning segment of the workforce loosely known as the gig economy. Approximately 150 million workers in North America and Western Europe have left the relatively stable confines of organizational life—sometimes by choice, sometimes not—to work as independent contractors. Some of this growth reflects the emergence of ride-hailing and task-oriented service platforms, but a recent report by McKinsey found that knowledge-intensive industries and creative occupations are the largest and fastest-growing segments of the freelance economy.

To learn what it takes to be successful in independent work, we recently completed an in-depth study of 65 gig workers. We found remarkably similar sentiments across generations and occupations: All those we studied acknowledged that they felt a host of personal, social, and economic anxieties without the cover and support of a traditional employer—but they also claimed that their independence was a choice and that they would not give up the benefits that came with it. Although they worried about unpredictable schedules and finances, they also felt they had mustered more courage and were leading richer lives than their corporate counterparts.

We discovered that the most effective independent workers navigate this tension with common strategies. They cultivate four types of connections—to *place, routines, purpose,* and *people*—that help them endure the emotional ups and downs of their work and gain energy and inspiration from their freedom. As the gig economy grows worldwide, these strategies are increasingly relevant. Indeed, we believe they may also be helpful to any corporate employees who are working more autonomously, from home or a remote office, or who feel they might one day want—or need—to jump into a freelance career.

Produce or Perish

The first thing we realized when we began interviewing independent consultants and artists was that the stakes of independent work are enormously high—not just financially but also existentially. Unshackled from managers and corporate norms, people can choose assignments that make the most of their talents and reflect their true interests. They feel ownership over what they produce and over their entire professional lives. One study participant told us, "I can be the most I've ever been myself in any job."

However, the price of such freedom is a precariousness that seems not to subside over time. Even the most successful, well-established people we interviewed still worry about money and reputation and sometimes feel that their identity is at stake. You can't keep calling yourself a consultant, for example, if clients stop asking for your services. A well-published writer told us, "You become your

Idea in Brief

Approximately 150 million people in North America and Western Europe now work as independent contractors, most of them in knowledge-intensive industries and creative occupations. The authors studied 65 of them in depth and learned that although they feel a host of personal, social, and economic anxieties without the cover and support of a traditional employer, they also say they chose independence and wouldn't give up the benefits that come with it.

Many of these workers have created a "holding environment" for themselves by establishing four connections: (1) place, in the form of idiosyncratic, dedicated workspaces that allow easy access to the tools of their owners' trades; (2) routines that streamline workflow and incorporate personal care; (3) purpose, to create a bridge between personal interests and motivations and a need in the world; and (4) people to whom they turn for reassurance and encouragement. These connections help independent workers sustain productivity, endure their anxieties, and even turn those feelings into sources of creativity and growth.

work. If you write a good book . . . it's really great, and when you don't achieve it, you have to accept . . . that failure might define who you are to yourself." An artist agreed: "There's no arriving. That's a myth."

For this reason, productivity is an intense preoccupation for everyone we interviewed. It provides self-expression and an antidote to precariousness. Interestingly, however, the people we talked with aren't just focusing on getting things done and sold. They care about both being *at work*—having the discipline to regularly generate products or services that find a market—and being *into their work:* having the courage to stay fully invested in the process and output of that labor.

Sustaining productivity is a constant struggle. Distress and distractions can erode it, and both impediments abound in people's working lives. One executive coach gave a poignant description of an unproductive day: "It's when there is so much to do that I'm disorganized and can't get my act together. [In the evening,] the same e-mails I opened in the morning are still open. The documents I wanted to get done are not done. I got distracted and feel like I wasted time." A day like that, he said, leaves him full of self-doubt.

When we asked interviewees the secret to getting through such days and ultimately sustaining productivity as they defined it, we discovered a paradox at the heart of their answers. They all want to preserve their independence and, in many cases, even their unsettledness (which one consultant described as the key to continued learning and "keeping my edge"), but they also spend a great deal of time developing a "holding environment"—a physical, social, and psychological space for their work.

This concept—first used by the British psychoanalyst Donald Winnicott to describe how attentive caregivers facilitate children's development by buffering them against distress and creating room for experimentation—has since been employed in the field of adult development to refer to conditions in which people can be their best and grow. Corporate employees, of course, can find them with a good boss in a solid organization. But for independent workers, a holding environment is less a gift than an accomplishment; it must be cultivated, and it can be lost.

So they create these environments for themselves by establishing and maintaining what we call "liberating connections"—because they both *free* people up to be individually creative and *bind* them to work so that their output doesn't wane.

The Four Connections

Place

Disconnected from a corporate office, the people we interviewed find places to work that protect them from outside distractions and pressures and help them avoid feeling rootless. Though many claimed their work was portable, they all still seemed to have somewhere to retreat. One writer told us, "People fail because they don't create a space and time to do whatever it is they need to do."

We visited many of these spaces in person and noticed several similarities among them. They feel confined—almost uncomfortably so in the case of some artists. They are used consistently for all substantive work. They allow easy access to the tools of the owner's trade and to little else. And they're dedicated to work; people usually leave them once their daily tasks are done. One software engineer, whose home office has all these features, described it as a "fighter pilot cockpit," where everything he needs is within arm's reach. "Sometimes it's claustrophobic," he explained, but "when I'm there, the open space is in my mind."

Despite these commonalities, each workspace is also unique, with a location, furniture, supplies, and decorations that reflect the idiosyncrasy of its owner's work. These places are not just protective cocoons for the working self—they evoke it, too. Karla, an independent consultant who initially told us she could do work "wherever I show up and am doing something that has positive impact in the world," eventually admitted that her home office is where she goes to avoid distraction and find inspiration, literally surrounded by her current and potential projects, arranged in visible and accessible piles. "When I walk through that door, I step into a space that embraces all the different aspects of myself," she told us. "I feel at home in there." Without that place and the space it gives her, Karla explained, she would probably be too sensitive to external demands and thus less focused and free.

Routines

In organizations, routines are often associated with safety or boring bureaucracy. However, a growing body of research has shown that elite athletes, scientific geniuses, popular artists, and even everyday workers use routines to enhance focus and performance. The professionals we spoke with tend to rely on them in the same way.

Some routines improve people's workflow: keeping a schedule; following a to-do list; beginning the day with the most challenging work or with a client call; leaving a sentence incomplete in an unfinished manuscript to make an easy start the next day; sweeping the studio floor while reflecting on a new piece. Other routines, usually involving sleep, meditation, nutrition, or exercise, incorporate personal care into people's working lives. Both kinds often have a ritual element that enhances people's sense of order and control in uncertain circumstances.

One consultant we interviewed takes a bath every morning and visualizes what she wants to accomplish while she soaks. Another consultant, Matthew, who specializes in helping boards focus on innovation, keeps a strict daily schedule: "I'm up at 6:00 and there's exercise. I pack my wife's lunch. We pray. She's out the door around 8:00. I'm in my office by 8:30, and I do work where there's deeper thought required—design or writing—in the morning. That's when I'm at my best. Then in the afternoon I schedule phone calls, more of the business or financial things that need to be done." This discipline even extends to his wardrobe: "I always get dressed for the office. Most days in summer I wear shorts when I'm not on the road, but still I shower and shave as if I were going to a workplace separate from home."

That may sound rigid, but it helps Matthew pour himself into his work. He and other successful independent workers seem to follow the advice of the French novelist Gustave Flaubert: "Be regular and orderly in your life . . . so that you may be violent and original in your work."

Purpose

For most people in our study, striking out on their own initially involved doing whatever work would allow them to find a footing in the market. But they were adamant that succeeding means taking only work that clearly connects to a broader purpose. All could articulate why their work, or at least their best work—be it to empower women through film, expose harmful marketing practices, sustain the American folk music tradition, or help corporate leaders succeed with integrity— is more than a means of earning a living. Purpose creates a bridge between their personal interests and motivations and a need in the world. Matthew, for example, said that although at first he felt "a certain desperation around having clients and making an income," over time his view of success shifted "to one that is a lot about living a life of service to others and making the planet a better place."

An executive coach we interviewed told us that purpose keeps her steady, inspired, and inspiring. "A big distinction between successful independents and the ones who aren't or go back [to corporate jobs] is getting to that place of knowing what you're meant to do. That gives me resilience for the ups and downs. It gives me the strength to decline work that isn't in alignment. It gives me a quality of authenticity and confidence that clients are drawn to. It's helpful to building or maintaining the business and serving the people I am here to serve."

We found that purpose, like the other connections, both binds and frees people by orienting and elevating their work.

People

Humans are social creatures. Studies in corporate settings have long demonstrated how important other people are to our careers—as role models who show us who we might become, and as peers who help us progress by sharing our path. Researchers have also warned about a "loneliness epidemic" hitting the workplace, for which independent workers can certainly be at even greater risk.

But those we interviewed are keenly aware of the dangers of social isolation and strive to avoid it. Though many are ambivalent about formal peer groups, which they often see as insipid substitutes for collegiality, all reported having people they turn to for reassurance and encouragement. Sometimes these are direct role models or supportive collaborators; in other cases they're family members, friends, or contacts in similar fields, who can't always offer specific work advice but nevertheless help our study participants push through challenging times and embolden them to take the risks their work entails.

Matthew, for example, noted that reaching out to people in his inner circle helps calm his anxiety: "If I were just left on my own, I could sit here in the office and go down a rat hole. You're left to your own inner voice, and it spirals down into ruminating." Karla told us that she, too, regularly turns to a handful of peers with whom she's close. "All the work I do in the independent economy comes through these connections," she said. But their help goes well beyond referrals. "My ability to process, develop, and grow as a human being and understand who I am in the work I'm doing comes from the conversations that I have with these folks," she explained. "These people are how I know what I'm supposed to be doing."

Redefining Success

In popular management tales, career success usually comes with security and equanimity. For independent workers, however, both are ultimately elusive. And yet most of those we studied told us they feel successful.

Our conclusion is that people in the gig economy must pursue a different kind of success—one that comes from finding a balance between predictability and possibility, between viability (the promise of continued work) and vitality (feeling present, authentic, and alive in one's work). Those we interviewed do so by building holding environments around place, routines, purpose, and people, which help them sustain productivity, endure their anxieties, and even turn those feelings into sources of creativity and growth. "There's a sense of confidence that comes from a career as a self-employed person," one consultant told us. "You can feel that no matter how bad it gets, I can overcome this. I can change it. I can operate more from a place of choice as opposed to a place of need."

Many we spoke to believe they wouldn't be able to find the same mental space or strength in a traditional workplace. Martha, the consultant who compared herself to a trapeze artist, recalled that she became "much more successful professionally" and "much more comfortable in my identity personally" when a trusted counselor helped her reframe—and own—her struggle, rather than seek ways to evade it. "She helped me understand that I could think of myself, which I now do, as a pioneer. I don't fit in any categories that exist in organizations, and it's more effective for me to be independent." Seen this way, discomfort and uncertainty were not just tolerable but affirming—signs that she was just where she needed to be.

When we spoke, she portrayed employment as no longer an anchor she missed but a shackle she'd been fortunate enough to break. "I don't know that I would frame [my new life] as precariousness anymore," she concluded. "I would frame it as really living."

Originally published in March–April 2018. Reprint R1802M

Managing Our Hub Economy

by Marco Iansiti and Karim R. Lakhani

THE GLOBAL ECONOMY IS COALESCING around a few digital super-powers. We see unmistakable evidence that a winner-take-all world is emerging in which a small number of "hub firms"— including Alibaba, Alphabet/Google, Amazon, Apple, Baidu, Facebook, Microsoft, and Tencent—occupy central positions. While creating real value for users, these companies are also capturing a disproportionate and expanding share of the value, and that's shaping our collective economic future. The very same technologies that promised to democratize business are now threatening to make it more monopolistic.

Beyond dominating individual markets, hub firms create and control essential connections in the networks that pervade our economy. Google's Android and related technologies form "competitive bottlenecks"; that is, they own access to billions of mobile consumers that other product and service providers want to reach. Google can not only exact a toll on transactions but also influence the flow of information and the data collected. Amazon's and Alibaba's marketplaces also connect vast numbers of users with large numbers of retailers and manufacturers. Tencent's WeChat messaging platform aggregates a billion global users and provides a critical source of consumer access for businesses offering online banking, entertainment, transportation, and other services. The more users who join these networks, the more attractive (and even necessary) it becomes for enterprises to offer their products and services through them. By driving increasing returns to scale and controlling crucial competitive bottlenecks, these digital superpowers can become even mightier, extract disproportionate value, and tip the global competitive balance.

Hub firms don't compete in a traditional fashion—vying with existing products or services, perhaps with improved features or lower cost. Rather, they take the network-based assets that have already reached scale in one setting and then use them to enter another industry and "re-architect" its competitive structure—transforming it from product-driven to network-driven. They plug adjacent industries into the same competitive bottlenecks they already control.

For example, the Alibaba spin-off Ant Financial does not simply offer better payment services, a better credit card, or an improved investment management service; it builds on data from Alibaba's already vast user base to commoditize traditional financial services and reorganize a good chunk of the Chinese financial sector around the Ant Financial platform. The three-year-old service already has over half a billion users and plans to expand well beyond China. Similarly, Google's automotive strategy does not simply entail creating an improved car; it leverages technologies and data advantages (many already at scale from billions of mobile consumers and millions of advertisers) to change the structure of the auto industry itself. (Disclosure: Both of us work or have worked with some of the firms mentioned in this article.)

If current trends continue, the hub economy will spread across more industries, further concentrating data, value, and power in the hands of a small number of firms employing a tiny fraction of the workforce. Disparity in firm valuation and individual wealth already causes widespread resentment. Over time, we can expect consumers, regulators, and even social movements to take an increasingly hostile stand against this concentration of value and economic connectivity. In a painfully ironic turn, after creating unprecedented opportunity across the global economy, digitization—and the trends it has given rise to—could exacerbate already dangerous levels of income inequality, undermine the economy, and even lead to social instability.

Idea in Brief

The Situation

A few digital superpowers, or hub firms, are capturing a dispropor-tionate and growing share of the value being created in the global economy.

The Challenge

This trend threatens to exacer-bate already dangerous levels of income inequality, undermine the economy, and destabilize society.

The Answer

While there are ways for com-panies that depend on hubs to defend their positions, the hubs themselves will have to do more to share economic value and sustain stakeholders.

Can these trends be reversed? We believe not. The "hub econ-omy," as we will argue, is here to stay. But most companies will not become hubs, and they will need to respond astutely to the growing concentration of hub power. Digitizing operating capabil-ities will not be enough. Digital messaging platforms, for example, have already dealt a blow to telecom service providers; invest-ment advisors still face threats from online financial-services companies. To remain competitive, companies will need to use their assets and capabilities differently, transform their core busi-nesses, develop new revenue opportunities, and identify areas that can be defended from encroaching hub firms and others rush-ing in from previously disconnected economic sectors. Some com-panies have started on this path—Comcast, with its new Xfinity platform, is a notable example—but the majority, especially those in traditional sectors, still need to master the implications of network competition.

Most importantly, the very same hub firms that are transforming our economy must be part of the solution—and their leaders must step up. As Mark Zuckerberg articulated in his Harvard commence-ment address in May 2017, "we have a level of wealth inequality that hurts everyone." Business as usual is not a good option. Witness the public concern about the roles that Facebook and Twitter played in the recent U.S. presidential election, Google's challenges with global regulatory bodies, criticism of Uber's culture and operating policies, and complaints that Airbnb's rental practices are racially discriminatory and harmful to municipal housing stocks, rents, and pricing.

Thoughtful hub strategies will create effective ways to share economic value, manage collective risks, and sustain the networks and communities we all ultimately depend on. If carmakers, major retailers, or media companies continue to go out of business, massive economic and social dislocation will ensue. And with governments and public opinion increasingly attuned to this problem, hub strategies that foster a more stable economy and united society will drive differentiation among the hub firms themselves.

We are encouraged by Facebook's response to the public outcry over "fake news"—hiring thousands of dedicated employees, shutting down tens of thousands of phony accounts, working with news sources to identify untrue claims, and offering guides for spotting false information. Similarly, Google's YouTube division invests in engineering, artificial intelligence, and human resources and collaborates with NGOs to ensure that videos promoting political extremists and terrorists are taken down promptly.

A real opportunity exists for hub firms to truly lead our economy. This will require hubs to fully consider the long-term societal impact of their decisions and to prioritize their ethical responsibilities to the large economic ecosystems that increasingly revolve around them. At the same time, the rest of us—whether in established enterprises or start-ups, in institutions or communities—will need to serve as checks and balances, helping to shape the hub economy by providing critical, informed input and, as needed, pushback.

The Digital Domino Effect

The emergence of economic hubs is rooted in three principles of digitization and network theory. The first is Moore's law, which states that computer processing power will double approximately every two years. The implication is that performance improvements will continue driving the augmentation and replacement of human activity with digital tools. This affects any industry that has integrated computers into its operations—which pretty much covers the entire economy. And advances in machine learning and cloud computing have only reinforced this trend.

The second principle involves connectivity. Most computing devices today have built-in network connectivity that allows them to communicate with one another. Modern digital technology enables the sharing of information at near-zero marginal cost, and digital networks are spreading rapidly. Metcalfe's law states that a network's value increases with the number of nodes (connection points) or users—the dynamic we think of as network effects. This means that digital technology is enabling significant growth in value across our economy, particularly as open-network connections allow for the recombination of business offerings, such as the migration from payment tools to the broader financial services and insurance that we've seen at Ant Financial.

But while value is being created for everyone, value capture is getting more skewed and concentrated. This is because in networks, traffic begets more traffic, and as certain nodes become more heavily used, they attract additional attachments, which further increases their importance. This brings us to the third principle, a lesser-known dynamic originally posited by the physicist Albert-László Barabási: the notion that digital-network formation naturally leads to the emergence of positive feedback loops that create increasingly important, highly connected hubs. As digital networks carry more and more economic transactions, the economic power of network hubs, which connect consumers, firms, and even industries to one another, expands. Once a hub is highly connected (and enjoying increasing returns to scale) in one sector of the economy (such as mobile telecommunications), it will enjoy a crucial advantage as it begins to connect in a new sector (automobiles, for example). This can, in turn, drive more and more markets to tip, and the many players competing in traditionally separate industries get winnowed down to just a few hub firms that capture a growing share of the overall economic value created—a kind of digital domino effect.

This phenomenon isn't new. But in recent years, the high degree of digital connectivity has dramatically sped up the transformation. Just a few years ago, cell phone manufacturers competed head-to-head for industry leadership in a traditional product market without appreciable network effects. Competition led to innovation and differentiation, with a business model delivering healthy profitability at scale for a dozen or so major competitors. But with the introduction of iOS and Android, the industry began to tip away from its hardware centricity to network structures centered on these multisided platforms. The platforms connected smartphones to a large number of apps and services. Each new app makes the platform it sits on more valuable, creating a powerful network effect that in turn creates a more daunting barrier to entry for new players. Today Motorola, Nokia, BlackBerry, and Palm are out of the mobile phone business, and Google and Apple are extracting the lion's share of the sector's value. The value captured by the large majority of complementors—the app developers and third-party manufacturers—is generally modest at best.

The domino effect is now spreading to other sectors and picking up speed. Music has already tipped to Apple, Google, and Spotify. E-commerce is following a similar path: Alibaba and Amazon are gaining more share and moving into traditional brick-and-mortar strongholds like groceries (witness Amazon's acquisition of Whole Foods). We've already noted the growing power of WeChat in messaging and communications; along with Facebook and others, it's challenging traditional telecom service providers. On-premise computer and software offerings are losing ground to the cloud services provided by Amazon, Microsoft, Google, and Alibaba. In financial services, the big players are Ant, Paytm, Ingenico, and the independent start-up Wealthfront; in home entertainment, Amazon, Apple, Google, and Netflix dominate.

Where are powerful hub firms likely to emerge next? Health care, industrial products, and agriculture are three contenders. But let's examine how the digital domino effect could play out in another prime candidate, the automotive sector, which in the United States alone provides more than seven million jobs and generates close to a trillion dollars in yearly sales.

Re-architecting the Automotive Sector

As with many other products and services, cars are now connected to digital networks, essentially becoming rolling information and transaction nodes. This connectivity is reshaping the structure of the automotive industry. When cars were merely products, car sales were the main prize. But a new source of value is emerging: the connection to consumers in transit. Americans spend almost an hour, on average, getting to and from work every day, and commutes keep getting longer. Auto manufacturers, responding to consumer demand, have already given hub firms access to dashboard screens in many cars; drivers can use Apple or Google apps on the car's built-in display instead of on their smartphones. If consumers embrace self-driving vehicles, that one hour of consumer access could be worth hundreds of billions of dollars in the U.S. alone.

Which companies will capitalize on the vast commercial potential of a new hour of free time for the world's car commuters? Hub firms like Alphabet and Apple are first in line. They already have bottleneck assets like maps and advertising networks at scale, and both are ready to create super-relevant ads pinpointed to the car's passengers and location. One logical add-on feature for autonomous vehicles would be a "Drive there" button that appears when an ad pops up (as already happens on Google's Waze app); pressing it would order the car to head to the touted destination.

In a future when people are no longer behind the wheel, cars will become less about the driving experience and more about the apps and services offered by automobiles as they ferry passengers around. Apart from a minority of cars actually driven for fun, differentiation will lessen, and the vehicle itself might well become commoditized. That will threaten manufacturers' core business: The car features that buyers will care most about—software and networks—will be largely outside the automakers' control, and their price premiums will go down.

The transformation will also upend a range of connected sectors—including insurance, automotive repairs and maintenance, road construction, law enforcement, and infrastructure—as the digital dominos continue to fall. (See the exhibit "The connected-car ecosystem.")

The connected-car ecosystem

Three software platforms—Android Auto, Apple CarPlay, and, to a lesser extent, OpenCar—dominate the market for integrating smartphone functionality into vehicles. They constitute powerful bottleneck assets because they have scores of supply-chain partners (left) and they enable other stakeholders (right) to reach consumers. (Note: The companies, apps, and regulators listed are selected examples only.)

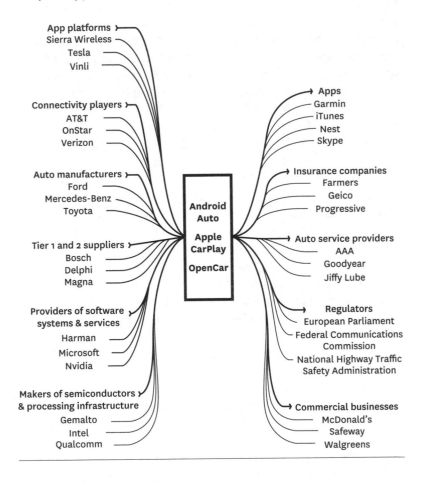

App platforms
Sierra Wireless
Tesla
Vinli

Connectivity players
AT&T
OnStar
Verizon

Auto manufacturers
Ford
Mercedes-Benz
Toyota

Tier 1 and 2 suppliers
Bosch
Delphi
Magna

Providers of software
systems & services
Harman
Microsoft
Nvidia

Makers of semiconductors
& processing infrastructure
Gemalto
Intel
Qualcomm

Android Auto
Apple CarPlay
OpenCar

Apps
Garmin
iTunes
Nest
Skype

Insurance companies
Farmers
Geico
Progressive

Auto service providers
AAA
Goodyear
Jiffy Lube

Regulators
European Parliament
Federal Communications
Commission
National Highway Traffic
Safety Administration

Commercial businesses
McDonald's
Safeway
Walgreens

For existing auto manufacturers, the picture is grim but not hopeless. Some companies are exploring a pay-per-use model for their cars and are acquiring, launching, or partnering with car-as-a-service providers. GM, for one, invested $500 million in the ride-sharing service Lyft, and its luxury-car division is now offering a monthly car subscription service. Daimler launched a car-sharing business called car2go. Several manufacturers have also invested in their own research into driverless vehicles or partnered with external providers.

Beyond these business-model experiments, automakers will need to play as the hubs do, by participating in the platform competition that will determine value capture in the sector. At least for the moment, alternatives to Google and Apple are scarce. One example is OpenCar, recently acquired by Inrix, a traditional auto supplier. Unlike Apple CarPlay and Google's Android Auto, which limit automaker-specific customization and require access to proprietary car data, the OpenCar framework is fully controlled by the car manufacturer. To take on the established giants, we believe that OpenCar and Inrix will have to develop an effective advertising or commerce platform or adopt some other indirect monetization strategy—and to do that, they'll probably need to partner with companies that have those capabilities.

To reach the scale required to be competitive, automotive companies that were once fierce rivals may need to join together. Here Technologies, which provides precision mapping data and location services, is an interesting example. Here has its roots in Navteq, one of the early online mapping companies, which was first bought by Nokia and later acquired by a consortium of Volkswagen, BMW, and Daimler (the multibillion-dollar price tag may have been too high for any single carmaker to stomach). Here provides third-party developers with sophisticated tools and APIs for creating location-based ads and other services. The company represents an attempt by auto manufacturers to assemble a "federated" platform and, in doing so, neutralize the threat of a potential competitive bottleneck controlled by Google and Apple. The consortium could play a significant role in preventing automotive value capture from tipping completely toward existing hub firms.

Of course, successful collaboration depends on a common, strongly felt commitment. So as traditional enterprises position themselves for a fight, they must understand how the competitive dynamics in their industries have shifted.

Increasing Returns to Scale Are Hard to Beat

Competitive advantage in many industries is moderated by *decreasing* returns to scale. In traditional product and service businesses, the value creation curve typically flattens out as the number of consumers increases, as we see in the exhibit "Profiting from a growing customer base." A firm gains no particular advantage as its user base continues to increase beyond already efficient levels, which enables multiple competitors to coexist.

Profiting from a growing customer base

For traditional product and service businesses, gaining additional customers does not continue adding commensurate value after a certain point. However, many platform businesses (Amazon, Facebook, and the like) become more and more valuable as more people and companies use them, connect with one another, and create network effects.

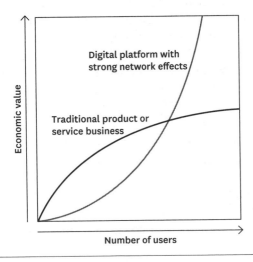

Some digital technologies, however, exhibit *increasing* returns to scale. A local advertising platform gets better and better as more and more users attract more and more ads. And as the number of ads increases, so does the ability to target the ads to the users, making individual ads more valuable. An advertising platform is thus similar to software platforms such as Windows, Linux, Android, and iOS, which exhibit increasing returns to scale—their growing value to consumers increases the number of available apps, while the value to app developers rises as the number of consumers rises. The more consumers, the greater the incentive for developers to build apps, and the more apps there are, the more motivated consumers are to use their digital devices.

These considerations are important to the nature of hub competition. The economics of traditional decreasing returns make it possible for several competitors to coexist and provide differentiated value to attract users. That's the dynamic in the auto industry today, with many car manufacturers competing with one another to offer a variety of differentiated products. But the increasing returns in digital assets like ad platforms (or possibly driverless-car technology) will heighten the advantage of the competitor with the largest scale, the largest network of users, or the most data. And this is where the hub firms will most likely leverage their large and growing lead—and cause value to concentrate around them.

In contrast with traditional product and service businesses, network-based markets exhibiting increasing returns to scale will, over time, tip toward a narrow set of players. This implies that if a conventional decreasing-returns business (say, telecom or media) is threatened by a new type of competitor whose business model experiences increasing returns, the conventional player is in for a rough ride. With increasing returns to scale, a digital technology can provide a bottleneck to an entire industrial sector. And left alone, competitive bottlenecks dramatically skew value capture away from traditional firms.

Pushing Back

Hub firms often compete against one another. Microsoft has made substantial investments in augmented reality in an effort to create a new hub and counterbalance the power that Google and Apple wield in the mobile space. Facebook acquired Oculus to force a similar structural shift in the emerging field of virtual reality. And a battle is looming in the smart-home arena, as Google, Apple, Microsoft, and Samsung attempt to reduce Amazon's early lead in voice-activated home technology.

But how does the rest of the economy deal with the increasing returns to scale of hub firms? With enough foresight and investment, traditional firms can resist by becoming hubs themselves, as we are seeing especially in the internet of things (IoT) space. GE is the classic example of this approach, with its investment in the Predix platform and the creation of GE Digital. [See the article "How I Remade GE," HBR, September–October 2017.] Other companies are following suit in different settings—for example, Verizon and Vodafone with their IoT platforms.

Firms can also shape competition by investing to ensure that there are multiple hubs in each sector—and even influencing which ones win. They can organize to support less-established platforms, thus making a particular hub more viable and an industry sector more competitive in the long term. Deutsche Telekom, for instance, is partnering with Microsoft Azure (rather than Amazon Web Services) for cloud computing in Central Europe.

Most importantly, the value generated by networks will change as firms compete, innovate, and respond to community and regulatory pressure. Multihoming—a practice enabling participants on one hub's ecosystem to easily join another—can significantly mitigate the rise of hub power. For example, drivers and passengers routinely multihome across different ride-sharing platforms, often checking prices on Uber, Lyft, and Fasten to see which is offering the best deal. Retailers are starting to multihome across payment systems, supporting multiple solutions (such as Apple Pay, Google Wallet, and Samsung Pay). If multihoming is common, the market is less likely to tip to a single player, preserving competition and diffusing value capture. Indeed, companies will need to make their products and services available on multiple hubs and encourage the formation of new hubs to avoid being held hostage by one dominant player. Take the wireless-speaker manufacturer Sonos: It has ensured that its music system seamlessly integrates with as many music services as possible, including Apple Music, Amazon Music Unlimited, Google Play Music, Pandora, Spotify, and Tidal.

Collective action can also restructure economic networks, shape value creation and capture, and ease competitive bottlenecks. In the 1990s the open-source community organized to compete against Microsoft Windows with the Linux operating system. That effort was actively supported by traditional players such as IBM and Hewlett-Packard and reinforced later by Google and Facebook. Today Linux (and Linux-related products) are firmly established in enterprises, consumer devices, and cloud computing. Similarly, the Mozilla open-source community and its Firefox browser broke Microsoft's grip on navigating the internet. Even Apple, notorious for its proprietary approach, relies on open-source software for its core operating systems and web services, and the infamous iPhone jailbreaking craze demonstrated both the extraordinary demand for third-party apps and the burgeoning supply of them.

Open source has grown beyond all expectations to create an increasingly essential legacy of common intellectual property, capabilities, and methodologies. Now collective action is going well beyond code sharing to include coordination on data aggregation, the use of common infrastructure, and the standardization of practices to further equilibrate the power of hubs. Efforts like OpenStreetMap are leading the way in maps, and Mozilla's Common Voice project is crowdsourcing global voice data to open up the speech-recognition bottleneck.

Collective action will be increasingly crucial to sustaining balance in the digital economy. As economic sectors coalesce into networks and as powerful hubs continue to form, other stakeholders will need to work together to ensure that hubs look after the interests of all network members. Cooperation will become more important for the rivals that orbit hubs; indeed, strategic joint action by companies that are not hubs may be the best competitive antidote to the rising power of hub firms.

The public is also raising concerns about privacy, online tracking, cybersecurity, and data aggregation. Solutions being suggested include requirements for social network and data portability similar to the requirements for phone number portability that telecommunications regulators instituted to increase competition among phone service providers.

The Ethics of Network Leadership

The responsibility for sustaining our (digital) economy rests partly with the same leaders who are poised to control it. By developing such central positions of power and influence, hub firms have become de facto stewards of the long-term health of our economy. Leaders of hub companies need to realize that their organizations are analogous to "keystone" species in biological ecosystems— playing a critical role in maintaining their surroundings. Apple, Alibaba, Alphabet/Google, Amazon, and others that benefit disproportionately from the ecosystems they dominate have rational and ethical reasons to support the economic vitality of not just their direct participants but also the broader industries they serve. In particular, we argue that hub companies need to incorporate value *sharing* into their business models, along with value creation and value capture.

Building and maintaining a healthy ecosystem is in the best interests of hub companies. Amazon and Alibaba claim millions of marketplace sellers, and they profit from every transaction those merchants make. Similarly, Google and Apple earn billions in revenue from the third-party apps that run on their platforms. Both companies already invest heavily in the developer community, providing programming frameworks, software tools, and opportunities and business models that enable developers to grow their businesses. But such efforts will need to be scaled up and refined as hub firms find themselves at the center of—and relying on—much larger and more-complex ecosystems. Preserving the strength and productivity of complementary communities should be a fundamental part of any hub firm's strategy.

Uber provides an interesting example of the repercussions of getting this wrong. Uber's viability depends on its relations with its drivers and riders, who have often criticized the company's practices. Under pressure from those communities—and from competitors that offer drivers the potential to earn more—Uber is making improvements. Still, its challenges suggest that no hub will maintain an advantage over the long term if it neglects the well-being of its ecosystem partners. Microsoft learned a hard lesson when it failed to maintain the health of its PC software ecosystem, losing out to the Linux community in cloud services.

But network ethics are not just about financial considerations; social concerns are equally important. Centralized platforms, such as Kiva for charitable impact investing and Airbnb for accommodation bookings, have been found to be susceptible to racial discrimination. In Airbnb's case, external researchers convincingly demonstrated that African-American guests were especially likely to have their reservation requests rejected. The pressure is now on Airbnb to fight bias both by educating its proprietors and by modifying certain platform features. Additionally, as Airbnb continues to grow, it must work to ensure that its hosts heed municipal regulations, lest they face a potentially devastating regulatory backlash.

Indeed, if hubs do not promote the health and sustainability of the many firms and individuals in their networks, other forces will undoubtedly step in. Governments and regulators will increasingly act to encourage competition, protect consumer welfare, and foster economic stability. Consider the challenges Google faces in Europe, where regulators are concerned about the dominance of both its search advertising business and its Android platform.

The centralizing forces of digitization are not going to slow down anytime soon. The emergence of powerful hub firms is well under way, and the threats to global economic well-being are unmistakable. All actors in the economy—but particularly the hub firms themselves—should work to sustain the entire ecosystem and observe new principles, for both strategic and ethical reasons. Otherwise, we are all in serious trouble.

Originally published in September–October 2017. Reprint R1705F

The Leader's Guide to Corporate Culture

by Boris Groysberg, Jeremiah Lee, Jesse Price, and J. Yo-Jud Cheng

STRATEGY AND CULTURE ARE AMONG the primary levers at top leaders' disposal in their never-ending quest to maintain organizational viability and effectiveness. Strategy offers a formal logic for the company's goals and orients people around them. Culture expresses goals through values and beliefs and guides activity through shared assumptions and group norms.

Strategy provides clarity and focus for collective action and decision making. It relies on plans and sets of choices to mobilize people and can often be enforced by both concrete rewards for achieving goals and consequences for failing to do so. Ideally, it also incorporates adaptive elements that can scan and analyze the external environment and sense when changes are required to maintain continuity and growth. Leadership goes hand-in-hand with strategy formation, and most leaders understand the fundamentals. Culture, however, is a more elusive lever, because much of it is anchored in unspoken behaviors, mindsets, and social patterns.

For better *and* worse, culture and leadership are inextricably linked. Founders and influential leaders often set new cultures in motion and imprint values and assumptions that persist for decades. Over time an organization's leaders can also shape culture, through both conscious and unconscious actions (sometimes with unintended consequences).

The best leaders we have observed are fully aware of the multiple cultures within which they are embedded, can sense when change is required, and can deftly influence the process.

Unfortunately, in our experience it is far more common for leaders seeking to build high-performing organizations to be confounded by culture. Indeed, many either let it go unmanaged or relegate it to the HR function, where it becomes a secondary concern for the business. They may lay out detailed, thoughtful plans for strategy and execution, but because they don't understand culture's power and dynamics, their plans go off the rails. As someone once said, culture eats strategy for breakfast.

It doesn't have to be that way. Our work suggests that culture can, in fact, be managed. The first and most important step leaders can take to maximize its value and minimize its risks is to become fully aware of how it works. By integrating findings from more than 100 of the most commonly used social and behavioral models, we have identified eight styles that distinguish a culture and can be measured. (We gratefully acknowledge the rich history of cultural studies—going all the way back to the earliest explorations of human nature—on which our work builds.) Using this framework, leaders can model the impact of culture on their business and assess its alignment with strategy. We also suggest how culture can help them achieve change and build organizations that thrive in even the most trying times.

Defining Culture

Culture is the tacit social order of an organization: It shapes attitudes and behaviors in wide-ranging and durable ways. Cultural norms define what is encouraged, discouraged, accepted, or rejected within a group. When properly aligned with personal values, drives, and needs, culture can unleash tremendous amounts of energy toward a shared purpose and foster an organization's capacity to thrive.

Culture can also evolve flexibly and autonomously in response to changing opportunities and demands. Whereas strategy is typically determined by the C-suite, culture can fluidly blend the

Idea in Brief

Executives are often confounded by culture, because much of it is anchored in unspoken behaviors, mindsets, and social patterns. Many leaders either let it go unmanaged or relegate it to HR, where it becomes a secondary concern for the business. This is a mistake, because properly managed, culture can help them achieve change and build organizations that will thrive in even the most trying times.

The authors have reviewed the literature on culture and distilled eight distinct culture styles: *caring*, focused on relationships and mutual trust; *purpose*, exemplified by idealism and altruism; *learning*, characterized by exploration, expansiveness, and creativity; *enjoyment*, expressed through fun and excitement; *results*, characterized by achievement and winning; *authority*, defined by strength, decisiveness, and boldness; *safety*, defined by planning, caution, and preparedness; and *order*, focused on respect, structure, and shared norms.

These eight styles fit into an "integrated culture framework"

according to the degree to which they reflect independence or interdependence (people interactions) and flexibility or stability (response to change). They can be used to diagnose and describe highly complex and diverse behavioral patterns in a culture and to model how likely an individual leader is to align with and shape that culture.

Through research and practical experience, the authors have arrived at five insights regarding culture's effect on companies' success: (1) When aligned with strategy and leadership, a strong culture drives positive organizational outcomes. (2) Selecting or developing leaders for the future requires a forward-looking strategy and culture. (3) In a merger, designing a new culture on the basis of complementary strengths can speed up integration and create more value over time. (4) In a dynamic, uncertain environment, in which organizations must be more agile, learning gains importance. (5) A strong culture can be a significant liability when it is misaligned with strategy.

intentions of top leaders with the knowledge and experiences of frontline employees.

The academic literature on the subject is vast. Our review of it revealed many formal definitions of organizational culture and a variety of models and methods for assessing it. Numerous processes exist for creating and changing it. Agreement on specifics is sparse across these definitions, models, and methods, but through a synthesis of seminal work by Edgar Schein, Shalom Schwartz, Geert Hofstede, and other leading scholars, we have identified four generally accepted attributes:

Shared

Culture is a group phenomenon. It cannot exist solely within a single person, nor is it simply the average of individual characteristics. It resides in shared behaviors, values, and assumptions and is most commonly experienced through the norms and expectations of a group—that is, the unwritten rules.

Pervasive

Culture permeates multiple levels and applies very broadly in an organization; sometimes it is even conflated with the organization itself. It is manifest in collective behaviors, physical environments, group rituals, visible symbols, stories, and legends. Other aspects of culture are unseen, such as mindsets, motivations, unspoken assumptions, and what David Rooke and William Torbert refer to as "action logics" (mental models of how to interpret and respond to the world around you).

Enduring

Culture can direct the thoughts and actions of group members over the long term. It develops through critical events in the collective life and learning of a group. Its endurance is explained in part by the attraction-selection-attrition model first introduced by Benjamin Schneider: People are drawn to organizations with characteristics similar to their own; organizations are more likely to select individuals who seem to "fit in"; and over time those who don't fit in tend to leave. Thus culture becomes a self-reinforcing social pattern that grows increasingly resistant to change and outside influences.

Implicit

An important and often overlooked aspect of culture is that despite its subliminal nature, people are effectively hardwired to recognize and respond to it instinctively. It acts as a kind of silent language.

Shalom Schwartz and E.O. Wilson have shown through their research how evolutionary processes shaped human capacity; because the ability to sense and respond to culture is universal, certain themes should be expected to recur across the many models, definitions, and studies in the field. That is exactly what we have discovered in our research over the past few decades.

Eight Distinct Culture Styles

Our review of the literature for commonalities and central concepts revealed two primary dimensions that apply regardless of organization type, size, industry, or geography: people interactions and response to change. Understanding a company's culture requires determining where it falls along these two dimensions.

People interactions

An organization's orientation toward people interactions and coordination will fall on a spectrum from highly independent to highly interdependent. Cultures that lean toward the former place greater value on autonomy, individual action, and competition. Those that lean toward the latter emphasize integration, managing relationships, and coordinating group effort. People in such cultures tend to collaborate and to see success through the lens of the group.

Response to change

Whereas some cultures emphasize stability—prioritizing consistency, predictability, and maintenance of the status quo—others emphasize flexibility, adaptability, and receptiveness to change. Those that favor stability tend to follow rules, use control structures such as seniority-based staffing, reinforce hierarchy, and strive for efficiency. Those that favor flexibility tend to prioritize innovation, openness, diversity, and a longer-term orientation. (Kim Cameron, Robert Quinn, and Robert Ernest are among the researchers who employ similar dimensions in their culture frameworks.)

By applying this fundamental insight about the dimensions of people interactions and response to change, we have identified eight styles that apply to both organizational cultures and individual leaders. Researchers at Spencer Stuart (including two of this article's authors) have interdependently studied and refined this list of styles across both levels over the past two decades.

Caring focuses on relationships and mutual trust. Work environments are warm, collaborative, and welcoming places where people help and support one another. Employees are united by loyalty; leaders emphasize sincerity, teamwork, and positive relationships.

Purpose is exemplified by idealism and altruism. Work environments are tolerant, compassionate places where people try to do good for the long-term future of the world. Employees are united by a focus on sustainability and global communities; leaders emphasize shared ideals and contributing to a greater cause.

Learning is characterized by exploration, expansiveness, and creativity. Work environments are inventive and open-minded places where people spark new ideas and explore alternatives. Employees are united by curiosity; leaders emphasize innovation, knowledge, and adventure.

Enjoyment is expressed through fun and excitement. Work environments are lighthearted places where people tend to do what makes them happy. Employees are united by playfulness and stimulation; leaders emphasize spontaneity and a sense of humor.

Results is characterized by achievement and winning. Work environments are outcome-oriented and merit-based places where people aspire to achieve top performance. Employees are united by a drive for capability and success; leaders emphasize goal accomplishment.

Authority is defined by strength, decisiveness, and boldness. Work environments are competitive places where people strive to gain personal advantage. Employees are united by strong control; leaders emphasize confidence and dominance.

Safety is defined by planning, caution, and preparedness. Work environments are predictable places where people are risk-conscious and think things through carefully. Employees are united by a desire to feel protected and anticipate change; leaders emphasize being realistic and planning ahead.

Order is focused on respect, structure, and shared norms. Work environments are methodical places where people tend to play by the rules and want to fit in. Employees are united by cooperation; leaders emphasize shared procedures and time-honored customs.

These eight styles fit into our integrated culture framework (see the exhibit "Integrated culture: The framework") according to the degree to which they reflect independence or interdependence (people interactions) and flexibility or stability (response to change). Styles that are adjacent in the framework, such as *safety* and *order,* frequently coexist within organizations and their people. In contrast, styles that are located across from each other, such as *safety* and *learning,* are less likely to be found together and require more organizational energy to maintain simultaneously. Each style has advantages and disadvantages, and no style is inherently better than another. An organizational culture can be defined by the absolute and relative strengths of each of the eight and by the degree of employee agreement about which styles characterize the organization. A powerful feature of this framework, which differentiates it from other models, is that it can also be used to define individuals' styles and the values of leaders and employees.

Inherent in the framework are fundamental trade-offs. Although each style can be beneficial, natural constraints and competing demands force difficult choices about which values to emphasize and how people are expected to behave. It is common to find organizations with cultures that emphasize both *results* and *caring,* but this combination can be confusing to employees. Are they expected to optimize individual goals and strive for outcomes at all costs, or should they work as a team and emphasize collaboration and shared success? The nature of the work itself, the business strategy, or the design of the organization may make it difficult for employees to be equally *results* focused and *caring.*

In contrast, a culture that emphasizes *caring* and *order* encourages a work environment in which teamwork, trust, and respect are paramount. The two styles are mutually reinforcing, which can be beneficial but can also present challenges. The benefits are strong loyalty, retention of talent, lack of conflict, and high levels of engagement.

Integrated culture: The framework

On the basis of decades of experience analyzing organizations, executives, and employees, we developed a rigorous, comprehensive model to identify the key attributes of both group culture and individual leadership styles. Eight charac-teristics emerge when we map cultures along two dimensions: how people inter-act (independence to interdependence) and their response to change (flexibility to stability). The relative salience of these eight styles differs across organiza-tions, though nearly all are strongly characterized by results *and* caring.

The spatial relationships are important. Proximate styles, such as safety *and* order, *or* learning *and* enjoyment, *will coexist more easily than styles that are far apart on the chart, such as* authority *and* purpose, *or* safety *and* learning. *Achieving a culture of* authority *often means gaining the advantages (and living with the disadvantages) of that culture but missing out on the advantages (and avoiding the disadvantages) of a culture of* purpose.

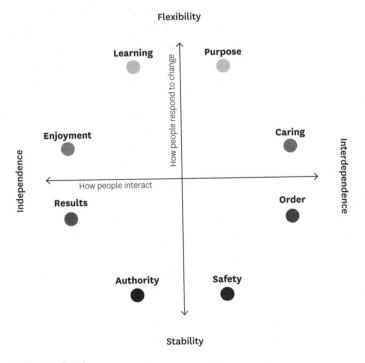

Source: Spencer Stuart.

Integrated culture: Leader statements

Top leaders and founders often express cultural sentiments within the public domain, either intentionally or unintentionally. Such statements can provide important clues to how these leaders are thinking about and leading their organizations' cultures.

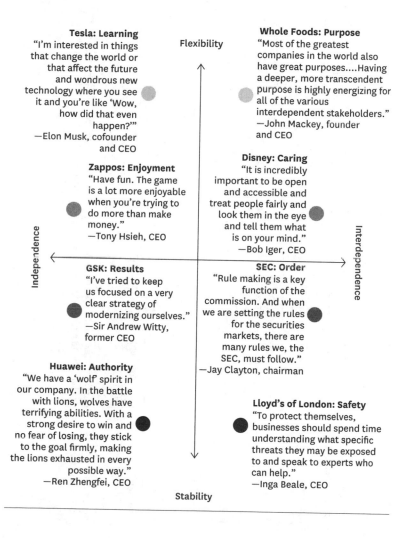

Tesla: Learning
"I'm interested in things that change the world or that affect the future and wondrous new technology where you see it and you're like 'Wow, how did that even happen?'"
—Elon Musk, cofounder and CEO

Flexibility

Whole Foods: Purpose
"Most of the greatest companies in the world also have great purposes....Having a deeper, more transcendent purpose is highly energizing for all of the various interdependent stakeholders."
—John Mackey, founder and CEO

Zappos: Enjoyment
"Have fun. The game is a lot more enjoyable when you're trying to do more than make money."
—Tony Hsieh, CEO

Disney: Caring
"It is incredibly important to be open and accessible and treat people fairly and look them in the eye and tell them what is on your mind."
—Bob Iger, CEO

Independence

Interdependence

GSK: Results
"I've tried to keep us focused on a very clear strategy of modernizing ourselves."
—Sir Andrew Witty, former CEO

SEC: Order
"Rule making is a key function of the commission. And when we are setting the rules for the securities markets, there are many rules we, the SEC, must follow."
—Jay Clayton, chairman

Huawei: Authority
"We have a 'wolf' spirit in our company. In the battle with lions, wolves have terrifying abilities. With a strong desire to win and no fear of losing, they stick to the goal firmly, making the lions exhausted in every possible way."
—Ren Zhengfei, CEO

Lloyd's of London: Safety
"To protect themselves, businesses should spend time understanding what specific threats they may be exposed to and speak to experts who can help."
—Inga Beale, CEO

Stability

The pros and cons of culture styles

Every culture style has strengths and weaknesses. The table below summarizes the advantages and disadvantages of each style and how frequently it appears as a defining culture characteristic among the companies in our study.

Culture style	Advantages	Disadvantages	Ranked 1st or 2nd
Caring Warm, sincere, relational	Improved teamwork, engagement, communication, trust, and sense of belonging	Overemphasis on consensus building may reduce exploration of options, stifle competitiveness, and slow decision making	63%
Purpose Purpose driven, idealistic, tolerant	Improved appreciation for diversity, sustainability, and social responsibility	Overemphasis on a long-term purpose and ideals may get in the way of practical and immediate concerns	9%
Learning Open, inventive, exploring	Improved innovation, agility, and organizational learning	Overemphasis on exploration may lead to a lack of focus and an inability to exploit existing advantages	7%
Enjoyment Playful, instinctive, fun loving	Improved employee morale, engagement, and creativity	Overemphasis on autonomy and engagement may lead to a lack of discipline and create possible compliance or governance issues	2%
Results Achievement driven, goal focused	Improved execution, external focus, capability building, and goal achievement	Overemphasis on achieving results may lead to communication and collaboration breakdowns and higher levels of stress and anxiety	89%

Authority Bold, decisive, dominant	Improved speed of decision making and responsiveness to threats or crises	Overemphasis on strong authority and bold decision making may lead to politics, conflict, and a psychologically unsafe work environment	4%
Safety Realistic, careful, prepared	Improved risk management, stability, and business continuity	Overemphasis on standardization and formalization may lead to bureaucracy, inflexibility, and dehumanization of the work environment	8%
Order Rule abiding, respectful, cooperative	Improved operational efficiency, reduced conflict, and greater civic-mindedness	Overemphasis on rules and traditions may reduce individualism, stifle creativity, and limit organizational agility	15%

Note: Sum of percentages is greater than 100 because styles were counted as dominant if they were ranked 1 or 2 overall.

The challenges are a tendency toward groupthink, reliance on consensus-based decisions, avoidance of difficult issues, and a calcified sense of "us versus them." Leaders who are more focused on *results* and *learning* may find the combination of *caring* and *order* stifling when they seek to drive entrepreneurship and change. Savvy leaders make use of existing cultural strengths and have a nuanced understanding of how to initiate change. They might rely on the participative nature of a culture focused on *caring* and *order* to engage team members and simultaneously identify a *learning*-oriented "insider" who has the trust of his or her peers to advocate for change through relationship networks.

The eight styles can be used to diagnose and describe highly complex and diverse behavioral patterns in a culture and to model how likely an individual leader is to align with and shape that culture. Using this framework and multilevel approach, managers can:

- Understand their organization's culture and assess its intended and unintended effects

- Evaluate the level of consistency in employees' views of the culture

- Identify subcultures that may account for higher or lower group performance

- Pinpoint differences between legacy cultures during mergers and acquisitions

- Rapidly orient new executives to the culture they are joining and help them determine the most effective way to lead employees

- Measure the degree of alignment between individual leadership styles and organizational culture to determine what impact a leader might have

- Design an aspirational culture and communicate the changes necessary to achieve it

The Link Between Culture and Outcomes

Our research and practical experience have shown that when you are evaluating how culture affects outcomes, the context in which the organization operates—geographic region, industry, strategy, leadership, and company structure—matters, as does the strength of the culture. (See "Context, Conditions, and Culture," the sidebar at the end of this article.) What worked in the past may no longer work in the future, and what worked for one company may not work for another.

We have arrived at the following insights:

When aligned with strategy and leadership, a strong culture drives positive organizational outcomes

Consider the case of a best-in-class retailer headquartered in the United States. The company had viewed its first priority as providing top-notch customer service. It accomplished this with a simple rule—Do right by the customer—that encouraged employees to use their judgment when providing service. A core HR training practice was to help every salesperson see customer interactions as an opportunity to create "service stories that become legendary." Employees were reminded to define service from the customer's perspective, to constantly engage customers with questions geared toward understanding their specific needs and preferences, and to go beyond their expectations.

In measuring the culture of this company, we found that like many other large retailers, it was characterized primarily by a combination of *results* and *caring*. Unlike many other retailers, however, it had a culture that was also very flexible, *learning* oriented, and focused on *purpose*. As one top executive explained, "We have freedom as long as we take good care of the customer."

Furthermore, the company's values and norms were very clear to everyone and consistently shared throughout the organization. As the retailer expanded into new segments and geographies over the years, the leadership strove to maintain an intense customer focus without diluting its cherished culture. Although the company had historically focused on developing leaders from within—who were natural culture carriers—recruiting outsiders became necessary as it grew. The company preserved its culture through this change by carefully assessing new leaders and designing an onboarding process that reinforced core values and norms.

Culture is a powerful differentiator for this company because it is strongly aligned with strategy and leadership. Delivering outstanding customer service requires a culture and a mindset that emphasize achievement, impeccable service, and problem solving through autonomy and inventiveness. Not surprisingly, those qualities have led to a variety of positive outcomes for the company, including robust growth and international expansion, numerous customer service awards, and frequent appearances on lists of the best companies to work for.

Selecting or developing leaders for the future requires a forward-looking strategy and culture

The chief executive of an agriculture business was planning to retire, spurring rumors about a hostile takeover. The CEO was actively grooming a successor, an insider who had been with the company for more than 20 years. Our analysis revealed an organizational culture that strongly emphasized *caring* and *purpose*. As one leader reflected, "You feel like part of a large family when you become an employee at this company."

The potential successor understood the culture but was far more risk-averse (*safety*) and respectful of traditions (*order*) than the rest of the company. Given the takeover rumors, top leaders and managers told the CEO that they believed the company needed to take a more aggressive and action-oriented stance in the future. The board decided to consider the internal candidate alongside people from outside the company.

Three external candidates emerged: one who was aligned with the current culture (*purpose*), one who would be a risk taker and innovative (*learning*), and one who was hard-driving and competitive (*authority*). After considerable deliberation, the board chose the highly competitive leader with the *authority* style. Soon afterward an activist investor attempted a hostile takeover, and the new CEO was able to navigate through the precarious situation, keep the company independent, and simultaneously begin to restructure in preparation for growth.

In a merger, designing a new culture on the basis of complementary strengths can speed up integration and create more value over time

Mergers and acquisitions can either create or destroy value. Numerous studies have shown that cultural dynamics represent one of the greatest yet most frequently overlooked determinants of integration success and postmerger performance.

For example, senior leaders from two merging international food retailers had invested heavily in their organizations' cultures and wanted to preserve their unique strengths and distinct heritages. An assessment of the cultures revealed shared values and areas of compatibility that could provide a foundation for the combined culture, along with important differences for which leaders would have to plan: Both companies emphasized *results, caring,* and *order* and valued high-quality food, good service, treating employees fairly, and maintaining a local mindset. But one operated in a more top-down manner and scored much higher on *authority,* especially in the behavior of leaders.

Because both companies valued teamwork and investments in the local community, the leaders prioritized *caring* and *purpose.* At the same time, their strategy required that they shift from top-down *authority* to a *learning* style that would encourage innovation in new-store formats and online retailing. As one senior leader said of the strategic aspiration, "We need to dare to do things differently, not play by the old rule books."

Once they had agreed on a culture, a rigorous assessment process identified leaders at both organizations whose personal style and values would allow them to serve as bridges to and champions for it. Then a program was launched to promote cultural alignment within 30 top teams, with an emphasis on clarifying priorities, making authentic connections, and developing team norms that would bring the new culture to life.

Finally, structural elements of the new organization were redesigned with culture in mind. A model for leadership was developed that encompassed recruitment, talent assessment, training and development, performance management, reward systems, and promotions. Such design considerations are often overlooked during organizational change, but if systems and structures don't align with cultural and leadership imperatives, progress can be derailed.

In a dynamic, uncertain environment, in which organizations must be more agile, *learning* gains importance

It's not surprising that *results* is the most common culture style among all the companies we have studied. Yet during a decade of helping leaders design aspirational cultures, we have seen a clear trend toward prioritizing *learning* to promote innovation and agility as businesses respond to increasingly less predictable and more complex environments. And although *learning* ranks fourth within our broader database, small companies (200 employees or fewer) and those in newer industries (such as software, technology, and wireless equipment) accord it higher values.

Consider one Silicon Valley–based technology company we worked with. Though it had built a strong business and invested in unique technology and top engineering talent, its revenue growth was starting to decline as newer, nimbler competitors made strides in a field exploding with innovation and business model disruption. Company leaders viewed the culture as a differentiator for the business and decided to diagnose, strengthen, and evolve it. We found a culture that was intensely *results* focused, team based (*caring*), and exploratory (a combination of *enjoyment* and *learning*).

After examining the overall business strategy and gaining input from employees, leaders aimed for a culture that was even more focused on *learning* and adopted our framework as a new language for the organization in its daily work. They initiated conversations between managers and employees about how to emphasize innovation and exploration. Although it takes time to change a culture, we found that the company had made notable progress just one year later. And even as it prepared for an impending sale amid ever greater competition and consolidation, employee engagement scores were on the rise.

A strong culture can be a significant liability when it is misaligned with strategy

We studied a Europe-based industrial services organization whose industry began to experience rapid and unprecedented changes in customer expectations, regulatory demands, and competitive dynamics. The company's strategy, which had historically emphasized cost leadership, needed to shift toward greater service differentiation in response. But its strong culture presented a roadblock to success.

We diagnosed the culture as highly *results* oriented, *caring,* and *order* seeking, with a top-down emphasis on *authority.* The company's leaders decided to shape it to be much more *purpose*-driven, enabling, open, and team based, which would entail an increase in *caring* along with *learning* and *purpose* and a decrease in *authority* and *results.*

This shift was particularly challenging because the current culture had served the organization well for many years, while the industry emphasized efficiency and *results.* Most managers still viewed it as a strength and fought to preserve it, threatening success for the new strategic direction.

Cultural change is daunting for any organization, but as this company realized, it's not impossible. The CEO introduced new leadership development and team coaching programs and training opportunities that would help leaders feel more comfortable with cultural evolution. When people departed, the company carefully selected new leaders who would provide supporting values, such as *caring,* and increased the emphasis on a shared *purpose.* The benefits of this strategic and cultural shift took the form of an increasingly diverse array of integrated service offerings and strong growth, particularly in emerging markets.

Four Levers for Evolving a Culture

Unlike developing and executing a business plan, changing a company's culture is inextricable from the emotional and social dynamics of people in the organization. We have found that four practices in particular lead to successful culture change:

Articulate the aspiration

Much like defining a new strategy, creating a new culture should begin with an analysis of the current one, using a framework that can be openly discussed throughout the organization. Leaders must understand what outcomes the culture produces and how it does or doesn't align with current and anticipated market and business conditions. For example, if the company's primary culture styles are *results* and *authority* but it exists in a rapidly changing industry, shifting toward *learning* or *enjoyment* (while maintaining a focus on *results*) may be appropriate.

An aspirational culture suggests the high-level principles that guide organizational initiatives, as at the technology company that sought to boost agility and flexibility amid increasing competition. Change might be framed in terms of real and present business challenges and opportunities as well as aspirations and trends. Because of culture's somewhat ambiguous and hidden nature, referring to tangible problems, such as market pressures or the challenges of growth, helps people better understand and connect to the need for change.

Select and develop leaders who align with the target culture

Leaders serve as important catalysts for change by encouraging it at all levels and creating a safe climate and what Edgar Schein calls "practice fields." Candidates for recruitment should be evaluated on their alignment with the target. A single model that can assess both organizational culture and individual leadership styles is critical for this activity.

Incumbent leaders who are unsupportive of desired change can be engaged and re-energized through training and education about the important relationship between culture and strategic direction. Often they will support the change after they understand its relevance, its anticipated benefits, and the impact that they personally can have on moving the organization toward the aspiration. However, culture change can and does lead to turnover: Some people move on because they feel they are no longer a good fit for the organization, and others are asked to leave if they jeopardize needed evolution.

Use organizational conversations about culture to underscore the importance of change

To shift the shared norms, beliefs, and implicit understandings within an organization, colleagues can talk one another through the change. Our integrated culture framework can be used to discuss current and desired culture styles and also differences in how senior leaders operate. As employees start to recognize that their leaders are talking about new business outcomes—innovation instead of quarterly earnings, for example—they will begin to behave differently themselves, creating a positive feedback loop.

Various kinds of organizational conversations, such as road shows, listening tours, and structured group discussion, can support change. Social media platforms encourage conversations between senior managers and frontline employees. Influential change champions can advocate for a culture shift through their language and actions. The technology company made a meaningful change in its culture and employee engagement by creating a structured framework for dialogue and cultivating widespread discussion.

Reinforce the desired change through organizational design

When a company's structures, systems, and processes are aligned and support the aspirational culture and strategy, instigating new culture styles and behaviors will become far easier. For example, performance management can be used to encourage employees to embody aspirational cultural attributes. Training practices can reinforce the target culture as the organization grows and adds new people. The degree of centralization and the number of hierarchical levels in the organizational structure can be adjusted to reinforce behaviors inherent to the aspirational culture. Leading scholars such as Henry Mintzberg have shown how organizational structure and other design features can have a profound impact over time on how people think and behave within an organization.

Putting It All Together

All four levers came together at a traditional manufacturer that was trying to become a full solutions provider. The change started with reformulating the strategy and was reinforced by a major brand campaign. But the president understood that the company's culture represented the biggest barrier to change and that the top leaders were the greatest lever for evolving the culture.

The culture was characterized by a drive for *results* followed by *caring* and *purpose,* the last of which was unusually strong for the industry. One employee described the company as "a talented and committed group of people focused on doing good for the planet, with genuine desire, support, and encouragement to make a difference in the community." Whereas the broader culture was highly collaborative, with flat decision making, leaders were seen as top-down, hierarchical, and sometimes political, which discouraged risk taking.

The top leaders reviewed their culture's strengths and the gaps in their own styles and discussed what was needed to achieve their strategic aspirations. They agreed that they needed more risk taking and autonomy and less hierarchy and centralized decision making. The president restructured the leadership team around strong business line leaders, freeing up time to become a better advocate for the culture and to focus more on customers.

The top team then invited a group of 100 middle managers into the conversation through a series of biannual leadership conferences. The first one established a platform for input, feedback, and the cocreation of an organizational change plan with clear cultural priorities. The president organized these managers into teams focused on critical business challenges. Each team was required to go outside the company to source ideas, to develop solutions, and to present its findings to the group for feedback. This initiative placed middle managers in change roles that would traditionally have been filled by vice presidents, giving them greater autonomy in fostering a *learning*-based culture. The intent was to create real benefits for the business while evolving the culture.

The president also initiated a program to identify employees who had positive disruptive ideas and working styles. These people were put on project teams that addressed key innovation priorities. The teams immediately began improving business results, both in core commercial metrics and in culture and engagement. After only one year employee engagement scores jumped a full 10 points, and customer Net Promoter Scores reached an all-time high—providing strong client references for the company's new and innovative solutions.

It is possible—in fact, vital—to improve organizational performance through culture change, using the simple but powerful models and methods in this article. First leaders must become aware of the culture that operates in their organization. Next they can define an aspirational target culture. Finally they can master the core change practices of articulation of the aspiration, leadership alignment, organizational conversation, and organizational design. Leading with culture may be among the few sources of sustainable competitive advantage left to companies today. Successful leaders will stop regarding culture with frustration and instead use it as a fundamental management tool.

What's Your Organization's Cultural Profile?

Before you begin an initiative to shape your organization's culture, it's important to explore where it is today. This worksheet and the questions that follow can help you formulate a preliminary assessment of your culture and get the conversation started.

Consider how your organization currently operates, what is valued, how people behave, and what unifies them. Partner with a colleague and independently rate each statement according to how well it describes your organization.

Add the two ratings in each row and then rank the eight styles. The higher the total, the stronger the match.

Compare your rankings with your colleague's and discuss the following questions:

- What do you like most about the current culture?

- What behaviors and mindsets might you evolve?

- How effective are your organization's leaders at role modeling the culture?

- What are the characteristics of people who are most successful in your culture?

- When new people don't succeed in your culture, what is the most common reason?

On a scale of 1-5, rate how well each of these statements describes your organization

1 = Not at all well 2 = Not very well 3 = Somewhat well 4 = Very well 5 = Extremely well

The organization is focused on:					The organization feels like:					Total
Collaboration and mutual trust					A big family					Caring
1	2	3	4	5	1	2	3	4	5	
Compassion and tolerance					An idealistic community or cause					Purpose
1	2	3	4	5	1	2	3	4	5	
Exploration and creativity					A dynamic project					Learning
1	2	3	4	5	1	2	3	4	5	
Fun and excitement					A celebration					Enjoyment
1	2	3	4	5	1	2	3	4	5	
Achievement and winning					A meritocracy					Results
1	2	3	4	5	1	2	3	4	5	
Strength and boldness					A competitive arena					Authority
1	2	3	4	5	1	2	3	4	5	
Planning and caution					A meticulously planned operation					Safety
1	2	3	4	5	1	2	3	4	5	
Structure and stability					A smoothly running machine					Order
1	2	3	4	5	1	2	3	4	5	

To see an expanded version of the assessment, go to this article at HBR.org.

How to Shape Your Culture

First you must identify culture targets. The best ones have some attributes in common: They align with the company's strategic direction; they're important to execute; and they reflect the demands of the external business environment. A good target should be both specific and achievable. For example, "We value our customers" can create ambiguity and lead to inconsistent choices regarding hiring, developing leaders, and running the company. A better version might be "We build genuine and positive relationships with customers; we serve our customers with humility; and we act as ambassadors for our rich brand heritage."

To Set a Culture Target:

Understand the current culture

Examine your culture—the company's founding and heritage, its espoused values, subcultures, leadership style, and team dynamics. (Use the preceding figure to start the conversation.)

Identify your culture's strengths and examine its impact on your organization today. Interview key stakeholders and influential members of the organization as needed.

Consider strategy and the environment

Assess current and future external conditions and strategic choices and determine which cultural styles will need to be strengthened or diminished in response.

Formulate a culture target according to which styles will support future changes.

Frame the aspiration in business realities

Translate the target into organizational change priorities. It should be framed not as a culture change initiative but in terms of real-world problems to be solved and solutions that create value.

Focus on *leadership alignment, organizational conversations,* and *organizational design* as the levers to guide the culture's evolution.

One Company's Experience

One large company used its search for a new director as an opportunity to bridge a problematic gap between the company's culture and the board's culture. To accomplish this, the leadership first diagnosed the two cultures along with its aspirations for the new director.

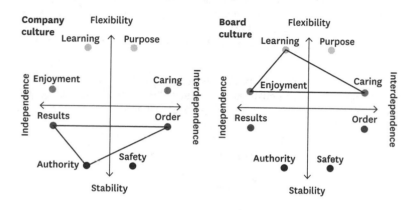

Whereas the company was highly *results* oriented and focused on *order,* discipline, and execution, the board was far more *learning* oriented, exploratory, inquisitive, and focused on *enjoyment*. A director who was *results* driven and curious would help bridge the two cultures.

Two years after an individual with the desired style was brought in, the board and the management team reported more-effective strategic planning activities and improved company performance.

Convergence Matters

When we compared employees' views on their organization's most salient cultural attributes, two types of organizations emerged: *low convergence* (employees rarely agreed on the most important cultural attributes) and *high convergence* (views were more closely aligned). In the two examples below, each dot represents one employee.

Note that in the low-convergence organization, seven of the eight cultural attributes were cited as most important, and every quadrant is represented. That means employees viewed their company in varying and often opposite ways. Some saw a *caring* organization, for example, while others saw one that emphasized *authority.*

Why is high convergence important? Because it correlates with levels of employee engagement and customer orientation. However, if the culture you have is not the one you want, high convergence will make it harder to change.

Company A: Low convergence

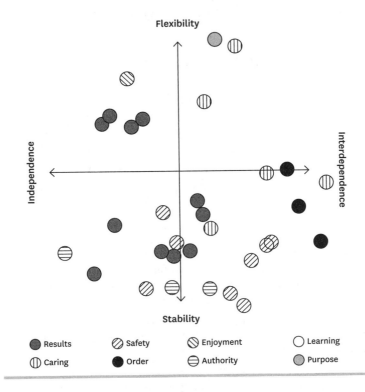

Company B: High convergence

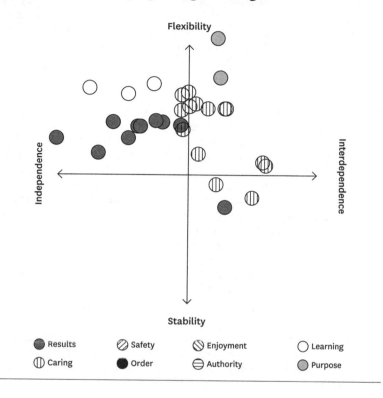

● Results	◐ Safety	◉ Enjoyment	○ Learning
⦶ Caring	● Order	⊖ Authority	◉ Purpose

Context, Conditions, and Culture

Context matters when assessing a culture's strategic effectiveness. Leaders must simultaneously consider culture styles and key organizational and market conditions if they want their culture to help drive performance. Region and industry are among the most germane external factors to keep in mind; critical internal considerations include alignment with strategy, leadership, and organizational design.

Region

The values of the national and regional cultures in which a company is embedded can influence patterns of behavior within the organization. (This linkage has been explored in depth by Geert Hofstede and the authors of the GLOBE study.) We find, for example, that companies operating in countries characterized by a high degree of institutional collectivism (defined as valuing equity within groups and encouraging the collective distribution of resources), such as France and Brazil, have cultures that emphasize *order* and *safety*. Companies operating in countries with low levels of uncertainty avoidance (that is, they are open to ambiguity and future uncertainty), such as the United States and Australia, place a greater emphasis on *learning, purpose,* and *enjoyment*. Such external influences are important considerations when working across borders or designing an appropriate organizational culture.

Industry

Varying cultural attributes may be needed to address industry-specific regulations and customer needs. A comparison of organizations across industries reveals evidence that cultures might adapt to meet the demands of industry environments.

Organizational cultures in financial services are more likely to emphasize *safety*. Given the increasingly complex regulations enacted in response to the financial crisis, careful work and risk management are more critical than ever in this industry. In contrast, nonprofits are far more purpose-driven, which can reinforce their commitment to a mission by aligning employee behavior around a common goal.

Culture styles ranked by industry

Based on an assessment of 230+ companies (industry) and a subsample of 25 companies (strategy)

Strategy

For its full benefit to be realized, a culture must support the strategic goals and plans of the business. For example, we find differences between companies that adopt a differentiation strategy and companies that pursue a cost leadership strategy. Although *results* and *caring* are key cultural characteristics at both types of companies, *enjoyment, learning,* and *purpose* are more suited to differentiation, whereas *order* and *authority* are more suited to cost leadership. Flexible cultures—which emphasize *enjoyment* and *learning*—can spur product innovation in companies aiming to differentiate themselves, whereas stable and predictable cultures, which emphasize *order* and *authority,* can help maintain operational efficiency to keep costs low.

Strategic considerations related to a company's life cycle are also linked to organizational culture. Companies with a strategy that seeks to stabilize or maintain their market position prioritize *learning,* whereas organizations operating with a turnaround strategy tend to prioritize *order* and *safety* in their efforts to redirect or reorganize unprofitable units.

Culture styles ranked by strategy

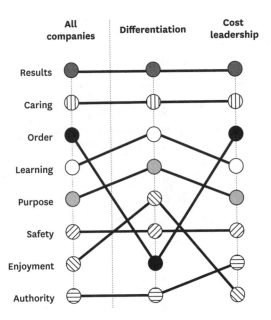

Based on an assessment of 230+ companies (industry) and a subsample of 25 companies (strategy)

Leadership

It is hard to overestimate the importance of aligning culture and leadership. The character and behaviors of a CEO and top executives can have a profound effect on culture. Conversely, culture serves to either constrain or enhance the performance of leaders. Our own data from executive recruiting activities shows that a lack of cultural fit is responsible for up to 68% of new-hire failures at the senior leadership level. For individual leaders, cultural fit is as important as capabilities and experience.

Organizational design

We see a two-way relationship between a company's culture and its particular structure. In many cases, structure and systems follow culture. For example, companies that prioritize teamwork and collaboration might design incentive systems that include shared team and company goals along with rewards that recognize collective effort. However, a long-standing organizational design choice can lead to the formation of a culture. Because the latter is far more difficult to alter, we suggest that structural changes should be aligned with the desired culture.

About the Research

We undertook a comprehensive study of organizational culture and outcomes to explore the link between them. We analyzed the cultures of more than 230 companies along with the leadership styles and values of more than 1,300 executives across a range of industries (including consumer discretionary, consumer staples, energy and utilities, financial and professional services, health care, industrials, and IT and telecommunications), regions (Africa, Asia, Europe, the Middle East, North America, Oceania, and South America), and organizational types (public, private, and nonprofit). We diagnosed those cultures using online survey responses from approximately 25,000 employees together with interviews of company managers.

Our analysis highlighted how strongly each of the eight styles defined the organizations in our study. *Results* ranked first, and *caring* second. This pattern is consistent across company types, company sizes, regions, and industries. *Order* and *learning* ranked among the third and fourth most common styles in many cultures.

Culture appears to most directly affect employee engagement and motivation, followed by customer orientation. To model its relationship to organizational outcomes, we assessed employee engagement levels for all the companies using widely accepted survey questions and arrived at customer-orientation scores with an online questionnaire. In many cases we also documented top leaders' individual styles and values.

We found that employee engagement is most strongly related to greater flexibility, in the form of *enjoyment, learning, purpose,* and *caring*. Similarly, we observed a positive relationship between customer orientation and those four styles plus *results*. These relationships, too, are surprisingly consistent across companies. We also found that engagement and customer orientation are stronger when employees are in close agreement about the culture's characteristics.

Our research was influenced by the work of countless scholars in this field, many of whom are mentioned in this article. In addition, we stand on the shoulders of giants such as David Caldwell, Jennifer Chatman, James Heskett, John Kotter, Charles O'Reilly, and many, many others who have inspired our thinking.

Originally published in January–February 2018. Reprint R1801B

The Error at the Heart of Corporate Leadership

by Joseph L. Bower and Lynn S. Paine

IN THE FALL OF 2014, the hedge fund activist and Allergan shareholder Bill Ackman became increasingly frustrated with Allergan's board of directors. In a letter to the board, he took the directors to task for their failure to do (in his words) "what you are paid $400,000 per year to do on behalf of the Company's owners." The board's alleged failure: refusing to negotiate with Valeant Pharmaceuticals about its unsolicited bid to take over Allergan—a bid that Ackman himself had helped engineer in a novel alliance between a hedge fund and a would-be acquirer. In presentations promoting the deal, Ackman praised Valeant for its shareholder-friendly capital allocation, its shareholder-aligned executive compensation, and its avoidance of risky early-stage research. Using the same approach at Allergan, he told analysts, would create significant value for its shareholders. He cited Valeant's plan to cut Allergan's research budget by 90% as "really the opportunity." Valeant CEO Mike Pearson assured analysts that "all we care about is shareholder value."

These events illustrate a way of thinking about the governance and management of companies that is now pervasive in the financial community and much of the business world. It centers on the idea that management's objective is, or should be, maximizing value for shareholders, but it addresses a wide range of topics—from performance measurement and executive compensation to share-holder rights, the role of directors, and corporate responsibility. This thought system has been embraced not only by hedge fund activists like Ackman but also by institutional investors more generally, along with many boards, managers, lawyers, academics, and even some regulators and lawmakers. Indeed, its precepts have come to be widely regarded as a model for "good governance" and for the brand of investor activism illustrated by the Allergan story.

Yet the idea that corporate managers should make maximizing shareholder value their goal—and that boards should ensure that they do—is relatively recent. It is rooted in what's known as agency theory, which was put forth by academic economists in the 1970s. At the theory's core is the assertion that shareholders own the corporation and, by virtue of their status as owners, have ultimate authority over its business and may legitimately demand that its activities be conducted in accordance with their wishes.

Attributing ownership of the corporation to shareholders sounds natural enough, but a closer look reveals that it is legally confused and, perhaps more important, involves a challenging problem of accountability. Keep in mind that shareholders have no legal duty to protect or serve the companies whose shares they own and are shielded by the doctrine of limited liability from legal responsibility for those companies' debts and misdeeds. Moreover, they may generally buy and sell shares without restriction and are required to disclose their identities only in certain circumstances. In addition, they tend to be physically and psychologically distant from the activities of the companies they invest in. That is to say, public company shareholders have few incentives to consider, and are not generally viewed as responsible for, the effects of the actions they favor on the corporation, other parties, or society more broadly. Agency theory has yet to grapple with the implications of the accountability vacuum that results from accepting its central—and in our view, faulty—premise that shareholders own the corporation.

The effects of this omission are troubling. We are concerned that the agency-based model of governance and management is being practiced in ways that are weakening companies and—if applied

Idea in Brief

The Problem

A widespread belief holds that "maximizing shareholder value" is the number one responsibility of boards and managers. But that's confused as a matter of corporate law and a poor guide for managerial behavior—and it has a huge accountability problem baked into it.

The Solution

A company's health—not its shareholders' wealth—should be the primary concern of those who manage corporations. That may sound like a small change, but it could make companies less vulnerable to damaging forms of activist investing—and make it easier for managers to focus on the long term.

even more widely, as experts predict—could be damaging to the broader economy. In particular we are concerned about the effects on corporate strategy and resource allocation. Over the past few decades the agency model has provided the rationale for a variety of changes in governance and management practices that, taken together, have increased the power and influence of certain types of shareholders over other types and further elevated the claims of shareholders over those of other important constituencies—without establishing any corresponding responsibility or accountability on the part of shareholders who exercise that power. As a result, managers are under increasing pressure to deliver ever faster and more predictable returns and to curtail riskier investments aimed at meeting future needs and finding creative solutions to the problems facing people around the world.

Don't misunderstand: We are capitalists to the core. We believe that widespread participation in the economy through the ownership of stock in publicly traded companies is important to the social fabric, and that strong protections for shareholders are essential. But the health of the economic system depends on getting the role of shareholders right. The agency model's extreme version of shareholder centricity is flawed in its assumptions, confused as a matter of law, and damaging in practice. A better model would recognize the critical role of shareholders but also take seriously the idea that corporations are independent entities serving multiple purposes and endowed by law with the potential to endure over time. And it would acknowledge accepted legal principles holding that directors and managers have duties to the corporation as well as to shareholders. In other words, a better model would be more company centered.

Before considering an alternative, let's take a closer look at the agency-based model.

Foundations of the Model

The ideas underlying the agency-based model can be found in Milton Friedman's well-known *New York Times Magazine* article of 1970 denouncing corporate "social responsibility" as a socialist doctrine. Friedman takes shareholders' ownership of the corporation as a given. He asserts that "the manager is the agent of the individuals who own the corporation" and, further, that the manager's primary "responsibility is to conduct the business in accordance with [the owners'] desires." He characterizes the executive as "an agent serving the interests of his principal."

These ideas were further developed in the 1976 *Journal of Financial Economics* article "Theory of the Firm," by Michael Jensen and William Meckling, who set forth the theory's basic premises:

- Shareholders own the corporation and are "principals" with original authority to manage the corporation's business and affairs.

- Managers are delegated decision-making authority by the corporation's shareholders and are thus "agents" of the shareholders.

- As agents of the shareholders, managers are obliged to conduct the corporation's business in accordance with shareholders' desires.

- Shareholders want business to be conducted in a way that maximizes their own economic returns. (The assumption that shareholders are unanimous in this objective is implicit throughout the article.)

Jensen and Meckling do not discuss shareholders' wishes regarding the ethical standards that managers should observe in conducting the business, but Friedman offers two views in his *Times* article. First he writes that shareholders generally want managers "to make as much money as possible while conforming to the basic rules of the society, both those embodied in law and those embodied in ethical custom." Later he suggests that shareholders simply want managers to use resources and pursue profit by engaging "in open and free competition without deception or fraud." Jensen and Meckling agree with Friedman that companies should not engage in acts of "social responsibility."

Much of the academic work on agency theory in the decades since has focused on ensuring that managers seek to maximize shareholder returns—primarily by aligning their interests with those of shareholders. These ideas have been further developed into a theory of organization whereby managers can (and should) instill concern for shareholders' interests throughout a company by properly delegating "decision rights" and creating appropriate incentives. They have also given rise to a view of boards of directors as an organizational mechanism for controlling what's known as "agency costs"—the costs to shareholders associated with delegating authority to managers. Hence the notion that a board's principal role is (or should be) monitoring management, and that boards should design executive compensation to align management's interests with those of shareholders.

The Model's Flaws

Let's look at where these ideas go astray.

1. Agency theory is at odds with corporate law: Legally, shareholders do not have the rights of "owners" of the corporation, and managers are not shareholders' "agents."
As other scholars and commentators have noted, the idea that shareholders own the corporation is at best confusing and at worst incorrect. From a legal perspective, shareholders are beneficiaries of

the corporation's activities, but they do not have "dominion" over a piece of property. Nor do they enjoy access to the corporate premises or use of the corporation's assets. What shareholders do own is their shares. That generally gives them various rights and privileges, including the right to sell their shares and to vote on certain matters, such as the election of directors, amendments to the corporate charter, and the sale of substantially all the corporation's assets.

Furthermore, under the law in Delaware—legal home to more than half the *Fortune* 500 and the benchmark for corporate law—the right to manage the business and affairs of the corporation is vested in a board of directors elected by the shareholders; the board delegates that authority to corporate managers.

Within this legal framework, managers and directors are fiduciaries rather than agents—and not just for shareholders but also for the corporation. The difference is important. Agents are obliged to carry out the wishes of a principal, whereas a fiduciary's obligation is to exercise independent judgment on behalf of a beneficiary. Put differently, an agent is an order taker, whereas a fiduciary is expected to make discretionary decisions. Legally, directors have a fiduciary duty to act in the best interests of the corporation, which is very different from simply doing the bidding of shareholders.

2. The theory is out of step with ordinary usage: Shareholders are not owners of the corporation in any traditional sense of the term, nor do they have owners' traditional incentives to exercise care in managing it.
This observation is even truer today than when it was famously made by Adolf Berle and Gardiner Means in their landmark 1932 study *The Modern Corporation and Private Property.* Some 70% of shares in U.S.-listed companies today are held by mutual funds, pension funds, insurance companies, sovereign funds, and other institutional investors, which manage them on behalf of beneficiaries such as households, pensioners, policy holders, and governments. In many instances the beneficiaries are anonymous to the company whose shares the institutions hold. The professionals who manage these investments are typically judged and rewarded each quarter

on the basis of returns from the total basket of investments managed. A consequence is high turnover in shares (seen in the exhibit "Average holding period for public company shares"), which also results from high-frequency trading by speculators.

The decisions of asset managers and speculators arise from expectations regarding share price over a relatively short period of time. As the economy passes through cycles, the shares of companies in entire industry sectors move in and out of favor. Although the shareholders of record at any given moment may vote on an issue brought before them, they need not know or care about the company whose shares they hold. Moreover, the fact that they can hedge or immediately sell their shares and avoid exposure to the longer-term effects

Average holding period for public company shares

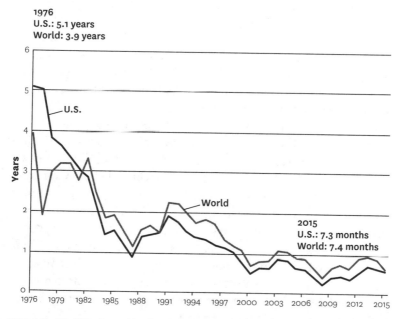

1976
U.S.: 5.1 years
World: 3.9 years

2015
U.S.: 7.3 months
World: 7.4 months

Source: The World Bank, World Federation of Exchanges Database.

of that vote makes it difficult to regard them as proprietors of the company in any customary sense.

The anonymity afforded the shares' beneficial owners further attenuates their relationship to the companies whose shares they own. Some 85% of publicly traded shares in the United States are held in the name of an institution serving as an intermediary—the so-called street name—on behalf of itself or its customers. And of the ultimate owners of those shares, an estimated 75% have instructed their intermediaries not to divulge their identities to the issuing company.

3. The theory is rife with moral hazard: Shareholders are not accountable as owners for the company's activities, nor do they have the responsibilities that officers and directors do to protect the company's interests.

The problem with treating shareholders as proprietors is exacerbated by the absence of another traditional feature of ownership: responsibility for the property owned and accountability—even legal liability, in some cases—for injuries to third parties resulting from how that property is used. Shareholders bear no such responsibility. Under the doctrine of limited liability, they cannot be held personally liable for the corporation's debts or for corporate acts and omissions that result in injury to others.

With a few exceptions, shareholders are entitled to act entirely in their own interest within the bounds of the securities laws. Unlike directors, who are expected to refrain from self-dealing, they are free to act on both sides of a transaction in which they have an interest. Consider the contest between Allergan and Valeant. A member of Allergan's board who held shares in Valeant would have been expected to refrain from voting on the deal or promoting Valeant's bid. But Allergan shareholders with a stake in both companies were free to buy, sell, and vote as they saw fit, with no obligation to act in the best interests of either company. Institutional investors holding shares in thousands of companies regularly act on deals in which they have significant interests on both sides.

In a well-ordered economy, rights and responsibilities go together. Giving shareholders the rights of ownership while exempting them from the responsibilities opens the door to opportunism, overreach, and misuse of corporate assets. The risk is less worrying when shareholders do not seek to influence major corporate decisions, but it is acute when they do. The problem is clearest when temporary holders of large blocks of shares intervene to reconstitute a company's board, change its management, or restructure its finances in an effort to drive up its share price, only to sell out and move on to another target without ever having to answer for their intervention's impact on the company or other parties.

4. The theory's doctrine of alignment spreads moral hazard throughout a company and narrows management's field of vision. Just as freedom from accountability has a tendency to make shareholders indifferent to broader and longer-term considerations, so agency theory's recommended alignment between managers' interests and those of shareholders can skew the perspective of the entire organization. When the interests of successive layers of management are "aligned" in this manner, the corporation may become so biased toward the narrow interests of its current shareholders that it fails to meet the requirements of its customers or other constituencies. In extreme cases it may tilt so far that it can no longer function effectively. The story of Enron's collapse reveals how thoroughly the body of a company can be infected.

The notion that managing for the good of the company is the same as managing for the good of the stock is best understood as a theoretical conceit necessitated by the mathematical models that many economists favor. In practical terms there is (or can be) a stark difference. Once Allergan's management shifted its focus from sustaining long-term growth to getting the company's stock price to $180 a share—the target at which institutional investors were willing to hold their shares—its priorities changed accordingly. Research was cut, investments were eliminated, and employees were dismissed.

5. The theory's assumption of shareholder uniformity is contrary to fact: Shareholders do not all have the same objectives and cannot be treated as a single "owner."

Agency theory assumes that all shareholders want the company to be run in a way that maximizes their own economic return. This simplifying assumption is useful for certain purposes, but it masks important differences. Shareholders have differing investment objectives, attitudes toward risk, and time horizons. Pension funds may seek current income and preservation of capital. Endowments may seek long-term growth. Young investors may accept considerably more risk than their elders will tolerate. Proxy voting records indicate that shareholders are divided on many of the resolutions put before them. They may also view strategic opportunities differently. In the months after Valeant announced its bid, Allergan officials met with a broad swath of institutional investors. According to Allergan's lead independent director, Michael Gallagher, "The diversity of opinion was as wide as could possibly be"—from those who opposed the deal and absolutely did not want Valeant shares (the offer included both stock and cash) to those who saw it as the opportunity of a lifetime and could not understand why Allergan did not sit down with Valeant immediately.

The Agency-Based Model in Practice

Despite these problems, agency theory has attracted a wide following. Its tenets have provided the intellectual rationale for a variety of changes in practice that, taken together, have enhanced the power of shareholders and given rise to a model of governance and management that is unrelenting in its shareholder centricity. Here are just a few of the arenas in which the theory's influence can be seen:

Executive compensation

Agency theory ideas were instrumental in the shift from a largely cash-based system to one that relies predominantly on equity. Proponents of the shift argued that equity-based pay would better align the interests of executives with those of shareholders. The same argument was used to garner support for linking pay more closely to stock performance and for tax incentives to encourage such "pay for performance" arrangements. Following this logic, Congress adopted legislation in 1992 making executive pay above $1 million deductible only if it is "performance based." Today some 62% of executive pay is in the form of equity, compared with 19% in 1980.

Disclosure of executive pay

Agency theory's definition of performance and its doctrine of alignment undergird rules proposed by the SEC in 2015 requiring companies to expand the information on executive pay and shareholder returns provided in their annual proxy statements. The proposed rules call for companies to report their annual total shareholder return (TSR) over time, along with annual TSR figures for their peer group, and to describe the relationships between their TSR and their executive compensation and between their TSR and the TSR of their peers.

Shareholders' rights

The idea that shareholders are owners has been central to the push to give them more say in the nomination and election of directors and to make it easier for them to call a special meeting, act by written consent, or remove a director. Data from FactSet and other sources indicates that the proportion of S&P 500 companies with majority voting for directors increased from about 16% in 2006 to 88% in 2015; the proportion with special meeting provisions rose from 41% in 2002 to 61% in 2015; and the proportion giving shareholders proxy access rights increased from less than half a percent in 2013 to some 39% by mid-2016.

The power of boards

Agency thinking has also propelled efforts to eliminate staggered boards in favor of annual election for all directors and to eliminate "poison pills" that would enable boards to slow down or prevent "owners" from voting on a premium offer for the company. From 2002 to 2015, the share of S&P 500 companies with staggered boards dropped from 61% to 10%, and the share with a standing poison pill fell from 60% to 4%. (Companies without a standing pill may still adopt a pill in response to an unsolicited offer—as was done by the Allergan board in response to Valeant's bid.)

Management attitudes

Agency theory's conception of management responsibility has been widely adopted. In 1997 the Business Roundtable issued a statement declaring that "the paramount duty of management and of boards of directors is to the corporation's stockholders" and that "the principal objective of a business enterprise is to generate economic returns to its owners." Issued in response to pressure from institutional investors, the statement in effect revised the Roundtable's earlier position that "the shareholder must receive a good return but the legitimate concerns of other constituencies also must have the appropriate attention." Various studies suggest ways in which managers have become more responsive to shareholders. Research indicates, for instance, that companies with majority (rather than plurality) voting for directors are more apt to adopt shareholder proposals that garner majority support, and that many chief financial officers are willing to forgo investments in projects expected to be profitable in the longer term in order to meet analysts' quarterly earnings estimates. According to surveys by the Aspen Institute, many business school graduates regard maximizing shareholder value as their top responsibility.

Investor behavior

Agency theory ideas have facilitated a rise in investor activism and legitimized the playbook of hedge funds that mobilize capital for the express purpose of buying company shares and using their position as "owners" to effect changes aimed at creating shareholder value. (The sidebar "The Activist's Playbook" illustrates how agency theory ideas have been put into practice.) These investors are intervening more frequently and reshaping how companies allocate resources. In the process they are reshaping the strategic context in which all companies and their boards make decisions.

The Activist's Playbook

For an understanding of the agency-based model in practice, there is no better place to look than an activist campaign. As a first step, the activist acquires shares in the targeted company—typically somewhere between 5% and 10%, but sometimes less than 1%. Shares in hand, he then claims the right to issue directives. (To leverage that power, he will often alert other hedge funds to his actions.) The language of ownership typically plays a prominent role. For example, in 2014, to advance a takeover of Allergan by Valeant Pharmaceuticals, Bill Ackman, of Pershing Square Capital Management, attacked Allergan's board for failing to do what the directors were paid to do "on behalf of the Company's owners." The activist may challenge the board's professionalism by appealing to agency theory norms of directorship. In one letter to the Allergan board, Ackman declared: "Your actions have wasted corporate resources, delayed enormous potential value creation for shareholders, and are professionally and personally embarrassing for you."

Although campaigns differ in their particulars, the activist's playbook for increasing shareholder value is fairly standard. As our colleagues Ian Gow and Suraj Srinivasan (with others) have documented in their study of nearly 800 campaigns at U.S. companies from 2004 to 2012, activists tend to focus on capital structure, strategy, and governance. They typically call for some combination of cutting costs, adding debt, buying back shares, issuing special dividends, spinning off businesses, reconstituting the board, replacing the CEO, changing the strategy, and selling the company or its main asset. Tax reduction is another element of many activist programs.

An activist whose demands go unheeded may initiate a proxy fight in an attempt to replace incumbent board members with directors more willing to do the activist's bidding. In a few instances, activists have even offered their chosen nominees special bonuses to stand for election or additional incentives for increasing shareholder value in their role as directors.

By most indications, hedge fund activists have been quite successful in effecting the changes they've sought. As reported by the industry, more companies are being targeted—473 worldwide in the first half of 2016 (including 306 in the United States), up from 136 worldwide in all of 2010—and activists' demands are frequently being met. In the United States in 2015, 69% of demands were at least partially satisfied, the highest proportion since 2010. Activists are also gaining clout in the boardroom, where they won 397 seats at U.S. companies in 2014 and 2015. Although activist hedge funds saw outflows of some $7.4 billion in the first three quarters of 2016, assets under management were estimated at more than $116 billion in late 2016, up from $2.7 billion in 2000.

Taken individually, a change such as majority voting for directors may have merit. As a group, however, these changes have helped create an environment in which managers are under increasing pressure to deliver short-term financial results, and boards are being urged to "think like activists."

Implications for Companies

To appreciate the strategic implications of a typical activist program, it is instructive to use a tool developed in the 1960s by the Boston Consulting Group to guide the resource-allocation process. Called the growth share matrix, the tool helped managers see their company as a portfolio of businesses with differing characteristics. One group of businesses might be mature and require investment only for purposes of modest expansion and incremental improvement. Assuming they have strong market share relative to their nearest competitors, those businesses are likely to be profitable and generate cash. Another group might also have leading positions but be in fast-growing markets; they, too, are profitable, but they require heavy investment to maintain or improve market share. A third group might have weak competitive positions in mature markets; these businesses require cash for survival but have no prospects for growth or increased profits. A final group might be in rapidly growing new markets where several companies are competitive and prospects are bright but risky.

The developers of the matrix called these four groups cash cows, stars, dogs, and bright prospects, respectively. The segmentation was meant to ensure that cash cows were maintained, stars fully funded, dogs pruned, and a limited number of bright prospects chosen for their longer-term potential to become stars. (See the exhibit "The growth share matrix.") When companies don't manage a portfolio in this holistic fashion, funds tend to get spread evenly across businesses on the basis of individual projects' forecasted returns.

It's a simple tool—but using it well is not simple at all. Managing a cash cow so that it remains healthy, nurturing star businesses in the face of emerging competition, fixing or divesting unpromising

---

The growth share matrix

BCG's growth share matrix enables companies to manage a portfolio of businesses: "cash cows," mature businesses that throw off cash; fast-growing "stars"; businesses with a weak position and few prospects for growth ("dogs"); and risky but big-upside businesses in fast-growing markets ("bright prospects").

Source: Boston Consulting Group.

---

businesses, and selecting one or two bright prospects to grow—all this takes talented executives who can function effectively as a team. Companies that succeed in managing this ongoing resource-allocation challenge can grow and reinvent themselves continually over time.

The growth share matrix illuminates the strategic choices managers face as they seek to create value indefinitely into the future. It's also useful for showing how to drive up a company's share price in the short term. Suppose a corporation were to sell off the dogs, defund the bright prospects, and cut expenses such as marketing and R&D from the stars. That's a recipe for dramatically increased earnings, which would, in turn, drive up the share price. But the corporation might lose bright prospects that could have been developed into the stars and cash cows of the future.

The activist investor Nelson Peltz's 2014 proposal for DuPont provides an example of this idea. At the core of his three-year plan for increasing returns to shareholders was splitting the company into three autonomous businesses and eliminating its central research function. One of the new companies, "GrowthCo," was to consist of DuPont's agriculture, nutrition and health, and industrial biosciences businesses. A second, "CyclicalCo/CashCo," was to include the low-growth but highly cash-generative performance materials, safety, and electronics businesses. The third was the performance chemicals unit, Chemours, which DuPont had already decided to spin off. In growth-share-matrix terms, Peltz's plan was, in essence, to break up DuPont into a cash cow, a star, and a dog—and to eliminate some number of the bright prospects that might have been developed from innovations produced by centralized research. Peltz also proposed cutting other "excess" costs, adding debt, adopting a more shareholder-friendly policy for distributing cash from CyclicalCo/CashCo, prioritizing high returns on invested capital for initiatives at GrowthCo, and introducing more shareholder-friendly governance, including tighter alignment between executive compensation and returns to shareholders. The plan would effectively dismantle DuPont and cap its future in return for an anticipated doubling in share price.

Value Creation or Value Transfer?

The question of whether shareholders benefit from such activism beyond an initial bump in stock price is likely to remain unresolved, given the methodological problems plaguing studies on the subject. No doubt in some cases activists have played a useful role in waking up a sleepy board or driving a long-overdue change in strategy or management. However, it is important to note that much of what activists call value creation is more accurately described as value transfer. When cash is paid out to shareholders rather than used to fund research, launch new ventures, or grow existing businesses, value has not been created. Nothing has been created. Rather, cash that would have been invested to generate future returns is simply being paid out to current shareholders. The lag time between when such decisions are taken and when their effect on earnings is evident exceeds the time frames of standard financial models, so the potential for damage to the company and future shareholders, not to mention society more broadly, can easily go unnoticed.

Given how long it takes to see the fruits of any significant research effort (Apple's latest iPhone chip was eight years in the making), the risk to research and innovation from activists who force deep cuts to drive up the share price and then sell out before the pipeline dries up is obvious. It doesn't help that financial models and capital markets are notoriously poor at valuing innovation. After Allergan was put into play by the offer from Valeant and Ackman's Pershing Square Capital Management, the company's share price rose by 30% as other hedge funds bought the stock. Some institutions sold to reap the immediate gain, and Allergan's management was soon facing pressure from the remaining institutions to accelerate cash flow and "bring earnings forward." In an attempt to hold on to those shareholders, the company made deeper cuts in the workforce than previously planned and curtailed early-stage research programs. Academic studies have found that a significant proportion of hedge fund interventions involve large increases in leverage and large decreases in investment, particularly in research and development.

The activists' claim of value creation is further clouded by indications that some of the value purportedly created for shareholders is actually value transferred from other parties or from the general public. Large-sample research on this question is limited, but one study suggests that the positive abnormal returns associated with the announcement of a hedge fund intervention are, in part, a transfer of wealth from workers to shareholders. The study found that workers' hours decreased and their wages stagnated in the three years after an intervention. Other studies have found that some of the gains for shareholders come at the expense of bondholders. Still other academic work links aggressive pay-for-stock-performance arrangements to various misdeeds involving harm to consumers, damage to the environment, and irregularities in accounting and financial reporting.

We are not aware of any studies that examine the total impact of hedge fund interventions on all stakeholders or society at large. Still, it appears self-evident that shareholders' gains are sometimes simply transfers from the public purse, such as when management improves earnings by shifting a company's tax domicile to a lower-tax jurisdiction—a move often favored by activists, and one of Valeant's proposals for Allergan. Similarly, budget cuts that eliminate exploratory research aimed at addressing some of society's most vexing challenges may enhance current earnings but at a cost to society as well as to the company's prospects for the future.

Hedge fund activism points to some of the risks inherent in giving too much power to unaccountable "owners." As our analysis of agency theory's premises suggests, the problem of moral hazard is real—and the consequences are serious. Yet practitioners continue to embrace the theory's doctrines; regulators continue to embed them in policy; boards and managers are under increasing pressure to deliver short-term returns; and legal experts forecast that the trend toward greater shareholder empowerment will persist. To us, the prospect that public companies will be run even more strictly according to the agency-based model is alarming. Rigid adherence to the model by companies uniformly across the economy could easily result in even more pressure for current earnings, less investment in R&D and in people, fewer transformational strategies and innovative business models, and further wealth flowing to sophisticated investors at the expense of ordinary investors and everyone else.

Toward a Company-Centered Model

A better model, we submit, would have at its core the health of the enterprise rather than near-term returns to its shareholders. Such a model would start by recognizing that corporations are independent entities endowed by law with the potential for indefinite life. With the right leadership, they can be managed to serve markets and society over long periods of time. Agency theory largely ignores these distinctive and socially valuable features of the corporation, and the associated challenges of managing for the long term, on the grounds that corporations are "legal fictions." In their seminal 1976 article, Jensen and Meckling warn against "falling into the trap" of asking what a company's objective should be or whether the company has a social responsibility. Such questions, they argue, mistakenly imply that a corporation is an "individual" rather than merely a convenient legal construct. In a similar vein, Friedman asserts that it cannot have responsibilities because it is an "artificial person."

In fact, of course, corporations *are* legal constructs, but that in no way makes them artificial. They are economic and social organisms whose creation is authorized by governments to accomplish objectives that cannot be achieved by more-limited organizational forms such as partnerships and proprietorships. Their nearly 400-year history of development speaks to the important role they play in society. Originally a corporation's objectives were set in its charter—build and operate a canal, for example—but eventually the form became generic so that corporations could be used to accomplish a wide variety of objectives chosen by their management and governing bodies. As their scale and scope grew, so did their power. The choices made by corporate decision makers today can transform societies and touch the lives of millions, if not billions, of people across the globe.

The model we envision would acknowledge the realities of managing these organizations over time and would be responsive to the needs of all shareholders—not just those who are most vocal at a given moment. Here we offer eight propositions that together provide a radically different and, we believe, more realistic foundation for corporate governance and shareholder engagement.

1. Corporations are complex organizations whose effective functioning depends on talented leaders and managers.
The success of a leader has more to do with intrinsic motivation, skills, capabilities, and character than with whether his or her pay is tied to shareholder returns. If leaders are poorly equipped for the job, giving them more "skin in the game" will not improve the situation

and may even make it worse. (Part of the problem with equity-based pay is that it conflates executive skill and luck.) The challenges of corporate leadership—crafting strategy, building a strong organization, developing and motivating talented executives, and allocating resources among the corporation's various businesses for present and future returns—are significant. In focusing on incentives as the key to ensuring effective leadership, agency theory diminishes these challenges and the importance of developing individuals who can meet them.

2. Corporations can prosper over the long term only if they're able to learn, adapt, and regularly transform themselves.
In some industries today, companies may need reinvention every five years to keep up with changes in markets, competition, or technology. Changes of this sort, already difficult, are made more so by the idea that management is about assigning individuals fixed decision rights, giving them clear goals, offering them incentives to achieve those goals, and then paying them (or not) depending on whether the goals are met. This approach presupposes a degree of predictability, hierarchy, and task independence that is rare in today's organizations. Most tasks involve cooperation across organizational lines, making it difficult to establish clear links between individual contributions and specific outcomes.

3. Corporations perform many functions in society.
One of them is providing investment opportunities and generating wealth, but corporations also produce goods and services, provide employment, develop technologies, pay taxes, and make other contributions to the communities in which they operate. Singling out any one of these as "the purpose of the corporation" may say more about the commentator than about the corporation. Agency economists, it seems, gravitate toward maximizing shareholder wealth as the central purpose. Marketers tend to favor serving customers. Engineers lean toward innovation and excellence in product performance. From a societal perspective, the most important feature of the corporation may be that it performs all these functions

simultaneously over time. As a historical matter, the original purpose of the corporation—reflected in debates about limited liability and general incorporation statutes—was to facilitate economic growth by enabling projects that required large-scale, long-term investment.

4. Corporations have differing objectives and differing strategies for achieving them.

The purpose of the (generic) corporation from a societal perspective is not the same as the purpose of a (particular) corporation as seen by its founders, managers, or governing authorities. Just as the purposes and strategies of individual companies vary widely, so must their performance measures. Moreover, companies' strategies are almost always in transition as markets change. An overemphasis on TSR for assessing and comparing corporate performance can distort the allocation of resources and undermine a company's ability to deliver on its chosen strategy.

5. Corporations must create value for multiple constituencies.

In a free market system, companies succeed only if customers want their products, employees want to work for them, suppliers want them as partners, shareholders want to buy their stock, and communities want their presence. Figuring out how to maintain these relationships and deciding when trade-offs are necessary among the interests of these various groups are central challenges of corporate leadership. Agency theory's implied decision rule—that managers should always maximize value for shareholders—oversimplifies this challenge and leads eventually to systematic underinvestment in other important relationships.

6. Corporations must have ethical standards to guide interactions with all their constituencies, including shareholders and society at large.

Adherence to these standards, which go beyond forbearance from fraud and collusion, is essential for earning the trust companies need to function effectively over time. Agency theory's ambivalence regarding corporate ethics can set companies up for destructive and even criminal behavior—which generates a need for the costly regulations that agency theory proponents are quick to decry.

7. Corporations are embedded in a political and socioeconomic system whose health is vital to their sustainability.
Elsewhere we have written about the damaging and often self-destructive consequences of companies' indifference to negative externalities produced by their activities. We have also found that societal and systemwide problems can be a source of both risk and opportunity for companies. Consider Ecomagination, the business GE built around environmental challenges, or China Mobile's rural communications strategy, which helped narrow the digital divide between China's urban and rural populations and fueled the company's growth for nearly half a decade. Agency theory's insistence that corporations (because they are legal fictions) cannot have social responsibilities and that societal problems are beyond the purview of business (and should be left to governments) results in a narrowness of vision that prevents corporate leaders from seeing, let alone acting on, many risks and opportunities.

8. The interests of the corporation are distinct from the interests of any particular shareholder or constituency group.
As early as 1610, the directors of the Dutch East India Company recognized that shareholders with a 10-year time horizon would be unenthusiastic about the company's investing resources in longer-term projects that were likely to pay off only in the second of two 10-year periods allowed by the original charter. The solution, suggested one official, was to focus not on the initial 10-year investors but on the strategic goals of the enterprise, which in this case meant investing in those longer-term projects to maintain the company's position in Asia. The notion that all shareholders have the same interests and that those interests are the same as the corporation's masks such fundamental differences. It also provides intellectual cover for powerful shareholders who seek to divert the corporation to their own purposes while claiming to act on behalf of all shareholders.

These propositions underscore the need for an approach to governance that takes the corporation seriously as an institution in society and centers on the sustained performance of the enterprise. They also point to a stronger role for boards and a system of accountability for boards and executives that includes but is broader than accountability to shareholders. In the model implied by these propositions, boards and business leaders would take a fundamentally different approach to such basic tasks as strategy development, resource allocation, performance evaluation, and shareholder engagement. For instance, managers would be expected to take a longer view in formulating strategy and allocating resources.

The new model has yet to be fully developed, but its conceptual foundations can be outlined. As shown in the exhibit "Contrasting approaches to corporate governance," the company-centered model we envision tracks basic corporate law in holding that a corporation is an independent entity, that management's authority comes from the corporation's governing body and ultimately from the law, and that managers are fiduciaries (rather than agents) and are thus obliged to act in the best interests of the corporation and its shareholders (which is not the same as carrying out the wishes of even a majority of shareholders). This model recognizes the diversity of shareholders' goals and the varied roles played by corporations in society. We believe that it aligns better than the agency-based model does with the realities of managing a corporation for success over time and is thus more consistent with corporations' original purpose and unique potential as vehicles for projects involving large-scale, long-term investment.

The practical implications of company-centered governance are far-reaching. In boardrooms adopting this approach, we would expect to see some or all of these features:

- greater likelihood of a staggered board to facilitate continuity and the transfer of institutional knowledge

- more board-level attention to succession planning and leadership development

- more board time devoted to strategies for the company's continuing growth and renewal

Contrasting approaches to corporate governance

Theory	Shareholder centered	Company centered
	Agency theory	*Entity theory*
Conception of the corporation	Legal fiction; nexus of contracts; pool of capital	Legal entity; social and economic organism; purposeful organization
Origins of the corporation	Private agreement among property owners to pool and increase capital	Created by lawmakers to encourage investment in long-term, large-scale projects needed by society
Functions of the corporation	Maximize wealth for shareholders	Provide goods and services; provide employment; create opportunities for investment; drive innovation
Purpose of specific corporations	Maximize shareholder value	Business purpose set by the particular company's board
Responsibilities to society	None (fictional entities can't have responsibilities)	Fulfill business purpose and act as a good corporate citizen
Ethical standards	Unclear: whatever shareholders want, or obey law and avoid fraud or collusion	Obey law and follow generally accepted ethical standards
Role of shareholders	Principals/owners of the corporation with authority over its business	Owners of shares; suppliers of capital with defined rights and responsibilities

Nature of shareholders	Undifferentiated, self-interested wealth maximizers	Diverse, with differing objectives, incentives, time horizons, and preferences
Role of directors	Shareholders' agents, delegates, or representatives	Fiduciaries for the corporation and its shareholders
Role of management	Shareholders' agents	Leaders of the organization; fiduciaries for the corporation and its shareholders
Management's objective	Maximize returns to shareholders	Sustain performance of the enterprise
Management's time frame	Present/near term (theory assumes the current share price captures all available knowledge about the company's future)	Established by the board; potentially indefinite, requiring attention to near, medium, and long term
Management performance metrics	Single: returns to shareholders	Multiple: returns to shareholders; company value; achievement of strategic goals; quality of goods and services; employee well-being
Strength	Simple structure permits clear economic argument	Consistent with law, history, and the realities facing managers
Weakness	Principles do not accord with law or good management; shareholders have power without accountability	Principles describe complex relationships and responsibilities; success is difficult to assess

- closer links between executive compensation and achieving the company's strategic goals

- more attention to risk analysis and political and environmental uncertainty

- a strategic (rather than narrowly financial) approach to resource allocation

- a stronger focus on investments in new capabilities and innovation

- more-conservative use of leverage as a cushion against market volatility

- concern with corporate citizenship and ethical issues that goes beyond legal compliance

A company-centered model of governance would not relieve corporations of the need to provide a return over time that reflected the cost of capital. But they would be open to a wider range of strategic positions and time horizons and would more easily attract investors who shared their goals. Speculators will always seek to exploit changes in share price—but it's not inevitable that they will color all corporate governance. It's just that agency theory, in combination with other doctrines of modern economics, has erased the distinctions among investors and converted all of us into speculators.

If our model were accepted, speculators would have less opportunity to profit by transforming long-term players into sources of higher earnings and share prices in the short term. The legitimizing argument for attacks by unaccountable parties with opaque holdings would lose its force. We can even imagine a new breed of investors and asset managers who would focus explicitly on long-term investing. They might develop new valuation models that take a broader view of companies' prospects or make a specialty of valuing the hard-to-value innovations and intangibles—and also the costly externalities—that are often ignored in today's models. They might want to hold shares in companies that promise a solid and continuing return and that behave as decent corporate citizens. Proxy advisers might emerge to serve such investors.

We would also expect to find more support for measures to enhance shareholders' accountability. For instance, activist shareholders seeking significant influence or control might be treated as fiduciaries for the corporation or restricted in their ability to sell or hedge the value of their shares. Regulators might be inclined to call for greater transparency regarding the beneficial ownership of shares. In particular, activist funds might be required to disclose the identities of their investors and to provide additional information about the nature of their own governance. Regulators might close the 10-day window currently afforded between the time a hedge fund acquires a disclosable stake and the time the holding must actually be disclosed. To date, efforts to close the window have met resistance from agency theory proponents who argue that it is needed to give hedge funds sufficient incentive to engage in costly efforts to dislodge poorly performing managers.

The time has come to challenge the agency-based model of corporate governance. Its mantra of maximizing shareholder value is distracting companies and their leaders from the innovation, strategic renewal, and investment in the future that require their attention. History has shown that with enlightened management and sensible regulation, companies can play a useful role in helping society adapt to constant change. But that can happen only if directors and managers have sufficient discretion to take a longer, broader view of the company and its business. As long as they face the prospect of a surprise attack by unaccountable "owners," today's business leaders have little choice but to focus on the here and now.

Further Reading

Below are some of the books and articles that examine themes touched on in this article.

- **Capitalism at Risk: Rethinking the Role of Business,** Joseph L. Bower, Herman B. Leonard, and Lynn S. Paine, Harvard Business Review Press, 2011

- **Firm Commitment: Why the Corporation Is Failing Us and How to Restore Trust in It,** Colin Mayer, Oxford University Press, 2013

- **Fixing the Game: Bubbles, Crashes, and What Capitalism Can Learn from the NFL,** Roger L. Martin, Harvard Business Review Press, 2011

- **The Shareholder Value Myth: How Putting Shareholders First Harms Investors, Corporations, and the Public,** Lynn Stout, Berrett-Koehler, 2012

- **"Focusing Capital on the Long Term,"** Dominic Barton and Mark Wiseman, HBR, January–February 2014

- **"A Global Leader's Guide to Managing Business Conduct,"** Lynn S. Paine, Rohit Deshpandé, and Joshua D. Margolis, HBR, September 2011

- **"The Incentive Bubble,"** Mihir Desai, HBR, March 2012

- **"Managing Investors: An Interview with Sam Palmisano,"** Justin Fox, HBR, June 2014

- **"What Good Are Shareholders?"** Justin Fox and Jay W. Lorsch, HBR, July–August 2012

Originally published in May–June 2017. Reprint R1703B

The CEO View: Defending a Good Company from Bad Investors

A conversation with former Allergan CEO David Pyott
by Sarah Cliffe

David Pyott had been the CEO of Allergan for nearly 17 years in April 2014, when Valeant Pharmaceuticals and Pershing Square Capital Management initiated the hostile takeover bid described in the accompanying article "The Error at the Heart of Corporate Leadership." He was the company's sole representative during the takeover discussions. When it became clear that the bid could not be fended off indefinitely, Pyott, with his board's blessing, negotiated a deal whereby Allergan would be acquired by Actavis (a company whose business model, like Allergan's, was growth oriented).

HBR: *Would you describe Allergan's trajectory in the years leading up to the takeover bid?*

Pyott: We'd experienced huge growth since 1998, when I joined as just the third CEO of Allergan and the first outsider in that role. We restructured when I came in and again 10 years later, during the recession. Those cuts gave us some firepower for investing back into the economic recovery. After the recession we were telling the market to expect double-digit growth in sales revenue and around the mid-teens in earnings per share.

Your investor relations must have been excellent.

They were. I am extremely proud to say that we literally never missed our numbers, not once in 17 years. We also won lots of awards from investor-relations magazines. You don't run a business with that in mind, but it's nice to be recognized.

In their article, Joseph Bower and Lynn Paine describe how difficult it is for any company to manage the pressure from investors who want higher short-term returns. You seem to have managed that well—until Valeant showed up. How?

Both buy-side and sell-side investors are like any other customer group. You should listen to what they say and respond when you can. But remember: Asking is free. If they say, "Hey, we want more," you have to be willing to come back with "This is what we can commit to. If there are better places to invest your funds, then do what you need to." Fortunately or unfortunately, I'm very stubborn.

Permit me a naive question: Since Allergan was going strong, why did it make sense to Valeant/Pershing Square to take you over and strip you down? I get that they'd make a lot of money, but wouldn't fostering continued growth make more in the long run?

Different business models. Valeant was a roll-up company; it wasn't interested in organic growth. Michael Pearson [Valeant's CEO] liked our assets—and he needed to keep feeding the beast. If he didn't keep on buying the next target, then the fact that he was stripping all the assets out of companies he'd already bought would have become painfully obvious.

He couldn't do it alone, given his already weak balance sheet, so he brought Ackman in—and Pershing Square acquired 9.7% of our stock without our knowledge. This was meant to act as a catalyst to create a "wolf pack." Once the hedge funds and arbitrageurs get too big a position, you lose control of your company.

I still thought we had a strong story to tell—and I hoped I could get long-term-oriented shareholders to buy new stock and water down the hedge funds' holdings. But almost nobody was willing to up their position. They all had different reasons—some perfectly good ones. It was a lesson to me.

That must have been disappointing.

Yes. It's poignant—some of those same people say to me now, "We miss the old Allergan. We're looking for high-growth, high-innovation stocks and not finding them." I just say, "I heartily agree with you."

Another thing that surprised and disappointed me was that I couldn't get people who supported what we were doing— who understood why we were not accepting the bid, which grossly undervalued the company—to talk to the press. Several people said they would, but then folks at the top of their companies said no. And the reporters who cover M&A don't know the companies well. The people who cover pharma are deeply knowledgeable—but once a company is in play, those guys are off the story day-to-day. So the coverage was more one-sided than we'd have hoped for.

Is the trend toward activist investors something that the market will eventually sort out?

Activist and hostile campaigns have been propelled by extraordinarily low interest rates and banks' willingness to accept very high leverage ratios. Recently investor focus has returned to good old-fashioned operational execution by management. But I do think that investment styles go in and out of fashion. I never would have guessed that when I went to business school.

Do you agree with Bower and Paine that boards and CEOs need to focus less on shareholder wealth and more on the well-being of the company?

Look at it from a societal point of view: A lot of the unrest we've seen over the past year is rooted in the idea that wealthy, powerful people are disproportionately benefiting from the changes happening in society. A lot of companies think that they need to make themselves look more friendly, not just to stockholders but to employees and to society. Having a broader purpose—something beyond simply making money—is how you do that and how you create strong corporate cultures.

I don't believe that strong performance and purpose are at odds, not at all. My own experience tells me that in order for a company to be a really high performer, it needs to have a purpose. Money matters to employees up to a point, but they want to believe they're working on something that improves people's lives. I've also found that employees respond really favorably when management commits to responsible social behavior. I used to joke with employees about saving water and energy and about recycling: "Look, I'm Scottish, OK? I don't like waste, and it saves the company money." That's a positive for employees.

Did that sense of purpose pay off when you were going through the takeover bid?

Absolutely. I left day-to-day operations to our president, Doug Ingram, that year. And we grew the top line 17%—more than $1 billion—the best operating year in our 62-year history. I remember an R&D team leader who came up to me in the parking lot and said, "Are you OK? Is there anything I can do?" I answered him, "Just do your job better than ever, and don't be distracted by the rubbish you read in the media." Employees all over the world outdid themselves, because they believed in the company.

What changes in government rules and regulations would improve outcomes for the full range of stakeholders?

My favorite fix is changing the tax rates. Thirty-five percent is woefully high relative to the rest of the world. If we got it down to 20%, we'd be amazed at how much investment and job creation happened in this country. The high rates mean that we're vulnerable to takeovers that have tax inversion as a motivator. We were paying 26%, and Valeant [headquartered in Canada] paid 3%. I think the capital gains taxes could be changed—in a revenue-neutral way—to incentivize holding on to stocks longer.

Shifting gears again: If a company wants to reorient itself toward long-term growth, what has to happen?

I think it's hard for a CEO to change his or her spots. Some can, but most can't. So in most cases you're going to need a new leader. And the board of directors really has to buy into it, because not only are you changing your strategy, you're changing your numbers. You must have a story to tell, for example: "For the next three years, we're not going to deliver 10% EPS growth. It's going to be 5% while we invest in the future. And that's not going to pay off until after three years, so you'll have to be patient." You have to be very, very clear about it.

And then everyone—the board, the investors, the lab technicians, the salespeople—will watch you to see if you're serious. It will take a lot of fortitude and determination. It's not impossible, but it's extremely difficult.

Originally published in May–June 2017. Reprint R1703B

Finally, Evidence That Managing for the Long Term Pays Off

by Dominic Barton, James Manyika, and Sarah Keohane Williamson

Companies deliver superior results when executives manage for long-term value creation and resist pressure from analysts and investors to focus excessively on meeting Wall Street's quarterly earnings expectations. This has long seemed intuitively true to us. We've seen companies such as Unilever, AT&T, and Amazon succeed by sticking resolutely to a long-term view. And yet we have not had the comprehensive data needed to quantify the payoff from managing for the long term—until now.

New research, led by a team from McKinsey Global Institute in cooperation with FCLT Global, found that companies that operate with a true long-term mindset have consistently outperformed their industry peers since 2001 across almost every financial measure that matters.

The differences were dramatic. Among the firms we identified as focused on the long term, average revenue and earnings growth were 47% and 36% higher, respectively, by 2014, and market

Firms focused on the long term exhibit stronger fundamentals and performance

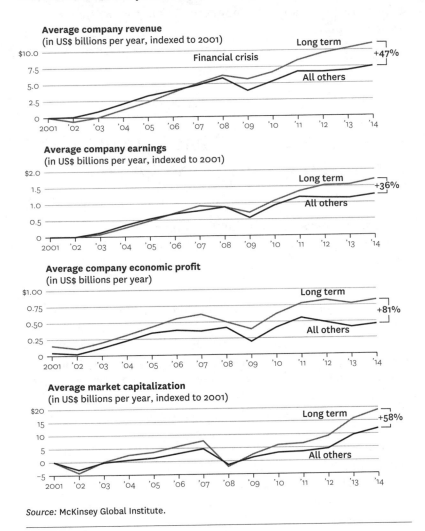

Average company revenue
(in US$ billions per year, indexed to 2001)

Long term

Financial crisis

+47%

All others

$10.0
7.5
5.0
2.5
0

2001 '02 '03 '04 '05 '06 '07 '08 '09 '10 '11 '12 '13 '14

Average company earnings
(in US$ billions per year, indexed to 2001)

Long term

All others

+36%

$2.0
1.5
1.0
0.5
0

2001 '02 '03 '04 '05 '06 '07 '08 '09 '10 '11 '12 '13 '14

Average company economic profit
(in US$ billions per year)

Long term

All others

+81%

$1.00
0.75
0.50
0.25
0

2001 '02 '03 '04 '05 '06 '07 '08 '09 '10 '11 '12 '13 '14

Average market capitalization
(in US$ billions per year, indexed to 2001)

Long term

All others

+58%

$20
15
10
5
0
-5

2001 '02 '03 '04 '05 '06 '07 '08 '09 '10 '11 '12 '13 '14

Source: McKinsey Global Institute.

capitalization grew faster as well. The returns to society and the overall economy were equally impressive. By our measures, companies that were managed for the long term added nearly 12,000 more jobs on average than their peers from 2001 to 2015. We calculate that U.S. GDP over the past decade might well have grown by an additional $1 trillion if the whole economy had performed at the level our long-term stalwarts delivered—and generated more than five million additional jobs over this period.

Who are these overachievers and how did we identify them? We'll dive into those answers shortly. But first, it's worth pausing to consider why finding conclusive data that establishes the rewards from long-term management has been so hard—and just how tangled the debate over this issue has been as a result.

In recent years we have learned a lot about the causes of short-termism and its intensifying power. We know from FCLT surveys, for example, that 61% of executives and directors say that they would cut discretionary spending to avoid risking an earnings miss, and a further 47% would delay starting a new project in such a situation, even if doing so led to a potential sacrifice in value. We also know that most executives feel the balance between short-term accountability and long-term success has fallen out of whack; 65% say the short-term pressure they face has increased in the past five years. We can all see what appear to be the results of excessive short-termism in the form of record levels of stock buybacks in the U.S. and historic lows in new capital investment.

But while measuring the increase in short-term pressures and identifying perverse incentives is fairly straightforward, assessing the ultimate impact of corporate short-termism on company performance and macroeconomic growth is highly complex. After all, "short-termism" does not correspond to any single quantifiable metric. It is a confluence of so many complex factors it can be nearly impossible to pin down. As a result, despite persistent calls for more long-term behavior from us and from CEOs who share our views, such as Larry Fink of BlackRock and Mark Wiseman, the former head of the Canada Pension Plan Investment Board, a genuine debate has continued to rage among economists and analysts over whether short-termism really destroys value.

Academic studies have linked the possible effects of short-termism to lower investment rates among publicly traded firms and decreased returns over a multiyear time horizon. Ambitious work has even attempted to quantify economic growth foregone due to cuts in R&D expenditure driven by short-termism, putting it in the range of about 0.1% per year. Other researchers, however, remain skeptical. How, they ask, could corporate profits in the U.S. remain so high for so long if short-termism were such a drag on performance? And isn't the focus on quarterly results a natural outgrowth of the rigorous corporate governance that keeps executives accountable?

What We Actually Measured—and the Limits of Our Knowledge

To help provide a better factual base for this debate, MGI, working with McKinsey colleagues from our Strategy & Corporate Finance practice as well as the team at FCLT Global, began last fall to devise a way to systemically measure short-termism and long-termism at the company level. It started with developing a proprietary Corporate Horizon Index. The data for this index was drawn from 615 non-finance companies that had reported continuous results from 2001 to 2015 and whose market capitalization in that period had exceeded $5 billion in at least one year. (We wanted to focus on companies large enough to feel the potential short-term pressures exerted by shareholders, boards, activists, and others.) Collectively, our sample accounts for about 60%–65% of total U.S. public market capitalization over this period. To further ensure valid results and to avoid bias in our sample, we evaluated all companies in our index only relative to their industry peers with similar opportunity sets and market conditions and tracked them over several years. We also looked at the proportional composition of the long-term and short-term groups to ensure they are approximately equivalent, so that the differential performance of individual industries cannot bias the overall results, and conducted other tests and controls to ensure statistical robustness.

One final caveat: While we firmly believe our index enables us to classify companies as "long-term" in an unbiased manner, our findings are descriptive only. We aren't saying that a long-term orientation causes better performance, nor have we controlled for every factor that could impact the relationship between those two.

All we can say is that companies with a long-term orientation tend to perform better than similar but short-term-focused firms. Even so, the correlation we uncovered between behaviors that typify a longer-term approach and superior historical performance deliver a message that's hard to ignore.

To construct our Corporate Horizon Index, we identified five financial indicators, selected because they matched up with five hypotheses we had developed about the ways in which long- and short-term companies might differ. These indicators and hypotheses were:

- **Investment.** The ratio of capex to depreciation. We assume long-term companies will invest more and more-consistently than other companies.

- **Earnings quality.** Accruals as a share of revenue. Our belief is that the earnings of long-term companies will rely less on accounting decisions and more on underlying cash flow than other companies.

- **Margin growth.** Difference between earnings growth and revenue growth. We assume that long-term companies are less likely to grow their margins unsustainably in order to hit near-term targets.

- **Earnings growth.** Difference between earnings-per-share (EPS) growth and true earnings growth. We hypothesize that long-term companies will focus less on things like Wall Street's obsession with earnings-per-share, which can be influenced by actions such as share repurchases, and more on the absolute rise or fall of reported earnings.

- **Quarterly targeting.** Incidence of beating or missing EPS targets by less than two cents. We assume long-term companies are more likely to miss earnings targets by small amounts (when they easily could have taken action to hit them) and less likely to hit earnings targets by small amounts (where doing so would divert resources from other business needs).

After running the numbers on these indicators, two broad groups emerged among those 615 large and midcap U.S. publicly listed companies: a "long-term" group of 164 companies (about 27% of the sample), which were either long-term relative to their industry peers over the entire sample or clearly became more long-term between the first half of the sample period and the second half, and a baseline group of the 451 remaining companies (about 73% of the sample). The performance gap that subsequently opened between these two groups of companies offers the most compelling evidence to date of the relative cost of short-termism—and the real payoff that arises from managing for the long term.

Trillions of Dollars of Value Creation at Stake

To recap, from 2001 to 2014, the long-term companies identified by our Corporate Horizons Index increased their revenue by 47% more than others in their industry groups and their earnings by 36% more, on average. Their revenue growth was less volatile over this period, with a standard deviation of growth of 5.6%, versus 7.6% for all other companies. Our long-term firms also appeared more willing to maintain their strategies during times of economic stress. During the 2008–2009 global financial crisis, they not only saw smaller declines in revenue and earnings but also continued to increase investments in research and development while others cut back. From 2007 to 2014, their R&D spending grew at an annualized rate of 8.5%, greater than the 3.7% rate for other companies.

Another way to measure the value creation of long-term companies is to look through the lens of what is known as "economic profit." Economic profit represents a company's profit after subtracting a charge for the capital that the firm has invested (working capital, fixed assets, goodwill). The capital charge equals the amount of invested capital times the opportunity cost of capital—that is, the return that shareholders expect to earn from investing in companies with similar risk. Consider, for example, Company A, which earns $100 of after-tax operating profit, has an 8% cost of capital and $800 of invested capital. In this case its capital charge is $800 times 8%, or $64. Subtracting the capital charge from profits gives $36 of economic profit. A company is creating value when its economic profit is positive, and destroying value if its economic profit is negative.

With this metric, the gap between long-term companies and the rest is even bigger. From 2001 to 2014 those managing for the long term cumulatively increased their economic profit by 63% more than the other companies. By 2014 their annual economic profit was 81% larger than their peers, a tribute to superior capital allocation that led to fundamental value creation.

No path goes straight up, of course, and the long-term companies in our sample still faced plenty of character-testing times. During the last financial crisis, for example, they saw their share prices take greater hits than their short-term counterparts. Afterward, however, the long-term firms significantly outperformed, adding an average of $7 billion more to their companies' market capitalization from 2009 and 2014 than their short-term peers did.

While we can't directly measure the cost of short-termism, our analysis gives an indication of just how large the value of what's being left on the table might be. As noted earlier, if all public U.S. companies had created jobs at the scale of the long-term-focused organizations in our sample, the country would have generated at least five million more jobs from 2001 and 2015—and an additional $1 trillion in GDP growth (equivalent to an average of 0.8 percentage points of GDP growth per year). Projecting forward, if nothing changes to close the gap between the long-term group and the others, then the U.S. economy could be giving up another $3 trillion in foregone GDP and job growth by 2025. Clearly, addressing persistent short-termism should be an urgent issue not just for investors and boards but also for policy makers.

Where Do We Go from Here?

Our research is just a first step toward understanding the scope and magnitude of corporate short-termism. For instance, our initial dataset was limited to the U.S., but we know the problem is a global one. How do the costs and drivers differ by regions? Our sample set consists only of publicly listed companies. How do the effects we discovered differ among private companies or among public companies with varying types of ownership structures? Are there metrics that can help predict when a company is becoming too short-term— and how do they differ among industries? Most important, what are the interventions that will prove most effective in shifting organizations onto a more productive long-term path?

On this last point, we and many others have identified steps that executives, boards, and institutional investors can take to achieve a better balance between hitting targets in the short term and operating with a persistent long-term vision and strategy. These range from creating investment mandates that reward long-term value creation, to techniques for "de-biasing" corporate capital allocation, to rethinking traditional approaches to investor relations and board composition. We will return to HBR in coming months with more data and insights into how companies can strengthen their long-term muscles.

The key message from this research is not only that the rewards from managing for the long term are enormous; it's also that, despite strong countervailing pressures, real change *is* possible. The proof lies in a small but significant subset of our long-term outperformers— 14%, to be precise—that didn't start out in that category. Initially, these companies scored on the short-term end of our index. But over the course of the 15-year period we measured, leaders at the companies in this cohort managed to shift their corporations' behavior sufficiently to move into the long-term category. What were the practical actions these companies took? Exploring that question will be a major focus for our research in the coming year. For now, the simple fact of their success is an inspiration.

Further Reading

- **"Capitalism for the Long Term,"** Dominic Barton, *Harvard Business Review*, March 2011

- **"Focusing Capital on the Long Term,"** Dominic Barton and Mark Wiseman, *Harvard Business Review*, January–February 2014

- **"Where Boards Fall Short,"** Dominic Barton and Mark Wiseman, *Harvard Business Review*, January–February 2015

- **"The Short Long,"** Andrew G. Haldane and Richard Davies, speech, Bank of England, May 2011

- **"Profits Without Prosperity,"** William Lazonick, *Harvard Business Review*, September 2014

- **"Does a Long-Term Orientation Create Value?"** Caroline Flammer and Pratima Bansal, *Strategic Management Journal*, February 2017

- **"Businesses Can and Will Adapt to the Age of Populism,"** the *Economist*, January 2017

Originally published in February 2017. Reprint H03GCC

Now What?

by Joan C. Williams and Suzanne Lebsock

FAREWELL TO THE WORLD where men can treat the workplace like a frat house or a pornography shoot. Since Hollywood producer Harvey Weinstein was accused of sexual misconduct in early October, similar allegations have been made about nearly 100 other powerful people. They all are names you probably recognize, in fields including media, technology, hospitality, politics, and entertainment. It's a watershed moment for workplace equality and safety; 87% of Americans now favor zero tolerance of sexual harassment.

Not only is this better for women, but it's better for most men. A workplace culture in which sexual harassment is rampant is often one that also shames men who refuse to participate. These men-who-don't-fit, like the mistreated women, face choices about whether and how to intervene without endangering their careers.

Still, it's unnerving for many men to see the numbers of those toppled by accusations grow ever higher. The recent summary dismissals of high-powered executives and celebrities have triggered worries that any man might be accused and ruined. Half of men (49%) say the recent furor has made them think again about their own behavior around women. Men wonder whether yesterday's sophomoric idiocy is today's career wrecker.

This is not a fight between men and women, however. One of the journalists to break the Weinstein story was Ronan Farrow, son of Mia Farrow and Woody Allen. Yes, that Woody Allen—the one who married his longtime girlfriend's daughter and is alleged to have sexually abused another daughter. "Sexual assault was an issue that had touched my family," said Farrow, who noted that this experience was instrumental in driving his reporting.

To repeat: This is not a fight between men and women. It's a fight over whether a small subgroup of predatory men should be allowed to interfere with people's ability to show up and do what they signed up for: work.

Several changes in the past decade have brought us to this startling moment. Some were technological: The internet enables women to go public with accusations, bypassing the gatekeepers who traditionally buried their stories. Other changes were cultural: A centuries-old stereotype—the Vengeful Lying Slut—was drained of its power by feminists who coined the term "slut shaming" and reverse-shamed those who did it. Just as important, women have made enough inroads into positions of power in the press, corporations, Congress, and Hollywood that they no longer have to play along with the boys' club; instead they can, say, lead the charge to force Al Franken's resignation or break the story on Harvey Weinstein.

The result of all these changes is what social scientists call a norms cascade: a series of long-term trends that produce a sudden shift in social mores. There's no going back. The work environment now is much different from what it was a year ago. To put things plainly, if you sexually harass or assault a colleague, employee, boss, or business contact today, your job will be at risk.

How the #MeToo Movement Changes Work

As commonplace as these dismissals have come to seem, we know that we are only beginning to scratch the surface of the harassment culture. In "You Can't Change What You Can't See: Interrupting Racial & Gender Bias in the Legal Profession," a forthcoming study of lawyers conducted by the Center for WorkLife Law (which Joan directs) for the American Bar Association, researchers found sexual harassment to be pervasive. Eighty-two percent of women and 74% of men reported hearing sexist comments at work. Twenty-eight

Idea in Brief

When Hollywood producer Harvey Weinstein was accused of sexual harassment, the dam broke. Allegations of sexual misconduct were raised against many powerful people, and millions of women shared their own stories of harassment. It's a watershed moment for equality, say Williams, a legal scholar, and Lebsock, a feminist historian. Now 87% of Americans favor zero tolerance of harassment. Half of men are rethinking their own behavior. Over 75% of people are more likely to report sexist treatment at work. Everything has changed, for a simple reason: Women are being believed. Such was not the case in 1991, when Anita Hill claimed harassment by Supreme Court justice nominee Clarence Thomas. Back then women who came forward were often discredited as "vengeful, lying sluts." But that stereotype has been drained of power by feminists who coined the term "slut-shaming" and reverse-shamed those who did it. As the #MeToo and Time's Up movements demonstrate, women will no longer be silenced. Translating outrage into action requires new norms of workplace conduct, which the authors outline. Firms are moving away from quiet settlements with victims and toward firing abusers. But employers still must follow due process and evaluate the credibility of reports. They need clear policies and fair procedures for handling harassment. No one's asking men to stop being men. But the reasonable assumption is that work relationships should be about work. You must not take one in a romantic direction if it's unwelcome, and the only way to safely tell what someone else wants is to ask. At the same time men shouldn't avoid women at work. That's unnecessary, unfair, and illegal: It deprives women of opportunities simply because of their gender. Women, if colleagues make you uncomfortable, tell them. If you're harassed, report it. The authors aren't sure they'd have said that before #MeToo, but they do now, and it signals that the world has changed.

percent of women and 8% of men reported unwanted sexual or romantic attention or touching at work. Seven percent of women and less than 1% of men reported being bribed or threatened with workplace consequences if they did not engage in sexual behavior. Fourteen percent of women and 5% of men said that they had lost work opportunities because of sexual harassment, which was also associated with delays in promotions, reduced access to high-profile assignments and sponsorship, bias against parents, and higher intent to leave. The three most acute types of harassment (excluding sexist remarks) were associated with reductions in income, demotions, loss of clients and office space, and removal from important committees.

These patterns hold true beyond the legal profession. According to a recent study by researchers at Oklahoma State University, the University of Minnesota, and the University of Maine, women who were sexually harassed were 6.5 times as likely to change jobs as women who weren't. "I quit, and I didn't have a job. That's it. I'm outta here. I'll eat rice and live in the dark if I have to," remarked one woman in the study.

Low-wage women, who often live paycheck to paycheck, and women who are working in the U.S. illegally are the most vulnerable. A survey of nearly 500 Chicago hotel housekeepers revealed that 49% had encountered a guest who had exposed himself. Janitors who work the graveyard shift and farmworkers have had trouble defending themselves against predatory supervisors. And restaurant workers experience it from three directions. A 2014 report aptly titled "The Glass Floor," which shares the findings of a survey of 688 restaurant workers from 39 states, reveals that nearly 80% of the female workers had been harassed by colleagues. Nearly 80% had been harassed by customers, and 67% had been harassed by managers—52% of them on a weekly basis. Workers found customer harassment especially vexing because they were loath to lose crucial income from tips. Small wonder that almost 37% of sexual harassment complaints filed by women with the Equal Employment Opportunity Commission in 2011 came from the restaurant industry.

The stories finally becoming public further highlight how sexual harassment subverts women's careers: Ashley Judd and Mira Sorvino found acting jobs harder to get after they rebuffed the voracious Weinstein. After Gretchen Carlson complained of a hostile work environment, she was assigned fewer hard-hitting interviews on *Fox & Friends* and, according to her legal complaint, was cut from her weekly appearances on the highly rated "Culture Warrior" segment of *The O'Reilly Factor*. Because word got out that Ninth Circuit judge Alex Kozinski sexually harassed clerks, many women did not apply for a clerkship at that court, which positions young lawyers to get clerkships at the U.S. Supreme Court—the biggest plum in the legal basket. When the ambitious congressional staffer Lauren Greene complained of sexual harassment by her boss, Representative Blake Farenthold, her career in politics evaporated. Today she works as a part-time assistant to a home builder.

A point often overlooked is that some sexual harassment victims are men. Men filed nearly 17% of sexual harassment complaints with the EEOC in 2016. Some men are harassed by women, but many are harassed by other men, some straight, some gay. A roustabout on an oil platform was harassed by coworkers on his eight-man crew, the U.S. Supreme Court found in 1998; the coworkers were offended by what they perceived as his insufficient machismo. Recently the Metropolitan Opera suspended longtime conductor James Levine after several men accused him of masturbation-heavy abuse that took place from the late 1960s to the 1980s, when his victims were 16 to 20 years old.

Such behavior is no longer seen as a "tsking" matter. Historically, it has been hard to win a sexual harassment suit, but rapidly shifting public perceptions may change that. Seventy-eight percent of women say they are more likely to speak out now if they are treated unfairly because of their gender. About the same percentage of men (77%) say they are now more likely to speak out if they see a woman being treated unfairly. It's a new day for a simple reason: Women are being believed.

Everything Is Changing

The strongest indicator that we're experiencing a norms cascade came when Senate Majority Leader Mitch McConnell stood up for the women—four of them at the time—who had come forward with revelations about senatorial candidate Roy Moore.

"I believe the women," McConnell said.

The statement stands in stark contrast to Anita Hill's treatment in 1991, when she testified before the Senate Judiciary Committee that Clarence Thomas, then a nominee to the Supreme Court, had sexually harassed her. Senators subjected her to a humiliating inquisition, watched by a rapt national television audience. Another former employee was waiting in the wings to describe how Thomas had sexually harassed her, too. But she was never called to testify. Instead, Hill withstood the all-male committee's bullying alone. After the hearings, opposition to Hill made her life at the University of Oklahoma so difficult that she left her tenured position—an object lesson on the risks facing anyone who dared to raise a charge of sexual harassment.

A recent poll by NPR dramatizes the sudden shift: 66% of Americans think that women who reported sexual harassment were generally ignored five years ago. Only 26% think that women are ignored today. When did we begin believing the women? What changed? And what are the implications for men?

We can trace the disbelief of—or at best, disregard for—women to the old stereotype we mentioned earlier, the one that holds women to be fundamentally irrational, vengeful, deceitful, and rampantly sexual.

An ancient version of this stereotype appears in Genesis, in which Eve commits the first sin and then drags Adam and the rest of humanity down with her for all time. Through the ages in Judeo-Christian tradition, authors expounded upon feminine evil. Among the most vivid prose stylists were two German friars, who in 1486 produced the classic book of witch lore *The Malleus Maleficarum* (or *The Hammer of Witches*). "What else is woman but a foe to friendship, an unescapable punishment, a necessary evil, a natural temptation, a desirable calamity, a domestic danger, a delectable detriment, an evil of nature, painted with fair colours!" they wrote. More to the point for us, perhaps, is their claim that a woman "is a liar by nature."

Although by the 19th century more-positive images of women arose, the stereotype of the Vengeful Lying Slut was too useful to die. It was imposed on entire classes of women, notably African-American women, as scholars have amply documented, and on working-class women pressured into sex by bosses. It was used to ostracize and humiliate high schoolers who found themselves suddenly disparaged as "easy." Whenever men, and sometimes boys, exploited women—or often girls—the stereotype of the Vengeful Lying Slut supplied the words to justify their behavior: She wanted it/asked for it/had it coming.

The stereotype alas persists. It underlies men's fears that they, too, will be brought down by false allegations. Some men have become so frightened that they now refuse to meet (or to eat with) a female colleague alone. When Roy Moore was accused of sexual assault, his campaign said he was the victim of a "witch hunt." That response is a telling and time-honored way of discrediting victims.

The #MeToo and Time's Up movements show that women can no longer be silenced by threats of slut shaming. When a manager at Google told one of the female engineers who worked there, "It's taking all my self-control not to grab your ass right now," she tweeted it out to the world. In the first 24 hours after actress Alyssa Milano suggested that victims of harassment reply "me too" to a tweet in October, 12 million women made #MeToo posts on Facebook. Instead of distancing themselves from those challenging sexual harassment, as might have happened in the past, actors and actresses wore black to the 2018 Golden Globes to signal their solidarity.

Translating outrage into action, however, requires moving beyond hashtags toward new norms of workplace conduct. It's a precarious moment, and a lot could go wrong. Just think what might have happened if the *Washington Post*, with admirable rigor, had not uncovered the truth when a woman approached it with a dramatic but false accusation against Roy Moore. Her purpose? To snooker the Post into publishing a bogus story and to thereby cast doubt on all mainstream media reporting the claims against Moore. But so far so good, with early signs that workplaces are indeed changing.

Firing Is the New Settlement

In the past companies often quietly paid to settle sexual harassment complaints against high-powered miscreants and tried to limit the damage through nondisclosure agreements. Incidents at Fox gave rise to at least seven settlements (some against Fox, some against individuals at Fox). Weinstein reportedly paid out eight. Despite getting large payouts, the plaintiffs were the ones who were forced to leave their companies, and many suffered career interruptions.

Quiet settlements are now becoming harder to justify. The unceremonious firings and forced resignations of famous men demonstrate that companies are moving away from that strategy. Settlements will likely continue in some circumstances, such as a first offense involving mild or ambiguous behavior or a situation that is consensual but violates company standards. But long strings of settlements in egregious cases will increasingly be seen as a breach of the directors' duty to the company. Boards of directors have never tolerated financial fraud and violations of the Foreign Corrupt Practices Act, and they are likely to adopt the same standards for harassment—firing without severance pay.

It's important to recognize that most of the firings have occurred at companies with sophisticated legal and HR departments, on the advice of counsel and with the involvement of senior management or the board or both. We should not assume that they are disclosing all the evidence they have. Companies have a strong motive not to release such evidence, lest the former employee use it as ammunition in a defamation or wrongful discharge suit. That's what companies do when they sack someone for cause, and that's what they are doing here.

Some worry that people will be fired too quickly and without due process. One point that's often overlooked: Due process isn't required of private employers, only public ones. What people are trying to insist on, quite properly, are fair procedures that uncover the truth. Companies should follow the same procedures they use when an employee has been accused of any type of serious misconduct. Typically, the employee is placed on leave while an investigation is performed. In most cases, although not all, that's what has been happening with sexual harassment cases.

Credibility assessments are, of course, important. Women are human beings, and sometimes human beings—male and female—lie. That's why we need to apply the standard methods we always use to assess credibility. Those methods are flawed, but they are all we have; if they will do for every other context, they will do for sexual harassment, too.

As we enter this new era, here's a comforting thought from someone who has spent his life thinking about how to ferret out the truth, the prominent evidence scholar Roger Park (a colleague of Joan's). His observation about sexual harassment is this: "Men have a motive to do it and lie, whereas women don't have a motivation to lie, considering what an ordeal it is." Making even *true* allegations of sexual harassment has historically been a poor career move.

That provides some assurance that reports of harassment are truthful. So do large numbers of people with similar stories. At least 42 women have come forward with allegations against Weinstein, and at least 10 against Ken Friedman, the New York restaurateur. At least a dozen people have made accusations against Kevin Spacey. Those numbers lend credibility to the allegations.

Employers who want to set up processes for handling harassment can begin with the standard sexual harassment policies. The Society for Human Resources has one; others are free online. Organizational training should spell out what's acceptable, which will vary from company to company. Some companies may want to add detail in light of recent events. Surprising as it sounds, some people seem to need a heads-up that porn, kissing, back rubs, and nudity are not appropriate at work.

How can this be? Here's a clue. At a dinner Judge Kozinski held with law clerks, he steered the conversation to the "voluptuous" breasts of a topless woman in a film, according to someone present. When one woman at the dinner reacted negatively, Kozinski responded that, well, he was a man.

Some men have an urgent need to preserve sexual harassment as a prerogative because, they feel, their manliness is at stake. But theirs is just one definition of manliness—a toxic and outdated one. It's time to move on.

The Workplace Today

Virtually all women and most men are now aligned against that toxic brand of masculinity. No one is asking men to stop being men or for people to stop being sexual beings. What's happened is that a small group of men are being required to abandon the stereotype that "real men" need to be unrelentingly sexual without regard to context or consent.

The not-unreasonable assumption is that work relationships should be about work. Some organizations have no-dating policies for that reason. If yours doesn't, remember that you must not take a relationship with a colleague in a romantic or sexual direction if doing so is unwelcome. Whether you can ask a colleague out is the source of much anxiety, especially in all-consuming work environments where people date coworkers because they spend so much time on the job that there's little opportunity to meet anyone else.

The only way to safely tell what someone else wants is to ask that person. Some men seem to have trouble discerning whether a woman is interested; Charlie Rose and Glenn Thrush said that they thought their feelings were reciprocated when women who received their overtures say they were not. This is not an unsolvable problem. If she's a work colleague and you'd like her to be something more, here's what to do: Imagine telling a woman who's been your friend forever that you'd like to take the relationship in a different direction. Ask in a way that gives her a chance to say that she prefers to remain a friend. No harm, no foul. What if your work colleague says no when she really means yes? Well, then, she's got to live with that. Let her. Let her change her mind if she wants to.

We all know that deals and crucial networking happen over lunch, dinner, and drinks. Socializing in this manner is fine. But if you do socialize with work colleagues, you need to realize that you can't behave inappropriately. Roy Price resigned from his job as head of Amazon Studios after Isa Hackett, an Amazon producer, publicly accused him of repeatedly propositioning her in a cab on the way to a work party, telling her, "You'll love my dick," and later at the gathering whispering "anal sex" loudly in her ear in the presence of others. Hollywood commentator Nellie Andreeva noted that in a post-Weinstein world Price's behavior would have hurt Amazon's ability to attract female showrunners and actors. He would have been "completely ostracized," an anonymous source told Andreeva.

Where the Law Draws the Line

by Joan C. Williams

Many of the sexual harassment cases making headlines involve criminal behavior. Sexual assault and related offenses are defined in different ways in different states. To take just one example, New York law prohibits "forcibly touching the sexual or other intimate parts of another person for the purpose of degrading or abusing such person or for the purpose of gratifying the actor's sexual desire." The statute helpfully adds that this "includes squeezing, grabbing or pinching." It should not be surprising or puzzling that such behavior is not acceptable.

Gentlemen, you already know not to invite a woman to discuss a job and then meet her wearing a bathrobe and expose yourself. Charlie Rose reportedly did that, and according to several women, Harvey Weinstein did that—and more. Masturbating in work contexts is not only unacceptable but illegal, yet that's what Louis C.K. did. One does not stick one's tongue down the throat of someone during a discussion of job prospects, as two women have claimed NPR's Michael Oreskes did. You do not kiss a colleague and lick her, as actor Andy Dick did.

Men do not expect to report to work and have their crotch grabbed. Women don't, either. It should not be frightening or confusing to be told this. But we understand why men are scared: Most sexual harassment does not involve sexual assault, and if you've ever told an off-color joke at work, asked out a colleague, or maybe been a little handsy at a holiday party (or know someone who has), we bet you've been thinking a lot about sexual harassment lately.

Employment law has a sober and balanced approach that is fully protective of the rights of men accused of sexual harassment. It defines two kinds of sexual harassment:

Quid Pro Quo Harassment

Making sexual favors a condition of any workplace opportunity is illegal under federal law. To win a lawsuit alleging it, a woman has to prove that someone with authority over her threatened to take a negative employment action unless she engaged in a sexual behavior—or promised her a promotion, raise, or other benefit if she did. Congressman John Conyers paid thousands of dollars to a staffer who said she was fired for refusing his sexual advances. According to accounts published in *New York* magazine, Roger Ailes tied women's work prospects to sex again and again: "If you want to play with the big boys, you have to lay with the big boys," he told a woman seeking a contract with the Republican National Committee in 1989. "No girls get a job here unless they're cooperative," he is reported to have said to a frightened 19-year-old in the sixties after he grabbed her and forcibly kissed her. Fifty years later, TV host Gretchen Carlson says, Ailes demoted and ultimately fired her for refusing to have sex with him. Fox settled Carlson's harassment case for $20 million. But it extended Bill O'Reilly's contract after O'Reilly settled a sexual harassment case against him for $32 million. Cases do not settle for that kind of money unless something has gone seriously wrong.

For men worried about *quid pro quo harassment,* the simplest approach is not to date someone you supervise. If you do, make sure it's consensual and remember that whether you stay together or break up, with respect to workplace issues you need to behave *exactly* as you would have if you'd never dated her. If you can't do that, don't date people you supervise. All this applies, of course, not only to men but also to women.

A Hostile Work Environment

Here again the legal test is quite protective of those accused of sexual harassment. To meet the legal definition the conduct must be unwelcome, the environment must be one that a reasonable person would consider hostile, the plaintiff herself must feel it to be hostile, and the behavior that makes the environment hostile must be severe or pervasive.

Moreover, plaintiffs very rarely win hostile environment cases that are based on a single "severe" incident. Almost invariably, they need to prove the behavior was "pervasive." How pervasive?

Very. In a 1993 Supreme Court case, a woman's boss made such comments as "You're a woman, what do you know?," "We need a man as the rental manager," and "Dumb-ass woman," and asked her in front of coworkers if she wanted to "go to the Holiday Inn" to negotiate a raise. He asked women to retrieve coins from the front pockets of his pants and threw objects on ground and asked women to pick them up. When the plaintiff complained to the boss about his conduct, he said he was joking and promised to stop, but he didn't. She quit, sued, and won: She had made it clear the behavior was unwelcome and that it personally offended her. The court found that a reasonable person would have felt the environment was hostile and that the hostility was pervasive.

This is so far beyond what most men would ever imagine is appropriate that they have little to fear. Still, the requirement that the plaintiff prove that she herself felt an environment to be hostile adds another layer of protection. So women need to speak up to demonstrate that they're personally experiencing that feeling, not just to show that an advance is unwelcome. "That makes me uncomfortable. We are at work" is enough.

It's OK to socialize with and date colleagues. But the law regarding "retaliation" requires that a colleague must be able to decline an invitation without consequences. The easiest way for a company to lose a sexual harassment suit is for a plaintiff to prove that she turned down an advance or complained of a hostile environment and then suffered retaliation.

A new textbook example comes from Uber. Susan Fowler's manager propositioned her on the company chat site. She took a screenshot of it and went to HR, which gave her a choice: Either she could transfer out of her team, or she could stay. But if she stayed, the people in HR said, her boss might give her a poor performance review and they could do nothing about it.

Here's the problem: Giving someone a poor review because she turned you down is retaliation, which is illegal. Fowler didn't want to transfer, because her team's project was a great match for her specific skills, but she decided to do so. Fortunately, she found other great work to do, but unfortunately, she continued to encounter sexist behavior, which she reported to HR. One day her boss called her in and threatened to fire her if she didn't stop making complaints. That's retaliation too—and it's illegal.

You can still compliment your colleagues. But there's a big difference between "I like that dress" and "You look hot in that dress." What if she really *does* look hot? Remember, she signed up to be your colleague, not your girlfriend. Treat her like a colleague unless by mutual consent, you change your relationship.

Don't let the pendulum swing too far the other way and bizarrely avoid women completely. That's unnecessary, unfair, and illegal: It deprives women of opportunities simply because they are women. You cannot refuse to have closed-door meetings with women unless you refuse to have closed-door meetings with men. Otherwise women will be denied access to all the sensitive information that's shared only behind closed doors, and that's a violation of federal law.

Moving forward, male allies will continue to play an important role in fighting harassment: If you see something, say something. It does take courage, but you can use a light touch. If you're standing around with a bunch of guys and a female colleague walks by, only to have someone say, "Wow, she's hot," you can say simply: "I don't think of her that way. I think of her as a colleague, and that's the way I suspect she'd like to be thought of."

Clear takeaways emerge for women, too. If a coworker tries to take a work relationship in a sexual direction, tell him clearly if that's unwelcome. If you face sexual joking that's making you uncomfortable, say, "This is making me uncomfortable" and expect it to stop. If you want to shame or jolly someone out of misbehavior while preserving your business relationships, consult Joan's *What Works for Women at Work*. Here's an approach that worked for one woman whose colleague proposed an affair: "I know your wife. She's my friend. You're married. There is just no way I would ever consider that. So let's not go there again."

But it's our final piece of advice that signals the tectonic shift: If you are being sexually harassed, report it. We're not sure if we would have advised that, in such a blanket and unnuanced way, even a year ago.

What we're seeing today is not the end of sex, or of seduction, or of *la différence*. What we're seeing is the demise of a work culture where women must submit to being treated, insistently and incessantly, as sexual opportunities. Most people, when they go to work, want to work. And now they can.

Originally published in January 2018. Reprint BG1801

The Omissions That Make So Many Sexual Harassment Policies Ineffective

by Debbie S. Dougherty

Our research began with a simple question: If 98% of organizations in the United States have a sexual harassment policy, why does sexual harassment continue to be such a persistent and devastating problem in the American workplace? As evidenced by recent headlines regarding ongoing sexual harassment in the National Park Service, Uber, and Fox News, it seems clear that sexual harassment policies have not stopped the problem they were designed to address.

Two bodies of research provided us with a possible direction as we explored the relationship between sexual harassment policies and outcomes. First, scholars convincingly argue that sexual harassment is embedded in organizational culture. In other words, sexual harassment serves an important cultural function for some organizations. And as any executive who has tried to lead cultural change knows, organizational culture can be immutable.

Second, organizational cultures are embedded in a larger national culture in which men have traditionally been granted privileges over women. It does not take a deep analysis to recognize this truth. Women are typically paid less, regardless of education, qualifications, or years of service. There are more CEOs named John leading big companies than there are female CEOs. The male-centric nature of our national culture is so pervasive that even many women are male-centered, aligning themselves with men and masculinity to tap into male privilege while attempting (usually unsuccessfully) to avoid the disadvantaged space that women occupy in the workplace.

All of this means that both men and women can react to sexual harassment by blaming other women for "making trouble" or "putting up with bad behavior," or by suggesting that the sexually harassed women should quit, without considering that perhaps the perpetrators instead of their targets should leave the organization. These attitudes have real consequences. Consider: In the Fox News harassment case, the alleged perpetrators received larger settlements than the targets. Cultures of sexual harassment are thus legitimized by drawing on the larger cultural imperative that privileges men over women.

Into this fraught cultural morass enters a well-intentioned document: the sexual harassment policy. To see how employees interpreted these policies, my colleague Marlo Goldstein Hode and I gave 24 employees of a large government organization a copy of the organization's sexual harassment policy, asking them to read it and then tell us about the policy. We asked them to talk about the policy in groups, and then we interviewed them individually.

We found that the actual words of the sexual harassment policy bore little resemblance to the employees' interpretations of the policy. Although the policy clearly focused on *behaviors* of sexual harassment, the participants almost universally claimed that the policy focused on *perceptions* of behaviors. Moreover, although the policy itself made clear that harassing behaviors were harassment regardless of either the gender or sexual orientation of the perpetrator or target, the employees focused almost exclusively on male-female heterosexual harassment. This shift is subtle but significant. For the participants, the policy was perceived as threatening, because any behavior could be sexual harassment if an irrational (typically female) employee perceived it as such. In this somewhat paranoid scenario, a simple touch on the arm or a nonsexual comment on appearance ("I like your hairstyle") could subject "innocent" employees (usually heterosexual males) to persecution as stipulated by the policy. As a result, the organization's sexual harassment policy was perceived as both highly irrational and as targeting heterosexual male employees. The employees shifted the meaning of the policy such that female targets of sexual harassment were framed as the perpetrators and male perpetrators were framed as innocent victims.

To accomplish this shift in meaning, the employees drew on assumptions of women being irrational and highly emotional and on assumptions of men being rational and competent. Through this intertwining of organizational policy, organizational culture, and national culture, the employees inverted the meaning of the sexual harassment policy, making it an ineffective tool in the fight against predatory sexual behavior in the workplace.

How can organizations combat the reinterpretation of sexual harassment policies? This question takes on urgency when we recognize that sexual harassment policies are table stakes in successfully managing the damaging behavior.

Remember that sexual harassment policies are not just legal documents. They are also culturally important, *meaning-making* documents that should play a role in defining, preventing, and stopping sexual harassment in an organization. The findings from our study suggest very specific language that may be useful in sexual harassment policies:

- **Include culturally appropriate, emotion-laden language in sexual harassment policies.** Our findings suggest that if you don't add this language, organizational members will include their own. For example, adding language such as "Sexual harassment is a form of predatory sexual behavior in which a person targets other employees" frames the behavior such that alternative interpretations may be more difficult to make. Using terms such as "predatory" instead of "perpetrator" and "target" instead of "victim" can shape how organizational members interpret the policy. Although policies tend to be stripped of emotions, it is essential for policy creators to recognize that policy creation is one of the most emotion-laden activities that organizational leaders are asked to accomplish. Because sexual harassment is such an emotionally laden topic, the creation of sexual harassment policies becomes even more emotionally challenging.

- **Sexual harassment policies should include bystander interventions as a required response to predatory sexual behavior.** Most policies place responsibility for reporting harassment exclusively on the target, which puts them in a vulnerable position. If they report the behavior, then they are likely to be viewed with suspicion by their colleagues, often becoming socially isolated from their coworkers. On the other hand, if they do not report the sexual harassment, then it is likely to continue unabated, creating harm for the targeted employee, and wider organizational ills, too. Mandating bystander intervention can relieve the target of their sole responsibility for reporting and stopping predatory sexual behavior, and rightly puts the responsibility of creating a healthier organizational culture on *all* members of the organization.

Sexual harassment is complicated. If it were a simple problem involving just two people, we would have resolved the issue decades ago. But sexual harassment is a complicated, entrenched problem. Systems theory tells us that solutions need to match the complexity of the problem. Writing a policy is complicated, as our study showed. But it's also just a start. No policy, no matter how well crafted, will prevent sexual harassment on its own, nor will it change a culture of sexual harassment. A policy is a first step that needs to be followed by persistent training, a willingness to listen to targets, and a readiness to fire employees who prey sexually on other employees—regardless of how important the predator may be in the organization.

Originally published in May 2017. Reprint H03ONZ

How Do Your Workers Feel About Harassment? Ask Them

by Andrea S. Kramer and Alton B. Harris

If your business is serious about eliminating the risk of sexual harassment—and it should be—you need to approach the problem comprehensively. This means recognizing that sexual harassment is part of a continuum of interconnected behaviors that range from gender bias to incivility to legally actionable assault. All these kinds of misconduct should be addressed collectively, because sexual harassment is far more likely in organizations that experience offenses on the "less severe" end of the spectrum than in those that don't.

There's no one-size-fits-all program for eliminating inappropriate gender-related behaviors; the best programs specifically address the characteristics of each workplace's culture. The vital first step, then, is to get an accurate picture of yours. How? Ask your employees directly. Do they see disparities in career opportunities? Are colleagues or supervisors rude to each other? Is there inappropriate sexual conduct? Do employees feel uncomfortable or unsafe at work?

The best way to find all this out is with a carefully designed employee survey. In this article we'll offer some key principles for fashioning one, along with a model survey that you can adapt (which incorporates some of the recommendations the EEOC made for surveys in its 2017 proposed enforcement guidance on harassment). Our advice is based on insights we developed while working with major business organizations and conducting several hundred gender-focused workshops and moderated conversations around the United States.

Though we think a workplace climate survey can be immensely valuable, we caution that managers and leaders should proceed only if they're fully committed to thoroughly and quickly addressing inappropriate behavior in their organizations. Once the surveys are undertaken, they'll create expectations of remedial action. They might also attract unwanted publicity or be used against the company in future litigation. Those risks, however, are substantially outweighed by the opportunity to develop a work environment that's free of sexual misconduct, gender bias, and incivility.

Step 1: Communicate with Employees

Inform your employees that you're undertaking an effort to understand how fair, courteous, and safe their workplace is. The goal is to encourage engaged and completely candid answers to the survey. For that reason, it should be anonymous and administered by a third party, not your HR department. Employees won't have faith that their answers are confidential if the survey is conducted in-house, and if you don't offer true anonymity, their responses are less likely to be honest.

It's crucial for employees to believe that management considers an unbiased and harassment-free workplace a priority and is sincere in its commitment to that objective. That will happen only if senior management openly endorses the initiative, communicates the importance of supporting it to the entire management team, and periodically speaks to all employees about it.

Employees also need to believe that the end result will be better policies for everyone. This last point can't be emphasized too strongly. If the steps you take to combat inappropriate gender-related behaviors are seen solely as efforts to "protect" women because of their vulnerability, the initiative will backfire.

The first organization-wide letter to employees might begin with a statement like this:

We are gathering information on a confidential basis to better understand our business's workplace climate. Our goal is to ensure that all employees receive equal opportunities, respect, and resources in a workplace that is free of incivility and does not toler-ate inappropriate sexual conduct.

The survey that you'll receive shortly is the first step toward achieving that objective.

We have hired a third-party administrator to conduct the survey on a strictly anonymous basis. Your answers and identity will be carefully protected from disclosure.

The administrator will contact you separately and detail its procedures for preserving anonymity.

The survey you'll receive is divided into four parts: gender bias, incivility, inappropriate sexual conduct, and overall workplace climate. All four areas are important, so please be as candid as possible in giving your views.

Employees should also be told that only the third-party adminis-trator will see the raw survey results and that it will provide an anal-ysis of those results to management. Once management receives that report, employees should be advised of the nature of and time-table for next steps.

We suggest that you emphasize that because the survey is anon-ymous, your organization cannot investigate or remedy specific claims raised by respondents—unless the incidents are separately reported in accordance with existing company procedures. Urge your employees to use those procedures if appropriate.

Step 2: Draw Up Your Survey

Whether you start with the assessment that we provide in this article or create your own questions, you should tailor your survey to your organization's culture and climate. Keep in mind the following:

- Avoid questions that could be used—or thought to be used—to identify participants, such as those about title, age, tenure with the company, responsibilities, and workplace location.

- Don't ask about marital or domestic status, sexual preference, children, or prior involvement in sexual misconduct investigations or proceedings. An inappropriate question in a job interview is equally inappropriate in a workplace climate survey.

- Keep the survey on point. Resist the temptation to use it as an opportunity to ask employees more broadly about their experiences, expectations, and future plans.

- Make the survey short and unambiguous. It should take no more than 10 minutes to finish. You may use true/false, multiple choice, or open-ended questions, but in our experience, the most useful approach is to incorporate a scale. Develop a series of statements that participants will be asked to indicate their degree of agreement with, using a scale of 1 (strongly disagree) to 7 (strongly agree). With statements that are intended to examine the frequency of specific behaviors, use a scale of 1 (very frequently) to 4 (never).

Step 3: Evaluate

A workplace climate survey needs no statistical evaluation beyond a simple tabulation. You're just attempting to determine whether some of your employees believe there are gender-related problems in your work environment and what those problems are.

Bear in mind that the survey is not an end in itself; it's a tool to identify whether you need new policies, practices, and procedures to eliminate inappropriate behavior and protect your employees against sexual harassment. Your results may indicate additional steps are necessary. You might need to assemble focus groups, conduct personal interviews, or host roundtable discussions. Since your goal is to ensure you have a welcoming, supportive, and productive workplace, the real work begins once you have a clear picture of your business's actual climate. Here is a template you can use when constructing your survey:

Model Workplace Climate Survey

Complete the following survey about your experience at XYZ Company, without referring to experiences at any prior organizations. The value of this survey depends directly on getting an accurate view of our workplace culture, so please answer all questions as honestly as possible.

1. Which of the following describes your gender?
   - Male
   - Female
   - Prefer to self-describe (specify)
   - Prefer not to say

Gender Bias

2. I feel valued by the organization.
   (1) Strongly disagree
   (2) Disagree
   (3) Slightly disagree
   (4) Neither agree nor disagree, or have no opinion
   (5) Slightly agree
   (6) Agree
   (7) Strongly agree

3. I believe my opportunities for career success are negatively affected by my gender.
   (1) Strongly disagree
   (2) Disagree
   (3) Slightly disagree
   (4) Neither agree nor disagree, or have no opinion
   (5) Slightly agree
   (6) Agree
   (7) Strongly agree

4. The people I work with treat me with respect and appreciation.
   (1) Strongly disagree
   (2) Disagree
   (3) Slightly disagree
   (4) Neither agree nor disagree, or have no opinion
   (5) Slightly agree
   (6) Agree
   (7) Strongly agree

5. My views are encouraged and welcomed by my supervisors and senior leaders without regard to my gender.
   (1) Strongly disagree
   (2) Disagree
   (3) Slightly disagree
   (4) Neither agree nor disagree, or have no opinion
   (5) Slightly agree
   (6) Agree
   (7) Strongly agree

6. Career-enhancing assignments and opportunities are disproportionately given to men.
   (1) Strongly disagree
   (2) Disagree
   (3) Slightly disagree
   (4) Neither agree nor disagree, or have no opinion
   (5) Slightly agree
   (6) Agree
   (7) Strongly agree

Civility

7. My coworkers are courteous and friendly.
   (1) Strongly disagree
   (2) Disagree
   (3) Slightly disagree
   (4) Neither agree nor disagree, or have no opinion
   (5) Slightly agree
   (6) Agree
   (7) Strongly agree

8. I'm aware of unpleasant and negative gossip in the workplace.
   (1) Strongly disagree
   (2) Disagree
   (3) Slightly disagree
   (4) Neither agree nor disagree, or have no opinion
   (5) Slightly agree
   (6) Agree
   (7) Strongly agree

9. I'm aware of abusive, disrespectful, or hostile treatment of employees.

(continued)

(1) Strongly disagree
(2) Disagree
(3) Slightly disagree
(4) Neither agree nor disagree, or have
no opinion
(5) Slightly agree
(6) Agree
(7) Strongly agree

10. I'm aware of bullying behavior in the
workplace.
(1) Strongly disagree
(2) Disagree
(3) Slightly disagree
(4) Neither agree nor disagree, or have
no opinion
(5) Slightly agree
(6) Agree
(7) Strongly agree

11. There are adverse consequences for senior leaders who are abusive, disrespectful, or hostile.
(1) Strongly disagree
(2) Disagree
(3) Slightly disagree
(4) Neither agree nor disagree, or have
no opinion
(5) Slightly agree
(6) Agree
(7) Strongly agree

12. I have been criticized for my personal
communication style or appearance.
(1) Very frequently
(2) Somewhat frequently
(3) Not at all frequently
(4) Never

13. All individuals are valued here.
(1) Strongly disagree
(2) Disagree
(3) Slightly disagree
(4) Neither agree nor disagree, or have
no opinion
(5) Slightly agree
(6) Agree
(7) Strongly agree

Inappropriate Sexual Conduct

14. I have experienced or witnessed unwanted
physical conduct in the workplace or by
coworkers away from the workplace.

(1) Very frequently
(2) Somewhat frequently
(3) Not at all frequently
(4) Never

15. I have witnessed or heard of offensive or
inappropriate sexual jokes, innuendoes,
banter, or comments in our workplace.
(1) Very frequently
(2) Somewhat frequently
(3) Not at all frequently
(4) Never

16. I have witnessed or heard of the
electronic transmission of sexually
explicit materials or comments by
coworkers.
(1) Very frequently
(2) Somewhat frequently
(3) Not at all frequently
(4) Never

17. I have received sexually inappropriate
phone calls, text messages, or social
media attention from a coworker.
(1) Very frequently
(2) Somewhat frequently
(3) Not at all frequently
(4) Never

18. I have been asked or have witnessed
inappropriate questions of a sexual
nature.
(1) Very frequently
(2) Somewhat frequently
(3) Not at all frequently
(4) Never

19. I have been the subject of conduct that
I consider to be sexual harassment.
(1) Very frequently
(2) Somewhat frequently
(3) Not at all frequently
(4) Never

20. Managers here tolerate or turn a blind
eye to inappropriate sexual conduct.
(1) Strongly disagree
(2) Disagree
(3) Slightly disagree
(4) Neither agree nor disagree, or have
no opinion
(5) Slightly agree
(6) Agree
(7) Strongly agree

21. I feel unsafe at work because of inappropriate sexual conduct by some individuals.
    (1) Strongly disagree
    (2) Disagree
    (3) Slightly disagree
    (4) Neither agree nor disagree, or have no opinion
    (5) Slightly agree
    (6) Agree
    (7) Strongly agree

22. I've seen career opportunities be favorably allocated on the basis of existing or expected sexual interactions.
    (1) Strongly disagree
    (2) Disagree
    (3) Slightly disagree
    (4) Neither agree nor disagree, or have no opinion
    (5) Slightly agree
    (6) Agree
    (7) Strongly agree

23. I would be comfortable reporting inappropriate sexual conduct by a coworker.
    (1) Strongly disagree
    (2) Disagree
    (3) Slightly disagree
    (4) Neither agree nor disagree, or have no opinion
    (5) Slightly agree
    (6) Agree
    (7) Strongly agree

24. I would be comfortable reporting inappropriate sexual conduct by a supervisor.
    (1) Strongly disagree
    (2) Disagree
    (3) Slightly disagree
    (4) Neither agree nor disagree, or have no opinion
    (5) Slightly agree
    (6) Agree
    (7) Strongly agree

Overall Workplace Climate

25. My productivity has been affected by inappropriate gender-related behavior in the workplace.
    (1) Strongly disagree
    (2) Disagree
    (3) Slightly disagree

(4) Neither agree nor disagree, or have no opinion
(5) Slightly agree
(6) Agree
(7) Strongly agree

26. I have considered leaving my job because of inappropriate gender-related behavior in the workplace.
    (1) Strongly disagree
    (2) Disagree
    (3) Slightly disagree
    (4) Neither agree nor disagree, or have no opinion
    (5) Slightly agree
    (6) Agree
    (7) Strongly agree

27. Star performers are held to the same standards as other employees with respect to inappropriate gender-related behavior.
    (1) Strongly disagree
    (2) Disagree
    (3) Slightly disagree
    (4) Neither agree nor disagree, or have no opinion
    (5) Slightly agree
    (6) Agree
    (7) Strongly agree

28. I have experienced or witnessed inappropriate gender-related behavior by third parties (such as customers, vendors, and suppliers) associated with our organization.
    (1) Very frequently
    (2) Somewhat frequently
    (3) Not at all frequently
    (4) Never

29. The organization's policies and processes with respect to prohibiting and reporting inappropriate gender-related behavior are easy to understand and follow.
    (1) Strongly disagree
    (2) Disagree
    (3) Slightly disagree
    (4) Neither agree nor disagree, or have no opinion
    (5) Slightly agree
    (6) Agree
    (7) Strongly agree

Originally published in January 2018. Reprint BG1801

Getting Men to Speak Up

by Michael S. Kimmel

In early November 1991, a month after Anita Hill's testimony about being sexually harassed by Supreme Court nominee Clarence Thomas, my mother invited me to dinner. After a long and pleasant meal, she told me that Hill's stories were all too familiar. When my mother was in graduate school, her mentor groped her. She left school the next day and didn't complete her PhD for 30 years.

Back in the 1990s, Hill wasn't believed when she bravely came forward. Instead she was vilified by the Senate Judiciary Committee as a woman scorned, as "a little bit nutty and a little bit slutty," as a now-contrite David Brock put it in his article smearing Hill. That response set the tone: Over the next 25 years, whenever a woman stood up to publicly accuse men like Bill Cosby or Bill Clinton of sexual assault, she usually ended up being the one on trial in the court of public opinion, charged with a lack of credibility.

But outside this public narrative, something started to shift: Women like my mother began to speak privately about their painful experiences. Mothers told their children, wives told their husbands, women told their friends, daughters told their parents. And they were believed.

Social scientists who study movements often speak of the three elements of revolution. First come the structural preconditions— long-term institutional changes that slowly build pressure, sometimes without even being noticed. In this case, those 25 years of simmering private conversations paved the way for today's widespread backlash against harassment. The second element of a revolution is precipitants—pivotal events that cause change to rapidly accelerate. One precipitant here was the 2016 release of the *Access Hollywood* videotape of Donald Trump bragging about kissing and groping women. After his election to the U.S. presidency despite this evidence, many women were both incredulous and furious.

Finally, there are trigger events that ignite a major explosion. In this case it was the rapid succession of revelations about Roger Ailes, Bill O'Reilly, and Harvey Weinstein. In what seemed like a first, the women's tales of abuse were not doubted—they were *believed*. And so #MeToo began, a reckoning so public that the women who spoke out were named Time magazine's people of the year in 2017.

We are in a new moment. For many of us, particularly men, it is scary and uncomfortable. Men are feeling vulnerable and afraid of false accusations (or perhaps true ones). They fear that things they did a long time ago will be reevaluated under new rules. They tell me they're walking on eggshells. Because of this, many men are staying silent rather than taking part in the conversation. And yet inaction isn't necessarily the right approach; there are important things men can do and say to support the women in their lives.

My experience studying masculinity and working with companies on sexual harassment has led me to focus on how men can take action to address this problem in the workplace. To do so effectively, we must come to terms with four questions: Why do men harass women? Don't they know it's wrong? How do they get away with it? And finally, what can we do about it?

Why Do Men Harass Women?

This one's easy. Men do it because they feel they can. It's hardly the case that men are so overcome by lust that they cannot restrain themselves, as some people have suggested. No, it's often about being in a position of power and feeling entitled to have access to women. These male harassers are emboldened to act by their privilege and authority and by the fact that their targets are in a weaker and more vulnerable position.

Don't They Know It's Wrong?

Nearly all of us know that grabbing a woman by her genitals, patting her butt, making lewd comments, or forcing her to engage in sexual activity is wrong. This is not some blurry line we have to negotiate. *We know.* "They let you do it" is the most telling quote from that *Access Hollywood* tape. Trump is saying, in effect, *You see what a big celebrity I am? Look what I can get away with.*

Some men, however, may not realize that the occasional shoulder massage, calling women "sweetie" or "honey," or making suggestive comments is also wrong. Men who are older tend to fall into this category. It's startling to remember that a mere two generations ago, white-collar workplaces looked like a lot like Don Draper's world on *Mad Men.* The offices with the windows and doors were occupied by men; the women were gathered in the secretarial pool in the center of the office, a sort of crude corral. Sexual access to them was considered a perk.

This might be why men in their sixties who are accused of behaving badly 30 years ago sometimes seem bewildered. They may feel they are being judged by contemporary standards for things they did under what they perceive as different rules. This is reflected in the data: According to a recent analysis by *The Economist,* "younger respondents were more likely to think that a behavior crossed the line than their older peers were."

This does not absolve younger guys of their own bad behavior, nor is it reason to forgive the older men being accused. Still, it's important to talk more about these generational issues and how they color our thinking about the way we treat women.

How Do They Get Away With It?

Complicit assent. Think again about the *Access Hollywood* tape. What might have happened had Billy Bush, the show's host at the time, responded with, *Donald, that's disgusting—not to mention illegal!* Or if the other guys on the bus had said, *That's gross.* What if Harvey Weinstein's brother, Bob, had grabbed him by the shoulders and yelled, *Harvey, stop it! I will throw you out of the company if you continue!*

Sexual harassment persists because of three factors: the sense of entitlement that some men feel toward the women they work with; the presumption that women won't report it or fight back; and the presumed support—even tacit support in the form of not calling out bad behavior—of other men.

What we've seen recently is the second leg of the stool getting kicked out. There's been an outpouring of resistance from women. Women are speaking out, loudly, and not stopping.

What Can We Do?

Now it's time to kick out the third leg. When men remain silent, it can be taken as a sign that we agree with the harasser, that we think the behavior is OK, and that we won't intervene. Men are complicit in a culture that enables sexual harassment, so it is up to us to actively, volubly speak up and let the perpetrators know that we are not OK with what they do.

I'll make one assertion here, which is backed by my experiences working with companies to promote gender equality over several decades: The overwhelming majority of men do not want to be jerks. We don't want to make women uncomfortable and don't want to say things that are offensive.

This puts a slightly more positive spin on the current male anxiety, which most assume is about being reported for harassment. But it also might be about the desire not to behave badly—and about not knowing exactly how to act.

We *can* act in a positive manner, however. Here's one scenario I suspect is remarkably common:

Adeline is sitting in a meeting. She is the only woman in the room. Rob is in the meeting, too, and he makes a sexist comment. The room goes silent. Everyone's attention is on Adeline: Is she going to do something, say something? *Oh, God, here she goes,* many of the other men are saying to themselves. Big eye roll. *She's gonna call him out and make everyone feel bad.* And Adeline has to decide if she's going to say something and make everyone miserable, or swallow it and stay miserable herself.

After the meeting, one of Adeline's colleagues, Fabrice, privately apologizes to her for Rob. "I'm really sorry about what he said in there," Fabrice says. "I didn't like that at all."

Fabrice thinks he's being supportive, but he's actually introducing another dilemma for Adeline. Does she nod politely and thank him? Or does she say, "Uh, where were you when I needed you?"

Men, what could you do differently? The obvious answer is that you could speak up, right then in the meeting, and say that you aren't comfortable with those kinds of statements. But typically we don't do that. Why not?

We're afraid that if we do, we'll be marginalized, kicked out of the men's club—that we'll become, in effect, "honorary women." Men know that doing the right thing sometimes carries costs, and most of us are worried about jeopardizing what we have. So we betray the women in the room, abandon our ethics, and slink away uncomfortably.

But think about that moment when Rob made his comment. I'm sure there were guys in the meeting who were looking down at their shoes, laughing uncomfortably, or shuffling the papers on the table. They didn't like it either but were too frightened to act.

Men, this is your chance. After the meeting, don't apologize to Adeline. Talk to one of the other guys who looked uneasy:

"Listen, Mateo, I hate it when Rob says things like that."

"So do I," says Mateo.

This is your opening: "The next time he does that, I'm going to say something. But as soon as I do, you have to jump right in and say that you don't like it either. Can I count on you?"

Because here is what we know. It might be too scary for one guy to risk marginalization by speaking up, even though failing to do the right thing will make him ashamed later. But when two guys call out sexism, that opens a space for more men to chime in. And the behavior that makes women feel uncomfortable and alone might stop right there.

A global insurance company I consulted with developed informal "male allies" training, teaching men how to develop strategies to support one another. Critically, they were not being asked to "rescue" women; they were charged with challenging other men. The men developed several approaches, including supporting one another when a child was sick or a family issue arose. Soon the company's male employees started talking more openly with one another about their experiences, their families, and their efforts to balance their lives. And after a year, the men reported higher levels of job satisfaction. Though it remains to be seen how these changes will affect sexual harassment at the company, the shared language and norms the men have developed will help them challenge one another and support men who speak out.

So, where do we go from here? After decades of accepting sexual harassment as the status quo, we have to take some of the weight off women's shoulders. It's simply not their responsibility alone to talk about and enforce workplace equality. We must call out the sexist behaviors of other men because it's wrong and because it undermines women's confidence and effectiveness in the workplace.

This is what it means to be allies, men. To stand up together and do the right thing. We know how to do it, and we're good at it most of the time. Brotherhood, teamwork, and camaraderie are the essence of the fraternity, the foxhole, and the sports team. Now we have to learn how to come together at work—and on the right side of things.

Originally published in January 2018. Reprint BG1801

About the Contributors

SUSAN ASHFORD is the Michael & Susan Jandernoa Professor of Management and Organizations at the University of Michigan.

DOMINIC BARTON is the global managing partner of McKinsey & Company. He is a coauthor of *Talent Wins: The New Playbook for Putting People First* (Harvard Business Review Press, 2018).

NICHOLAS BLOOM is the William Eberle Professor of economics at Stanford University and a codirector of the Productivity, Innovation and Entrepreneurship program at the National Bureau of Economic Research.

JOSEPH L. BOWER is the Donald K. David Professor Emeritus at Harvard Business School. He is the coauthor (with Lynn S. Paine and Herman B. Leonard) of *Capitalism at Risk: Rethinking the Role of Business* (Harvard Business Review Press, 2011).

AARON K. CHATTERJI is an associate professor at Duke University's Fuqua School of Business and Sanford School of Public Policy.

J. YO-JUD CHENG is a doctoral candidate in the strategy unit at Harvard Business School.

SARAH CLIFFE is editorial director, *Harvard Business Review*.

THOMAS H. DAVENPORT is the President's Distinguished Professor of Information Technology and Management at Babson College, a research fellow at the MIT Initiative on the Digital Economy, and a senior adviser at Deloitte Analytics.

DEBBIE S. DOUGHERTY is a Professor in the Department of Communication at the University of Missouri and Editor Elect of the *Journal of Applied Communication Research*.

HEIDI K. GARDNER is a distinguished fellow at Harvard Law School and the author of *Smart Collaboration: How Professionals and Their*

Firms Succeed by Breaking Down Silos (Harvard Business Review Press, 2017). Her research, teaching, and advisory work focus on leadership and collaboration in professional services firms.

BORIS GROYSBERG is the Richard P. Chapman Professor of Business Administration at Harvard Business School and a coauthor, with Michael Slind, of *Talk, Inc.* (Harvard Business Review Press, 2012). Twitter: @bgroysberg.

ALTON B. HARRIS is a law partner at Nixon Peabody. He has worked to promote gender equality in the workplace for more than 30 years. He is the coauthor (with Andrea S. Kramer) of *Breaking Through Bias: Communication Techniques for Women to Succeed at Work* (Bibliomotion, 2016). Learn more at andieandal.com or on Twitter: @AndieandAl.

JAMES E. HEPPELMANN is the president and CEO of PTC, a leading maker of industrial software.

MARCO IANSITI is the David Sarnoff Professor of Business Administration at Harvard Business School, where he heads the Technology and Operations Management Unit and the Digital Initiative.

MICHAEL S. KIMMEL is the SUNY Distinguished Professor of Sociology and Gender Studies at Stony Brook University, where he founded the Center for the Study of Men and Masculinities, and the author of *Angry White Men* (Nation Books, 2013).

ANDREA S. KRAMER is a law partner at McDermott Will & Emery. She has worked to promote gender equality in the workplace for more than 30 years. She is the coauthor (with Alton B. Harris) of *Breaking Through Bias: Communication Techniques for Women to Succeed at Work* (Bibliomotion, 2016). Learn more at andieandal.com or on Twitter: @AndieandAl.

KARIM R. LAKHANI is a professor of business administration at Harvard Business School and the founding director of the Harvard Innovation Science Laboratory.

SUZANNE LEBSOCK is the Emeritus Board of Governors Professor of History at Rutgers University, where she cofounded the top-ranked graduate program in the history of women and gender. Lebsock's books include *A Murder in Virginia* (W.W. Norton, 2003) and *The Free Women of Petersburg* (W.W. Norton, 1984).

JEREMIAH LEE leads innovation for advisory services at Spencer Stuart. He is a cofounder of two culture-related businesses.

JAMES MANYIKA is the San Francisco–based director of the McKinsey Global Institute (MGI), the business and economics research arm of McKinsey & Company.

MARK MORTENSEN is an associate professor and the chair of the Organizational Behaviour Area at INSEAD. He researches, teaches, and consults on issues of collaboration, organizational design and new ways of working, and leadership.

LYNN S. PAINE is the John G. McLean Professor of Business Administration at HBS. She is the coauthor (with Joseph L. Bower and Herman B. Leonard) of *Capitalism at Risk: Rethinking the Role of Business* (Harvard Business Review Press, 2011).

GIANPIERO PETRIGLIERI is an associate professor of organizational behavior at INSEAD.

MICHAEL E. PORTER is a University Professor at Harvard, based at Harvard Business School.

JESSE PRICE is a leader in organizational culture services at Spencer Stuart. He is a cofounder of two culture-related businesses.

DAVID PYOTT is a philanthropist and the former CEO of Allergan.

RAJEEV RONANKI is a principal at Deloitte Consulting, where he leads the cognitive computing and health care innovation practices. Some of the companies mentioned in his article are Deloitte clients.

RAFFAELLA SADUN is the Thomas S. Murphy Associate Professor of Business Administration at Harvard Business School.

MICHAEL W. TOFFEL is the Senator John Heinz Professor of Environmental Management at Harvard Business School.

JOHN VAN REENEN is the Gordon Y. Billard Professor in MIT's department of economics and its Sloan School of Management.

MAXINE WILLIAMS is Facebook's global director of diversity.

JOAN C. WILLIAMS is Distinguished Professor of Law and Founding Director of the Center of WorkLife Law at the University of California, Hastings College of the Law. Her newest book is *White Working Class: Overcoming Class Cluelessness in America* (Harvard Business Review Press, 2017).

SARAH KEOHANE WILLIAMSON is CEO of FCLT Global.

AMY WRZESNIEWSKI is a professor of organizational behavior at the Yale School of Management.

Ackman, Bill, 165, 177, 181, 194
action logics, 136
activism
  CEO, 47–65
  investor, 176–177, 180–182, 195
after-sales services, 98
agency-based governance model,
  165–182
  compared with company-
    centered model, 188–189
  flaws in, 166–167, 169–174
  foundations of, 168–169
  implications for companies of,
    178–180
  and investor activism, 176–177
  and moral hazard, 172–173, 182
  in practice, 174–178
  and value creation/transfer,
    180–182
  See also company-centered gover-
    nance model
agency costs, 169
agency theory, 166, 168–186, 190
agile environment, 148–149
Ailes, Roger, 217–218, 233
Airbnb, 120, 131
algorithms, 72–73
Ali, Mohamad, 58
Alibaba, 117, 118, 122, 130. See also
  hub firms
Allen, Woody, 207–208
Allergan, 165, 172, 174, 177, 181,
  193–197
Alphabet, 117, 123. See also hub
  firms
Amazon, 117, 122, 128, 130. See also
  hub firms
American Civil Liberties Union,
  53
Ant Financial, 118, 122
Anthem, 79, 81–82, 121
Anti-Defamation League, 53

Apple, 55–57, 117, 122, 123, 125, 128,
  130. See also hub firms
artificial intelligence (AI), 67–84
  business benefits of, 70
  challenges of, 71, 75
  future of, 82–83
  job losses from, 83, 105
  pilot projects, 78–81
  portfolio of projects for, 76–78
  scaling up use of, 81–82
  technology selection, 78
  types of, 68–75
  understanding technologies of,
    75–76
  use of, 67–68, 77
Ashford, Susan, 109–116
asset managers, 170–172, 190–191
augmented reality (AR), 85–108
  about, 86–90
  applications, 86, 87, 101–104
  capabilities of, 90–93
  cost savings from, 100
  creation and management of,
    100–102
  deployment of, 101–104
  digital content for, 102–103
  to enhance decision making, 89
  hardware, 103–104
  impact of, 85–86, 90, 105, 108
  and physical environment, 103
  as product feature, 94–95
  and strategy, 99–101
  and value chain, 95–99
  value creation by, 94–99
  and virtual reality, 93–94
  workings of, 106–107
authority cultural style, 138, 143
automation, 68–71, 75, 78, 105
automotive sector, 123–126
awareness raising, by CEO activists,
  51–52
AZEK, 97, 102

Baidu, 117. *See also* hub firms
Barton, Dominic, 197–204
bathroom law controversy, 49, 50, 53, 62
Becton, Dickinson, 74, 79
Benioff, Marc, 48, 49, 50, 52, 55, 56, 62
Berni, Arrigo, 31
bias
  in performance reviews, 43, 44
  racial, 37–45
  unconscious, 37
big data, 20, 42, 75, 83
Blankfein, Lloyd, 51–52
Bloom, Nicholas, 19–35
boards of directors, 169, 170, 175–176, 187, 195
Boeing, 91
Bosch Rexroth, 91
bottlenecks, 76, 117–118, 129
Bower, Joseph L., 165–192
boycotts, 63–64. *See also* CEO activists
bright prospects, 178–180. *See also* growth share matrix
Brock, David, 231
business-process redesign, 79–81

capital gains taxes, 196
caring cultural style, 138, 139, 142, 144
Carlson, Gretchen, 210, 218
cash cows, 178–180. *See also* growth share matrix
Cathy, Dan, 50, 52
CEO activists, 47–65
  effectiveness of, 53–55, 63–64
  examples of, 50
  implications for democracy of, 62
  increasing numbers of, 47–49

and internal stakeholders, 63
issues for, 57–58, 61
motivations of, 49, 51
playbook for, 57–64
responses to, 58–61, 63–64
risks and rewards for, 54–57
tactics of, 48, 51–54
timing for, 61
change, responses to, 137–139. *See also* corporate culture
chatbots, 73–74, 78
Chatterji, Aaron K., 47–65
Cheng, J. Yo-Jud, 133–164
Chick-fil-A, 56. *See also* boycotts
chief executive officers (CEOs)
  activism by, 47–65
  in family-run firms, 30–31
  and management practices, 34
China Mobile, 186
Cliffe, Sarah, 193–197
climate change, 52
cloud services, 122
coaching, augmented reality for, 91–92
cognitive distance, 89
cognitive engagement, 73–74
cognitive insight, 72–73
cognitive load, 89
cognitive technology. *See* artificial intelligence (AI)
cognitive technology projects, 68
collaboration among firms, 125–126. *See also* multiteaming
collectivism, 160
Comcast, 119
communication, with stakeholders, 101
company-centered governance model, 182–191. *See also* agency-based governance model
competitive advantage, 19, 126–127

competitive bottlenecks, 117–118, 129
computer-aided design (CAD), 95–96
connected-car ecosystem, 123–124
connectivity, 121, 122
content-publishing model, 104. *See also* augmented reality (AR)
context, for corporate culture, 160–163
contract employees, 5, 109–116
convergence, 158–159
Conyers, John, 217. *See also* sexual harassment
Cook, Tim, 48, 55–58
Cornetta, Hallie, 41. *See also* Facebook
corporate culture, 133–164
  changing, 149–152
  context for, 160–163
  and convergence, 158–159
  defining, 134–137
  effect of, 135
  evolution of, 134–135
  future leaders and, 146–147
  integrated cultural framework, 135, 139–141
  and leadership, 133–134, 145–146, 162
  management of, 134
  and management practices, 32–34
  and mergers, 147–148
  organizational conversations about, 151
  and organizational design, 151–152, 163
  and outcomes, 145–149
  and people interactions, 137
  profile of, 154–155
  purpose of, 133
  research on, 164
  and responses to change, 137–139
  and sexual harassment, 221–222
  shaping your, 156–157
  and strategy, 145–146, 149, 161–162
  styles of, 135, 137–144
corporate governance. *See* governance
Corporate Horizon Index, 200–203
corporate law, 169–170
corporate social responsibility, 168, 169, 183
corporations
  as complex organizations, 183–184
  culture of (*see* corporate culture)
  ethical standards of, 185–186
  interests of, 186
  as legal constructs, 183
  long-term prosperity of, 184, 196, 197–204
  objectives and strategies of, 185
  political and socioeconomic environment of, 186
  political role of, 47–48
  societal functions of, 184–185
  value creation by, 185
cost savings
  from AR, 100 (*see also* augmented reality)
  from multiteaming, 7
cross-functional teams, 44–45
cultural change, 149–152
cultural norms, 134, 145
culture. *See* corporate culture
customer base, growth of, 126–127
customer experience, and augmented reality, 97
customer feedback and AR, 100. *See also* augmented reality (AR)
customer harassment, 210. *See also* sexual harassment

Daimler, 125
Danaher Business System (DBS), 29, 32
data scientists, 75–76
Davenport, Thomas H., 67–84
decision making, augmented reality for enhanced, 89. *See also* augmented reality (AR)
deep learning, 72–73, 75, 78
Democrats, responses to CEO activism by, 58, 59
Department of Homeland Security, 94
DHL, 97, 98–99
Dick, Andy, 217. *See also* sexual harassment
digital content, 102–103
digital domino effect, 120–122
digital revolution, 105
digital technology, 121, 127
digitization, 118, 120, 132
discrimination, 37–45, 131
Disney, 141
diversity, promotion of, 38–45
dogs, 178–180. *See also* growth share matrix
Dougherty, Debbie S., 221–224
DuPont, 180
Dutch East India Company, 186

earnings growth, 201
Ecomagination, 186
e-commerce, AR applications for, 97. *See also* augmented reality (AR)
economic issues, 58
economic power, leveraging of, 52–54
economic profit, 202–203
Emmert, Mark, 52–53
employees

AR, 100–101 (*see also* augmented reality)
contract, 5, 109–116
feedback from, 29
multiteaming, 1–17
skill deficits in, 31–32
surveying about sexual harassment, 225–231
from underrepresented groups, 37–45
employment law, 217–219
enjoyment cultural style, 138, 142
Enron, 173
entry barriers, 122
equity-based pay, 174–175
ethical standards, 185–186
ethics, of network leadership, 130–131
executive compensation, 174–175, 181–182
expert systems, 75

Facebook, 44–45, 74, 117, 119, 120, 122, 128. *See also* hub firms
family-run firms, 29–31
Farrow, Mia, 207. *See also* sexual harassment
Farrow, Ronan, 207–208. *See also* sexual harassment
feedback
  customer, 100
  employee, 29
flexibility, 137. *See also* corporate culture
Ford Motor Company, 94
Fowler, Susan, 219. *See also* sexual harassment
Fox News, 213, 218, 222
Franken, Al, 208. *See also* sexual harassment
Frazier, Kenneth, 52, 56, 61, 63

freelancers, 109–116
Friedman, Ken, 215. *See also* sexual harassment
Friedman, Milton, 168, 169, 183

Gardner, Heidi K., 1–17
General Electric (GE), 128
General Motors (GM), 33, 125
gig economy, 109–116
global economy, 117
global financial crisis, 202
Gokaldas Exports, 30
good governance model, 166. *See also* governance
Google, 117–120, 122, 123, 125, 128, 130, 131. *See also* hub firms
Gordon, Robert, 20
governance
    agency-based model of, 165–182
    company-centered model of, 182–191
    good, 166
    structure, 29–31
government regulations, 196
Green, Barbara, 50
Green, David, 50, 51
Greene, Lauren, 211. *See also* sexual harassment
growth share matrix, 178–180
Groysberg, Boris, 133–164
GSK, 141

Hackett, Isa, 216. *See also* sexual harassment
Harris, Alton B., 225–231
hedge funds, 165–166, 177, 181–182, 191
Heppelmann, James E., 85–108
high-convergence organizations, 158–159

Hill, Anita, 211–212, 231. *See also* sexual harassment
hiring practices, bias in, 37–45
hostile work environment, 218–219
Huawei, 141
hub economy, 117–132
    digital domino effect, 120–122
    ethical leadership in, 130–131
    returns to scale in, 126–127
    spread of, 118–119
hub firms, 117–132
    in automotive sector, 123–126
    criticisms of, 119–120
    leaders of, 130–131
    opportunity for, 120
    pushing back against, 127–130
human capital, interdependence, 13–15
human interactions, for freelancers, 115. *See also* freelancers
human resources, AR applications for, 98–99. *See also* augmented reality (AR)
humans, future of, 105, 108

Iansiti, Marco, 117–132
Iconics, 96
IKEA, 97, 102
Immelt, Jeff, 51
immigration issue, 47, 53, 55, 56, 58
income inequality, 118, 119
independent contractors, 109–116
industry context, 160–161
information processing, 89
Ingenico, 122
Inrix, 125
institutional investors, 165–166, 172
instructional aids, 91–92
integrated cultural framework, 135, 139–141
intelligent agents, 73–74, 78, 79

interaction, with SCPs, 92–93
internet of things (IoT), 128
investor activism, 176–177, 180–182, 195

Jensen, Michael, 168–169, 183
job losses, from AI, 83, 105. *See also* artificial intelligence (AI)
Judd, Ashley, 210. *See also* sexual harassment

Kimmel, Michael S., 231–237
Kiva, 131
knowledge transfer, 2, 7, 14, 15–16
Kozinski, Alex, 211, 215. *See also* sexual harassment
KPN, 98
Kramer, Andrea S., 225–231

Lakhani, Karim R., 117–132
leaders
    activism by corporate, 47–65
    corporate, 183–184
    for cultural change, 150–151
    cultural statements by, 141
    developing future, 146–147
    of hub firms, 130–131
    organizational, 13–17
    team, 6, 8
leadership
    corporate, 183–184
    and culture, 133–134, 145–146, 162
    errors in, 165–206
    network, 130–131
    and strategy, 133
learning cultural style, 138, 139, 142, 144, 148–149
learning environment, 11–12
Lebsock, Suzanne, 207–220

Lee, Jeremiah, 133–164
Lee Company, 92
Levine, James, 211. *See also* sexual harassment
Lewis, Peter, 50
limited liability doctrine, 166, 172
Linux, 129, 131
Lloyd's of London, 141
logistics, and augmented reality, 96–97
long-term value creation, 197–204
Louis C.K., 217. *See also* sexual harassment
low-convergence organizations, 158
Lyft, 53, 125

machine learning, 72–73, 75, 77, 105. *See also* artificial intelligence (AI)
Mackey, John, 50
male privilege, 221. *See also* sexual harassment
management attitudes, 176
management practices
    causes of differences in, 27–34
    core, 22
    false perceptions about, 27–29, 34
    in family-run firms, 29–31
    importance of, 19–20
    for long-term growth, 197–204
    and organizational culture, 32–34
    and performance, 25–26
    quality of, 25
    research on, 20–27
    skill deficits in, 31–32
    undervaluing competent, 19–35
    variations in, 23–27
managers
    as agents of shareholders, 168
    alignment of interests of with shareholders, 173

corporate, 183–184
ethical standards of, 169
as fiduciaries, 170, 187
overconfidence by, 27–28
role of, 169–170
manufacturing, and augmented
reality, 96. *See also* augmented
reality (AR)
Manyika, James, 197–204
marginalized groups, bias and
discrimination against,
37–45
marketing, and augmented reality,
97. *See also* augmented reality
(AR)
McConnell, Mitch, 211. *See also*
sexual harassment
MD Anderson Cancer Center, 67
Meckling, William, 168–169, 183
meetings, team, 11
men
and sexual harassment, 207–220,
222–223, 231–237
and toxic masculinity, 215
mental capacity, 89
Merck, 61
mergers, 147–148
Metcalfe's law, 121
#MeToo movement, 208–211, 213,
233
Microsoft, 117, 122, 127–128, 131. *See
also* hub firms
Milano, Alyssa, 213. *See also* sexual
harassment
Moleskine, 31
Moore, Roy, 211, 213
Moore's law, 120–121
moral hazard, 172–173, 182
Mortensen, Mark, 1–17
motivation, boosting, 12–13
Moynihan, Brian, 48, 49
Mozilla, 129

multihoming, 128–129
multiteaming, 1–17
advantages of, 1–3, 5
disadvantages of, 2, 3, 5–6
goals of, 7
managing challenges of, 6–17
reasons for use of, 2–5
research on, 4
Murdoch, James, 53

NASA, 70–71
national culture, 160, 221
Navteq, 125
Netflix, 122
network competition, 117–119
network connectivity, 121, 122
network effects, 121, 122
network hubs, 121
network leadership, 130–131
network theory, 120
Nordstrom, 64
norms cascade, 208, 211–213

Oculus, 128
Oesterle, Bill, 52
OpenCar, 125
open-source software, 129
OpenStreetMap, 129
operational effectiveness,
19–20, 23
operational management, 22
opportunity cost of capital, 202
Oracle, 56
order cultural style, 139, 143, 144
O'Reilly, Bill, 218, 233. *See also*
sexual harassment
Oreskes, Michael, 217. *See also*
sexual harassment
organizational culture. *See* corporate culture

organizational leaders
   priorities for, 13–17
   See also leaders
organizational politics, 32–34
organizational structure, 151–152, 163
organizations, use of multiteaming
   in, 1–17

Paine, Lynn S., 165–192
Paytm, 122
Pearson, Michael, 194
Peltz, Nelson, 180
Pence, Mike, 53
people analytics, 38–45
people interactions, 137. *See also*
   corporate culture
performance
   and culture, 145–149
   false perceptions about, 27–29
   and management practices, 25–26
   monitoring, 22
performance-based compensation,
   175, 181–182
performance reviews, bias in, 43, 44
Pershing Square Capital Management, 193–197
Petriglieri, Gianpiero, 109–116
Pfizer, 77
pilot projects, for AI, 78–81. *See also*
   artificial intelligence (AI)
Plank, Kevin, 54–55, 56
"poison pills," 175–176
political issues, 47, 48, 49, 58
Polman, Paul, 50
Porter, Michael E., 19, 85–108
Price, Jesse, 133–164
Price, Roy, 216
process automation, 68–71, 75, 78,
   105
process improvements, from multiteaming, 7

product demonstrations, 97
product development, and
   augmented reality, 95–96.
   See also augmented reality
   (AR)
product differentiation, 99–100
productivity
   growth, 20
   of independent contractors,
   111–112
public company shares, 170–172
purpose, for freelancers, 114–115
purpose cultural style, 138, 142
Pyott, David, 193–197

qualitative analysis, 43–44
quid pro quo harassment, 217–218.
   See also sexual harassment

racial discrimination, 37–45, 131
Reality Editor, 92–93
Red Ventures, 40–41, 43
regional culture, 160
Religious Freedom Restoration Act
   (RFRA), 50, 52–57
Republicans, responses to CEO
   activism by, 58, 59
resource allocation, 178–180
resource utilization, and multiteaming, 7
results cultural style, 138, 139, 142,
   144, 148
returns to scale, 126–127, 128
revenue growth, 201
robotic process automation (RPA),
   68–71, 75, 78, 105
Rogers, Jim, 50
Ronanki, Rajeev, 67–84
Rose, Charlie, 217. *See also* sexual
   harassment

routines, of freelancers, 113–114. *See also* freelancers

Sadun, Raffaella, 19–35
safety cultural style, 138, 139, 143
sales, and augmented reality, 97. *See also* augmented reality (AR)
Salesforce, 55
Samsung, 128
Scangos, George, 51–52
Schulman, Dan, 49, 53
Schultz, Howard, 48, 55, 58
SCPs. *See* smart, connected products (SCPs)
SEBank, 74
Securities and Exchange Commission (SEC), 141
self-employment, 109–116
sexual harassment, 207–220
 allegations of, 214–215
 bystander intervention for, 224
 elimination of, 225
 employee survey on, 225–231
 firings and settlements, 213–215
 laws on, 217–219
 male victims of, 211
 men speaking up about, 231–237
 new norms around, 208, 211–213, 231–233
 policies, 215, 221–224
 reasons for, 233
 and today's workplace, 215–216, 219–220
shareholders
 accountability of, 166–167, 172–173, 191
 interests of, 186
 rights of, 175
 role of, 167–172
 uniformity of, 174
 wishes of, 168–169, 174

shareholder value, 165–168, 176, 177, 180–182, 185, 195
short-term returns, 194, 199–200, 203–204. *See also* shareholder value
skills
 deficits, 31–32
 mapping team members', 9–10
"slut shaming," 208, 213. *See also* sexual harassment
smart, connected products (SCPs), 85, 86, 90, 92–93, 98, 99, 105
smart glasses, 86, 92, 95, 96, 104
social connections, for freelancers, 115. *See also* freelancers
social issues, 47, 48, 49, 51–52, 58
software applications, for AR, 104. *See also* augmented reality (AR)
Sonos, 129
Sorvino, Mira, 210. *See also* sexual harassment
speculators, 171–172, 190
Spotify, 122
stability, 137. *See also* corporate culture
stakeholders
 communication with, 101
 multiple, 185
Starbucks, 55
stars, 178–180. *See also* growth share matrix
stereotypes, 208, 212–213
strategy
 and augmented reality, 99–101
 and competitive advantage, 19
 and culture, 145–146, 149, 161–162
 and leadership, 133
 and operational excellence, 20, 34–35
 purpose of, 133
success, redefining, in gig economy, 116. *See also* freelancers

talent management, 22
Target, 63–64
target setting, 22
team leaders, priorities for, 6, 8
team members
    boosting motivation of, 12–13
    creating learning environment
        for, 11–12
    interpersonal connections
        between, 8–9
    mapping skills of, 9–10
teams
    buffers against shocks in, 16–17
    cross-functional, 44–45
    interdependence among, 13–15
    launching, 8–9
    managing, 6, 8–13
    meetings, 11
    multiteaming, 1–17
    time management for, 10–11
technology
    artificial intelligence, 67–84
    augmented reality, 85–108
    digital, 121, 127
    visualization, 90–91
Tencent, 117. See also hub firms
Tesla, 141
Thomas, Clarence, 212, 231. See also
    sexual harassment
time management, across teams,
    10–11
Time's Up movement, 213. See also
    sexual harassment
Toffel, Michael W., 47–65
total shareholder return (TSR), 175
Toyota Production System, 33
training, augmented reality for,
    91–92. See also augmented real-
    ity (AR)
Trump, Donald, 52–56, 61, 64, 234
Twitter, 51–52, 119

Uber, 119–120, 131, 219
Ulukaya, Hamdi, 50, 58
unconscious bias, 37
Under Armour, 54–55
underrepresented groups, bias and
    discrimination against, 37–45
use cases, for AI, 77. See also artifi-
    cial intelligence (AI)
user experience or user interface
    (UX/UI) design, 100
user interfaces, and augmented
    reality, 92–93. See also aug-
    mented reality (AR)

Valeant Pharmaceuticals, 165, 172,
    174, 177, 181, 193–197
valuation models, 190. See also gov-
    ernance
value capture, 121. See also hub
    economy
value chain, and augmented reality,
    95–99
value concentration, 118. See also
    hub economy
value creation
    by augmented reality, 94–99.
        See also augmented reality
        (AR)
    by corporations, 185
    and investor activists, 180–182
    long-term, 197–204
value transfer, 180–182
Vanguard, 73–74, 79–81
Van Reenen, John, 19–35
Vengeful Lying Slut stereotype,
    208, 212–213. See also sexual
    harassment
Videojet, 32–33
virtual reality (VR), 93–94
visualization technology, 90–91

warehouse operations and AR,
96–97. *See also* augmented
reality (AR)
Watson, 77
Wayfair, 97, 102
Wealthfront, 122
WeChat, 117, 122
Weinstein, Harvey, 207, 208, 210,
213, 215, 216, 217, 233, 234–235.
See also sexual harassment
Whole Foods, 141
Williams, Joan C., 207–220
Williams, Maxine, 37–45
Williamson, Sarah Keohane,
197–204
women
and sexual harassment, 207–224,
231–237
stereotypes of, 208, 212–213
work environment

and #MeToo movement, 208–211
hostile, 218–219
workers. *See* employees
workplace climate survey, 225–231
workplace discrimination, 37–45
work relationships, 215–220
workspaces, for freelancers, 112–113.
See also freelancers
Wrzesniewski, Amy, 109–116

Xerox, 98

YouTube, 120

Zappos, 141
Zuckerberg, Mark, 119

The most important management ideas all in one place.

We hope you enjoyed this book from *Harvard Business Review*. Now you can get even more with HBR's 10 Must Reads Boxed Set. From books on leadership and strategy to managing yourself and others, this 6-book collection delivers articles on the most essential business topics to help you succeed.

HBR's 10 Must Reads Series

The definitive collection of ideas and best practices on our most sought-after topics from the best minds in business.

- Change Management
- Collaboration
- Communication
- Emotional Intelligence
- Innovation
- Leadership
- Making Smart Decisions

- Managing Across Cultures
- Managing People
- Managing Yourself
- Strategic Marketing
- Strategy
- Teams
- The Essentials

hbr.org/mustreads

Buy for your team, clients, or event.
Visit hbr.org/bulksales for quantity discount rates.